Beyond the Walls

Also by Paul Wilkes

Paul Wilkes

Image Books

Doubleday

New York London Toronto

Sydney Auckland

Beyond the Walls

Monastic Wisdom for

Everyday Life

AN IMAGE BOOK
PUBLISHED BY DOUBLEDAY
a division of Random House, Inc.
1540 Broadway, New York, New York 10036

IMAGE, DOUBLEDAY, and the portrayal of a deer drinking from a stream are
trademarks of Doubleday, a division of Random House, Inc.

Beyond the Walls was originally published in hardcover by Doubleday in 1999.
Psalms quoted are from *The Abbey Psalter* (Mahwah, N.J.: Paulist Press, 1981).

Book design by Dana Leigh Treglia

The Library of Congress has cataloged the Doubleday hardcover as follows:

Wilkes, Paul, 1938–
    Beyond the walls: monastic wisdom for everyday life / Paul Wilkes. — 1st ed.
      p. cm.
    I. Abbey of Our Lady of Mepkin (Moncks Corner, S.C.). 2. Trappists—
Spiritual life. [I. Wilkes, Paul, 1938– .] I. Title.
    BX2525.A33W58   1999
    271'.125075793—dc21   99-22808
                        CIP

ISBN 0-385-49436-X
Copyright © 1999 by Paul Wilkes

All Rights Reserved
Printed in the United States of America
First Image Books Edition: October 2000

10 9 8 7 6 5 4 3 2

To the Members

of My Community

TRACY

NOAH

DANIEL

Contents

Historical Note

When Constantine ended the persecution of Christians in 313 C.E., the enfranchisement granted this small but growing religious movement was viewed by some of them as nothing short of a curse. In a still very pagan world, how would Christians be able to practice heroic virtue and express their total commitment to the way of Christ that had indelibly imprinted the early church? How could they properly honor their God now that secular and religious life—once considered anathema to each other—had been bidden to live in harmony?

One way of preserving this purity of belief was unwittingly born in those days of Constantine when Antony, a prosperous Egyptian peasant, abandoned his comfortable home and life and unaccountably walked into the desert. He wanted to live as Christ had lived—in radical simplicity, poverty, and charity—and saw no way to do this within the villages and cities of his day. He had no desire to start a new expression of Christianity; he sought only to find his God and save his soul. Antony barricaded himself in a deserted fort, ate sparingly, and prayed for the next twenty-one years.

His example and the wisdom the desert taught him drew other disciples, both women and men, who sought God while living alone. "The single ones" they began to be called—*monos* in Greek; monks. They dedicated their lives to prayer and contemplation, providing refuge and rest for those who came seeking their wisdom as well as for the wayfarer.

Soon small communities informally began to gather both to ameliorate an extraordinarily arduous lifestyle and—as the Roman Empire collapsed and barbarian hordes pillaged and destroyed much of the then-civilized world—for mutual support. Various sets of guidelines and practices were formulated to give structure to their lives. But it was not until the sixth century that Benedict—who also had begun his search for God as a hermit—wrote what became known as the *Rule of St. Benedict*, or simply the *Rule*. It was a document that would change the face of Western spirituality—and the world.

The *Rule*, asking neither for heroic bodily privation nor marathons of prayer, carefully ordered a monk's day. *Ora et labora*, prayer and work, were apportioned in healthy and sensible balance. It was, essentially, an ordinary lay person's way to God. Priests were given no special place; all were brethren, equal. Monastic life, as ordained by the *Rule*, promised both community support for the spiritual journey and the time and latitude necessary for individual assent to God. Belonging and solitude. Voices raised to God in prayer and opportunity for utter silence.

Benedict's small communities, or monasteries, quickly spread throughout Europe. Although his followers sought unpopulated areas, villages and even sizable towns grew up around their primitive monasteries as people sought their wisdom, grace, and—eventually—protection. Monasteries proved to be exemplary models of true Christian community life. They were not only centers of sanctity but of scholarship, devoting considerable resources to the transcription of ancient texts. Because of their stability in an unstable time, they also became repositories for documents and art, in essence preserving the fragments of Western culture. Monasteries, those communities of seekers after God who had left behind the claims of human society, ironically became the lasting lights of civilization as the long shadows of the Dark Ages crept across the centuries.

In this vacuum of both cultural and temporal authority, abbots eventually became formidable secular princes, ruling over enormous estates and controlling great wealth. Benedict's simple way was gradually obscured as extravagant liturgies praised God and meat graced monastic tables; furs and soft garments enfolded monks sworn to the most austere of lives. Serfs did much of the work on monastic estates, and some monks found the companionship that was supposed to have been sought in the community in the arms of concubines instead. Physical pleasure, not spiritual sustenance, was sought with alarming diligence.

Yet within these communities there were those who could see that convenience, wealth, and carnality did not mark a path to God. They yearned to return to the simple community life that Benedict espoused.

In the year 1098, a small band of twenty-one Benedictine monks left the splendor of their monastery at Molesme. Led by Robert, Alberic, and Stephen Harding, they traveled to a wild and desolate spot in the densely forested, insect-infested French lowlands at Cîteaux, near present-day Dijon. There, they found a small chapel. Gathering boughs and branches, they erected crude shelters and began their effort to live the *Rule* to the full, to live as Benedict had promised: "We shall run on the path of God's commandments, our hearts overflowing with the inexpressible delight of love." Distinguished by their coarse, unbleached woolen garments, so unlike the reverential black of the Benedictines, they became known as the "white" monks.

A few years later, Bernard of Clairvaux gathered thirty fellow noblemen and family members and joined this struggling community, then called simply *Novum Monasterium* (the "New Monastery"). Because of the monastery's location at Cîteaux, Bernard and the many who would follow him began to be called Cistercians. This was somewhat troubling; after all, their original intention was nothing other than to be good Benedictines, providing by example a way to reform and refocus the order. It soon became clear, however, that they had already set out upon a different path. For unlike the Benedictines, who accepted children given over to their care for a variety of reasons—a thank offering to God, physical or mental illness, a second or third son who would never receive sufficient inheritance—the Cistercians only accepted grown men, most of them men of the world. Soldiers, nobles, and courtiers, the landed and the landless, all came in ever-increasing numbers. They came in the full knowledge that much would be demanded of them—but convinced that the promise of both an earthly and a heavenly paradise would there be within their grasp.

As Antony was not alone in seeking God in the desert, the Cistercians were not the only reformers dedicating themselves to reclaiming the Benedictine life of simplicity, contemplative prayer, silence, and manual labor. But the Cistercians had something the others did not; they had Bernard. It was Bernard's genius to marry the asceticism of early Benedictine life with a much warmer and intimate union with Christ, inspiring a community life that would come to be called a "school of charity." In other words, by living daily in harmony and with love for one another, Cistercian monks were replicating the divine plan and prefiguring what eternal bliss might be.

This way of life was so attractive to men and women of his day that Bernard founded an average of two new monasteries each year of his life. By the thirteenth century, seven hundred and fifty Cistercian monasteries had been founded. At the time, they formed perhaps the most important network of learning, writing, and theological study in the world.

As the Cistercians had sought to reform the Benedictine traditions, in turn the Cistercians themselves would be called to reform. History repeated itself, even within these cloistered walls; the Cistercians found that as they tried directly to influence social, economic, even political and ecclesiastical life, their core contemplative life was given short shrift—and their impact waned. In the seventeenth century, Armand de Rance surveyed the Cistercian landscape and found it crowded with well-endowed land-holding monasteries. Monks lived in a splendor that rivaled the ostentatious decadence of the French court. Like Bernard before him, de Rance could see that these monks had lost their once holy vision.

De Rance's was a penitential interpretation of the *Rule of St. Benedict*, demanding that sinful bodies be ground to holiness under an abbot's pestle in a monastic mortar. So rigorous was the lifestyle he demanded as abbot of La Trappe, the monastery near Rouen, that the average monk's life span there was but seven years. His reformulation of contemplative monastic life attracted many, who would soon be popularly known as Trappists.

The French Revolution almost annihilated monasticism, Trappists included. Of the one thousand five hundred monasteries that once dotted the countryside, only thirty survived the antireligious fervor. A handful of Trappist refugees came from France to America in 1803 and attempted to establish a foundation. They found conditions too harsh—even for monks used to extreme privation—and returned home. It was not until 1848 that the first American Trappist monastery was finally established in Gethsemani, Kentucky, a densely wooded, insect-ridden area not dissimilar from that of Cîteaux.

Seemingly unaffected by currents within the church and without, the Trappists continued to live a rigorous, almost medieval life well into the twentieth century. One of the Gethsemani monks, Thomas Merton, wrote eloquently about the life in *The Seven Storey Mountain*, a surprising post–World War II bestseller, the publication of which coincided with a surge of vocations to the Trappist life.

It was not until after the Second Vatican Council of 1962–1965 that some Trappist practices—such as absolute silence and abstinence from even eggs, cheese, and fish—were somewhat relaxed, in keeping with the council's summons to look to "the primitive inspiration" of religious orders, "and their adaptation of the changed conditions of our time."[1] This was also a period that saw both a decline in vocations and the departure of hundreds of monks from monasteries they had once sworn would be their last home on Earth. After an extraordinary, century-long revival, the Trappists faced retrenchment and uncertainty once again.

[1] *Perfectae Caritatis*, n. 2

But even as the numbers of Trappists were declining, monastic life was experiencing an amazing transformation. The age of the monastery as spiritual source and spiritual home was at hand. Men and women of the world looked to these otherworldly places for sustenance and guidance in a confusing time—as earlier generations, in various ways and for various reasons, had in the centuries before. Monasticism—born of a hunger for solitude, unified in the need for community, once a pillar of scholarship and order—was now looked to as a spiritual beacon by those outside its walls. In a strange way, monasticism was beginning to have a broader, more profound, yet exquisitely subtle impact on American culture and individual lives.

And no order had down through the centuries kept a truer vision of monasticism's ascent to holiness and practical approach to everyday life than the Trappists. Theirs was a repository of holiness and spirituality whose riches were desired by many a seeker. Small groups of lay people began to affiliate themselves with certain monasteries. But most people—while admiring and visiting these places—could not see ways to incorporate the verities at the core of monasticism into their own lives.

Trappist life is a hundred and fifty years old in America; but it is a spiritual path with ancient roots, and a rich and variegated history. In the United States, there are presently some 469 men and 114 women living in seventeen Trappist communities (five convents and twelve monasteries). One of these monasteries, founded in 1949 when Gethsemani could not contain all those who aspired to the life, is Our Lady of Mepkin, set in a rural area some fifty miles west of Charleston, South Carolina.

Currently, Mepkin has twenty-seven monks, about the same number it had at its foundation.

INTRODUCTION

Monasteries

From the time I pulled up to the gates of the Abbey of Gethsemani in a coral pink Ford convertible, a high school senior in search of Thomas Merton with stale beer on my breath and a deep yearning in my callow heart, monasteries have always played a major part in the minor drama of my life. Through the thick and shifting fog of teenage hormones that otherwise obscured my vision, I had read Merton's *The Seven Storey Mountain* and unexpectedly found exactly who it was I wanted to be and how it was I wanted to live. Yes, the monastic life demanded across-the-spectrum renunciation of the highest order, in all material and sensual categories; but equally it held out the promise of an excellence so noble, brave, and focused.

Lost in a world of youthful excess, my soul cried out for boundaries and purpose. "Meaning" was not a word in popular use then, but it was what I sought. I could see no more perfect a place on earth than a monastery, and I longed to hear my name called at Gethsemani so that I might enter. But the call never came. The great voice all of us want to hear never summoned me to that or any other great task, so I melted into the workaday, nonmonastic world that the vast majority of humans populate. But I never forgot that place and that man—whom I was never to meet in person.

Then came years when I married and lived outside the Catholic Church into which I was born and once could never have imagined leaving. Outwardly I was a Protestant, but inwardly I had not left the church at all. I sang the Wesleys' splendid hymns, but Gregorian chant echoed deep in my being. My tenuous link to monasticism—which could be sustained without any outward appearance of clinging to this distinctive form of spirituality—was the amazingly large and varied Merton oeuvre, some forty books in all. Then there were others—Aelred of Rievaulx, Pachomius, William of St. Thierry, and of course the grand pillars of monasticism, Benedict and Bernard. I read deeply, hungrily, secretly.

When my marriage and self simultaneously foundered *in extremis*, I steered immediately toward the only true beacon I knew, in hopes of regaining my bearings. One day I simply packed a small bag and headed for New York's Port Authority bus station to begin a midlife pilgrimage that would eventually take me to a rich sampling of monasteries, in one of which I had hoped to find my soul. Of course, my soul was in my body, but in one of these places at least I found a place where I was at rest. It was, like Gethsemani, a Trappist monastery. The circle was complete, in a way. But actually a new, and tighter circle was starting to form.

Years of unbridled hedonism—not serious spiritual pursuit—followed this pilgrimage, strangely punctuated by visits to the monastery, St. Joseph's, which occupied the crest of one of central Massachusetts rolling hills near the town of Spencer. When finally I was so sick of myself I couldn't go on, and so frightened of a wonderful woman who had come into my life that I ran from her, I went back to St. Joseph's—seeking its protective shadow like a scared animal. After being the most public and outrageous of men, I lived as a hermit for nearly a year, yielding to the gentle rhythms of the monastic day and trying to abide God's seasons of both weather and heart.

I desperately wanted to join the Trappists, to finally hear God's call to be a monk. Instead, I heard another call. One day, I abruptly left my holy sanctuary, bought an engagement ring and, traveling south at horrifying speed, proposed to that woman in an advertising agency office overlooking the then tawdry expanse of New York's Times Square. When we eventually found a permanent home, it was hardly by coincidence but minutes from the monastery at Spencer. The call was still there, though certainly faint and filtered through the mesh of married life. I harbored the hope of living a dual life. It never quite happened. Two sons were born. Monasticism was a diorama on the other side of a very thick piece of glass. I could view it so clearly; I could not enter into it.

But the desire to live life on some higher plain, with some greater goal—more spiritually, more monastic—would not leave me. It was strange: monasticism had spoken to my life in so many ways, although I had never been a monk. I continually referred to the practices and values of the monastic community as practices and values that made sense in the outside world. Detachment, both from the slavery of material possessions and from the adoration of each passing emotion. A healthy balance of honest work with time for prayer and things of the spirit world: *ora et labora*. The continuing effort to renew, make ourselves better people. The practice of communal love and hospitality. If money, sex, and power were the cornerstones of secular culture, I had found that the poverty, chastity, and obedience of the monks ultimately offered far greater satisfaction. And I sensed that monastic life and the example of the monastic community had much to say not only to my own life, but to other lives outside the walls as well.

When our family moved to the South some years later I quickly found another monastery. Like a pilot fish needing its whale (or was I more like a barnacle?) I attached myself to this much larger creature as it traveled its steady, almost instinctual course through the swirling, murky waters of late-twentieth-century America. Something strange and, to me, extraordinary began to happen. No other monastery that I had ever visited affected me in quite the same way. For it was at Mepkin Abbey, set on an old rice plantation on the banks of South Carolina's Cooper River, that I began to see what I once regarded as a wall separating the monastic from the mundane world—a wall as thick as those surrounding monasteries—as a sheer, thin membrane. At Mepkin I began to see more clearly that monastic life and my life—our lives—are not so dissimilar after all. Many people sense there is a bit of the monk within them that yearns to be fulfilled; from time to time it cries out, not allowing us to rest until it is recognized and embraced. I believe this; but, of course, this belief is nothing extraordinary. After all, the monastic way is really nothing more or less than a way of seeking unity and relationship with God, and which utterly disregards anything that prevents our true happiness and human fulfillment. Monasticism is spirituality laid bare; it is the human yearning to open one's self to the divine spirit within, a yearning that pulsates throughout every human culture.

I believe this yearning is not only a matter for monks; for if the integrity and happiness with which monks live and the peace we feel at these holy places is somehow limited to monasteries, then the God who has inspired generation upon generation of monks has played a devious trick on the rest of us. It must be possible to incorporate monastic values, monastic principles into everyday life, if only because it was out of everyday life and ordinary people that monasticism was shaped. Benedict himself was a layman and was never ordained; in essence, monasticism began as a lay movement.

Although my hope here is to offer up monasticism's example for our time and lives, I would be the last to attempt launching some sort of New Catholic Triumphalism. There were and are other valid expressions of monasticism, both Christian and non-Christian: Neoplatonic, Buddhist, Hindu, Jaina, and Anglican among them. Yet it is a sad fact that Catholic monastic spirituality (which forms much of the bedrock of Western spirituality) has been ghettoized and marginalized—and dismissed as impractical by lay Catholics and non-Catholics alike. I look upon the wisdom of Catholic monastic life as a treasure buried beneath too many layers of misunderstanding and even fear. Monasticism is not about dogma; it is about God and an authentic spirituality. Its simple truths beckon to be rediscovered. Especially today, as we cast about for "new" spiritualities and seek answers in exotic places, here is a clear and well-marked path to a spirituality that can both bring us closer to God and infuse our everyday lives. That was and is the monk's goal. Is it not the goal of many of us as well?

For myself, I can only say that the monastic thread has woven through my life—sometimes seen, sometimes not, but ever there.

Seeking to plumb the secrets and mysteries of the Christian monastic tradition is not easy. Neither is it a matter of simple transference of principles lived in a setting certainly different from that of our secular lives. But then, what achievement of lasting importance has ever been easy or uncomplicated? All of us have had our fill of quick fixes and instant remedies. For the seeker who truly wants both the greatest possible fullness of human life and a meaningful relationship with the transcendent yet immanent ground of our being—which many of us know as God—the demands, though great, promise the reward of life rich beyond telling.

This book is one man's effort to listen to monastic wisdom and to be alert to life's lessons about what it is to be human—and, one hopes, holy. It is an attempt to apply monastic wisdom to everyday life. Ever aware of my inadequacy, yet all the while open to the workings of God at this place called Mepkin, I began what would turn out to be a year of monthly visits.

And like many pilgrims beginning a spiritual journey, I started out on exactly the wrong foot.

Indirection

Finding the True Path

It is a strange and wondrous place—as monasteries typically are; too sensuous and exquisite a setting for a life considered austere, marginal, or irrelevant to that which we know as "the real world." Egrets flying in from the Cooper River marshes sail through air sweetly fragrant with magnolia and gardenia blossoms. Lining the grand approach to what was once a fine rice plantation are giant live oaks, their thick branches draped with Spanish moss like so many boas casually flung over the shoulders of substantial but elegant cotillion belles. The air may at first seem quiet, but echoes break through time to be carried along in the muggy stillness. The throaty call of the chieftain and medicine man at the campfire, over a deerskin drum's steady beat; the wail of slaves far from home, softly wafting a spiritual toward a heaven that offered their only relief; the confident laughter of a press baron and his friends, thick with well-mixed martinis, sated with the quail shot that day.

Some fifty years ago, the latest of the settlers came. Their voices would be hushed, raised only to their Divine Spirit. This was a strange breed of men, sprung from a swamp in France, driven by the desire to conquer themselves and create a heavenly kingdom on earth. They sought God— God alone. A noble quest. Few persevere, but the ideal lives on.

Cistercian life is not as it was in the malarial swamps of Cîteaux, where monks worked and slept in their garments and ate (and sometimes gladly vomited) the bitter vetch that passed for sustenance. Today, these monks have e-mail and a microwave, eat frozen food and wear synthetic fibers; but the quest is still very much the same. And that is why people like myself come here, to experience the timeless, the idealistic, the impractical.

It does not matter what hour of day or time of year I arrive, for the Trappists laugh at time, bending it to their resolute wills by obeying it precisely. They gather for prayer at 3:20, 5:30, 7:30 A.M., noon, 6:00 and 7:40 P.M.; meals and work periods begin and conclude at similarly uniform times. There is no other place in my life so comforting in its sameness.

I came to the Trappists this June day—as is often the case when we arrive at a monastery—on a fool's mission. Our desire is genuine, but our methods too rooted in that so-called real world. We approach the monastery directly, banging on the gates, demanding that it release its secrets. We know the questions; we are sincere; we have not taken the easy way. Should not the answers then follow quickly? God should stand ready to speak to us. I come seeking peace. And answers. May I please have some? *Now!*

I arrived that morning like a Marine storming a beach, fierce, intentional, armed with a battle plan. For some reason that was overwhelmingly important at the time, I felt I needed to stop skirting around the edges of monastic life and get right to its essence. I wanted to find out how monks experienced God. Wasn't this why monks came to monasteries, why we visit them? What better place could there be to hear about the experience of God than in a Trappist monastery?

"God. That's a tough one to talk about," said Brother Edward quizzically when I saw him on the path just outside the church as I arrived early in the morning. Edward is a Trappist of forty years, having entered after a tour in the Navy when the immensity and the quiet of the ocean summoned him to a journey upon an expanse even more vast and uncharted. He joined the community at Gethsemani when Thomas Merton was there—although with the strict silence that was then practiced, he never exchanged more than eye contact with the great spiritual master. Edward is a handsome man, sixty-nine years old, with silvery hair, a trimmed silver beard, and a ready Polish smile—which he flashed, showing well-spaced teeth; then he was off.

Monks don't leave questing pilgrims standing there with a stupid question on their lips; instead, they gently move the venue. The venue on Edward's mind was the tremendously successful presentation of "The Dream of Gerontius" that had been staged at the monastery as one of the special events of Piccolo Spoleto, part of Spoleto Festival USA. While many events are staged in Charleston, still other concerts take place, as the festival's brochure notes, in "the churches, the parking lots, the storefronts and wherever people might gather." Monasteries are not the usual gathering spots, at least not for most people; but I had long ago learned that monks, while rigid about certain aspects of life, were far from literal minded.

Mepkin's abbot, Father Francis Kline—a Julliard-trained musical marvel who had mastered all of Bach by the age of fifteen—had been the organist for Sir Edward Elgar's composition, its text by John Henry Cardinal Newman sung by a superb chorus. But it was not only interest in Francis's sterling performance and the packed house that brought us together; it was a pursuit that we especially shared that Edward wanted to talk about. I had spent more hours with Edward over the past few years than any other of the Mepkin monks, not in any great spiritual pursuit or dialogue but in the refectory kitchen as we prepared a series of Sunday lunch extravaganzas for the community. Not a half-bad cook myself, it was a small contribution I could make. Edward talked of the smoked salmon, fresh asparagus and mesquite salad around which the after-concert meal centered as if it were a sacred oblation, manna in the desert, holy food. He spoke of Celia Cerasoli, proprietor of a fine Charleston restaurant, with the hushed respect due venerable abbots—or abbesses. Day in, day out, their vegetarian fare might march to an all too familiar beat, but Trappist monks still know, savor, and pay homage to great food when it is offered. If great spiritual masters are honored within this tradition, so are great culinary masters.

Edward had blunted the planned assault. The chapel bells were ringing; it was time for Mass. Talking about the experience of God would have to wait so that we might try to have such an experience instead.

The abbey church at Mepkin is built in the Cistercian style, in the shape of a cross, with a high-vaulted ceiling soaring over what is a quite narrow *palus*, the vertical portion of Christianity's cosmic tree. There are no adornments or diversions such as stained glass windows or fine liturgical art to lure the mind, only a stark granite altar at the front, with a simple crucifix on a stand and four candles at its corners. A square granite holy-water font sits before it, symbolizing the continuing purification that must take place in the life of the seeker. "God alone" reads the stark call to arms above the entrance to more than a few Trappist monasteries; this quiet place is testimony to that noble pursuit. All things unnecessary to that end are muted in Cistercian life, so that the interior journey to the heart of God and into the depths of one's own soul may be pursued without distraction.

As an overnight visitor, I was invited to sit with the monks in the two rows of varnished-pine choir stalls aligned against each long wall. In their midst that morning I found myself both praying fervently—for help in my "experience of God" venture—and daydreaming hopelessly. During one of the readings, with my mind floating about the airy spaces overhead, my eyes wandered upwards to a circular window high in the cupola in which a cross—or simply two pieces of molding (in such a place, the seeker finds symbolism everywhere)—had been placed. The sun was now high enough to give the sky that pure blue shade it achieves best when the day (or one's mind) is fresh. Clouds, like meringue puffs, scudded across this serene tableau. I realized how well I could see their movement, how rich was the color of the sky, limited as I was to taking in one infinitesimally small fraction of the broad sweep that offered itself fully just outside those walls.

Such it is with the monastic life; so restricted, a small, pure peephole on the universe—but what a view! Profound, rich, more than enough for human eyes to behold. We need to restrict the view in order to better see the movement of God; by seeing everything, we see nothing at all. I was living proof of that.

How I wanted this vantage point to be the perspective from which I could see all of life. That is why I have come to monasteries all my life, seeking to see intensely and clearly, hoping to take that keener acuity in all things. But if my monastic visits usually imparted a sense of peace and a view of life at once detached and yet more passionate, if moments of such insight send chills of recognition through me, I had proved an utter failure in making the monastic experience real and accessible when I was outside the monastery.

Lost in my reverie, my face turned upward, I was brought back to earth at that moment by one of the most irritating voices I had ever heard. It was the sing-songy voice of one of the monks, reading the gospel. All the intonations were wrong, the emphases falling on the wrong words, the voice too loud, too jarring, too embarrassingly *jejune*. All I could hear were tones, not words; it was as though someone were jabbing at my eardrums with an ice pick. Was I alone in my irritation? Hadn't this man ever been told how he was ruining what should have been a sublime moment for his brother monks—and for fervent pilgrims?

After mass I went to the cell that had been assigned to me, which was next to the abbot's. It was, like all the cells, a simple but quite comfortable eight-by-twelve-foot room with a bed, desk, its own air-conditioning unit, and a small private bath. On the bluff just outside my room, which over-looked a broad expanse of the Cooper River, I picked two huge, aromatic magnolia blossoms and put them in a glass, arranging a bed of Spanish moss before them. Searching for the perfect cross to place upon it, the nearest approximation I could find in nature was a droopy Y-shaped stick. Symbolism reigned; a metaphor for my life. Next to my tiny makeshift shrine was my notebook, opened to the first of many questions with which

I had readied myself to talk to the monks about their experience of God. Reading them again, I could only be embarrassed. Did I actually write these?

Realizing I would only make a still greater fool of myself if I troubled yet another monk with those questions about God, I knew I needed to rethink my approach. There is no requirement for visitors at Trappist monasteries to do anything structured at all—attendance at mass, the various hours of prayer throughout the day, even meals are optional. So, after a quick stop in the monastery library to see what might unintentionally but more beneficially fall into my hands, I began to walk, hoping that clarity would somehow come.

The tiny window of my cell and the unsettling voice of my own chagrin faded quickly as I lost myself in reading an article, an odd one for *Cistercian Studies Quarterly*, the order's scholarly journal. It was a recounting of what is known about the seven Trappist monks of Our Lady of Atlas in Algeria who had been kidnapped and killed by Muslim fundamentalists in 1996. The article only further confirmed my love for this order and its at once humble and yet brave insertion into a world that may not comprehend it—and which, in such cases as the monks of Atlas, sometimes violently rejects it. My feet trod the familiar asphalt of the narrow road leading out from the cloistered buildings, as my heart soared with the words of one Father Christian de Chergé, written in advance of a death he knew well could be his, addressed directly to his murderer, a man who would slit his throat:

> And . . . you, the friend of my final moment, who would not be aware of what you were doing.
>
> Yes, I also say this Thank You and this A-Dieu to you, in whom I see the face of God.[1]

Was this not true heroism, true love of the enemy, true embodiment of the Christian message? In that horrible face, the face of God? Astounding.

[1]"Testament of Dom Christian," Appendix 1 in Donald McGlynn, "Atlas Martyrs," *Cistercian Studies Quarterly* 32(2) (1997), 189.

Father Christian's bravery caused me to ponder: what should we dedicate ourselves to? Should we cling to our life, our desires—or be ready to give them away? Of course, these might be categorized as typically "Catholic" personal interrogations; but I'm sure that such questions steal across many minds each day. "What are we here for, anyhow?" And in Trappist monasteries, where men and women have so clearly cut themselves off from the eyes, comforts, acclaim, and reassurance of the world, such questions are as much part of life as taking the next breath. It is why people come to monasteries—to confront themselves and the meaning of who they are.

Such heroic bravery and vaunted piety had been at the very core of my Catholic education, held up as basic to any life worthily lived, from the time I was very young until the moment of reading those words; and yet I knew I would not be going off to Algeria to take Father Christian's place and offer myself as a sacrifice. Instead, the next day I would be getting into my car—air conditioned against the assault of the muggy tidewater climate—and driving back to my life as a married man, husband, father, and provider. I found this disquietingly mundane, pathetically small, ordinary. I trudged on.

There was another article in that issue of *Cistercian Studies*, bubbling with its own graces, perhaps more accessible than martyrdom in the Algerian desert. It told of the discernment—that wonderful, sensible, patient word—going on within the Trappists and other orders to share the gifts of monastic life with the larger world. In this article, the abbot general of the Trappists, Father Bernardo Olivera, signaled a new openness, and a few groups of lay people who had established affiliations with monasteries spoke of their fledgling experiences.

A strange phenomenon was occurring. At the very time the number of Trappist vocations were declining, the outside world was hungering even more for authentic spiritual tradition, the wisdom of spiritual masters. There was a treasure trove tended to by fewer and older men and women; meanwhile the spiritually impoverished had little access to it.

It was a theme that Abbot Francis had explored in a recent book with the rather ethereal title of *Lovers of the Place*, which carried the equally woolly subtitle *Monasticism Loose in the Church*. The Mepkin abbot was holding up the monastic life, witness, and technique as a time-tested spiritual path, but saying that it had to be constantly renewed. The time may have come, the abbot averred, for monasticism to be lived not only within the cloister—as Cistercians had been doing it for nine hundred years—but by people in everyday life. Yes, Father Francis, I agreed. But how? Again, I was knocking.

I looked up from this self-addressed inquiry and found myself near the end of the road that winds around back to the Cooper River. It is here that Henry and Clare Booth Luce are buried, in the isolation afforded only to the wealthy and the poor. Their Carrara marble tombstone is set in the midst of what once was the formal gardens of their 7,000-acre hunting preserve, 3,200 acres of which they gave to the Trappists. A statue of the Blessed Virgin faithfully watches over their graves.

Clare was a much-heralded convert to Catholicism (her mentor was Bishop Fulton Sheen, whose prime time television program was an astounding success in the 1950s). Hank, although the child of Protestant missionaries to China, was more private about his religious leanings. Mepkin was their jewel, a place where world and business leaders were brought to hunt and be feted by the Luces. Two dozen staff worked year-round to keep the grounds in pristine condition and the guesthouses and main house—designed by Edward Durell Stone—in readiness for a Luce visit.

But these subtly undulating hills, the mammoth trees, and the surging tidal river all lost their magic when Clare Booth Luce's nineteen-year-old daughter, Anne Clare Brokaw, was killed in an automobile accident. Soon after, Clare gave the land and buildings for a new Trappist foundation— both a generous gift and a touching memorial to her only child, who is buried beside her. When the Abbey of Gethsemani founded Mepkin, so great was the astounding post-war embrace of monastic life that the novices were obliged to sleep in tents. Twenty-nine of them came, founders of a different kind of refuge—a number only a little larger than the retinue of those who had once worked here so a handful of the chosen might enjoy beauty and rest.

As I gazed out from a low stone wall near the Luces' graves to the ponds below, with huge bullfrogs sunning themselves on the far bank and an alligator lurking in the slimy green waters near the shore, I concluded there was no more appropriate place to pray. After all, I was on already holy ground, additionally consecrated for people of my profession by the presence of a couple canonized in American journalism and letters.

I have a propensity to pray, especially when I am confused. And confusion was certainly the order of that day. So I prayed. Such thoughts hurled heavenward when put to paper sometimes sound hollow, but they ran something like this:

Experience of God? Lord, somehow I don't think I'm going about this too well. There's something else here, something else I'm seeking. What? Help me to find it.

You've brought me through so many times before. Let me believe in you. Sometimes my faith in you is so real; I have confidence you'll guide me on the right path. Then I doubt, and nothing seems possible. Let me see you working in my life. If you are breaking me down so that something else can be built up, please be gentle with me.

Help me in my time here at Mepkin to be open to you. Help me to be a good man, not the headstrong fool that I can so easily be. Help me to be kind to my children and my wife. After all, it doesn't matter what great thoughts I have here, if I can't bring their application into daily life.

I spent the next few minutes in quiet, listening. But for me, as for most of us, prayer is a monologue; prayers are not answered merely because they have been offered. The turtles languished in the hot Carolina sun, the gnarled lump of the alligator's head remained unmoved. I trudged back toward the monastery buildings to get that notebook and talk to another monk.

It was Brother Paul, stooped by the calcium-deficient diet of his early Trappist days, arthritic, yet graced by a countenance of the smoothest, most radiant skin. Yes, there was such a thing as the "experience of God," this angelic man, now confined to a wheelchair, gently allowed as I asked one of those hollow questions.

"But don't go at it so . . . so . . . *frontally,*" he said. "God will let you experience his love, but this is never to be desired. That would be prideful. In fact, it can be harmful to approach God so adamantly. Rather, I think," he said, in a voice of tentative innocence, not that of an expert who as a monk has sought God for almost sixty years, "the whole idea is to cooperate with the little graces every day brings. God lets you know if you are pleasing him or offending him. Monks seek the supernatural, but that is rooted in the natural, in natural relationships, living within the 'School of Charity'—that phrase of Aelred of Rievaulx, which so well describes what a monastery really is about. Everybody has their own 'school'; this is ours, and we are constantly learning in it. You have yours and it will teach you. If you allow it."

But our relationship with God? I blundered on. How did we go about having one? "Oh, there is prayer and fasting and *lectio divina,* but really it comes down to some pretty simple things," the good brother said. "Honesty," he offered, his eyes sparkling. "Just that we be completely honest and forthcoming with him; that is enough. We know when we fail. The best thing is to be honest about it, right away, then pick yourself up and go on, with confidence and love, a bit more humble than before."

It didn't matter whether you were monk or non-monk, this good and beautiful creature said, nor was it important at what stage a person's spirituality seemed to be; what mattered was to quickly admit one's faults and to go on. With humility. "Great trust and confidence in God are basic," he said, with a smile of enviable surety. "Jesus loves to be trusted all out. He loves when we are honest with him about who we are and what we are doing."

As I left his room in the infirmary, I realized we had talked not so much about the experience of God, but rather the experience of life.

I stumbled through a few more interviews with willing and patient monks that afternoon. It was not until the next day that a tiny light flickered through the morning Eucharist, illuminating another path.

The Eucharist has always been at the very center of my spiritual life;

after all, this is the real presence of God in our midst, according to my religious tradition. The Eucharist's luminous afterglow is the time for lofty thoughts, for "sweet communion," grand intentions. Being seated in the choir of a Trappist monastery, surrounded by men whose lives combined centuries of holy pursuit, and sensing through their lives even more centuries of rich monastic tradition, surely compounded and magnified the moment.

But I knew this would not last. Inevitably I am uplifted by each monastic sojourn, propelled along for a few hours or days by its momentum. But just as inevitably I lose not the monastic promise, not the charism or memory, but that more immediate contact. It is not that my life falls apart; it does not. But it no longer has access to these unique nutrients, the power to continually inform and inspire my life.

That morning, as I sat in the stilled abbey church, it dawned on me that I had already gathered here the seeds for planting within that richly fertile, fragile ecosystem that is the garden of a soul. This is the way that God often works. It is called grace. It is as prevalent as the rich aroma of gardenia and magnolia at Mepkin. A person need only to inhale. Saints and the enlightened—and Brother Paul—know this.

It is harder work for the rest of us.

In the quiet of my room after mass I found my eyes fixed on words of Jean Leclercq, a wise monk-historian I was fortunate to meet some years before. Writing of the man who unwittingly gave birth to the Cistercians by directing monasticism back to its purity of purpose, Leclercq noted: "All of Bernard's teaching is concerned with the passage from 'flesh' to 'spirit' . . . to an openness of the whole of creation as a result of going beyond oneself, of surpassing that instinctive self, as yet unliberated by grace."[2]

Exactly! ". . . as yet unliberated by grace." If there were five words that summed me up, these would do quite well. I wanted to live, as I rounded the bend of late middle age and headed back to the beginning of the circle we must all complete, in the way Jan Van Deenen, a Dutch Jesuit,

[2]Jean Leclercq, Introduction to *Bernard of Clairvaux: Selected Works*, trans. G. R. Evans (New York: Paulist, 1987), 38.

had described: "Between one activity and another, there's a moment when it's possible to reenter the stream of God's life, so that in moving between activities I am still in touch with the God who is constantly speaking to all of us . . . finding God in all things."[3]

Actually, this is not so dissimilar from a monk's spiritual journey. While monks live intentional lives in a far more concentrated form, reinforced by many periods of daily prayer, reflection, reading, and communal support, theirs, too, is a continual struggle to be good and to be close to God. I have known enough monks to realize that their struggle—while on a different level and in a seemingly rarefied environment—is still human, real, and immediate.

The monks have their community, their "school of charity," in which they can test lofty thoughts and aspirations in the crucible of daily life. And, as Brother Paul had reminded me, I had mine. A home that I share with my wife and two sons, aged thirteen and eleven. The streets of Wilmington, North Carolina, where I live. The university where I teach, stores where I shop. All these were other "schools" where I might learn and practice.

The vague idea was becoming enfleshed. With regular trips to the monastery as my touchstones, I would try to take into my life whatever precious grains of monastic wisdom I gleaned during each visit. I loved the idea. I loved its quiet challenge.

But what became increasingly troubling once the initial bliss wore off, which it did by mid-morning, was that I also knew myself. I knew how the best intentions with which I drove out through the monastery gate simply evaporated when confronted by the first car poking along in front of this terribly impatient man, or by an insistent son demanding I take him to buy yet another CD whose sound I did not yearn to hear. Bills, a balky transmission, poison ivy, unreturned phone calls, criticism, the tone of my wife's voice—the multiple annoyances of life.

I am a Catholic born to the old ways of certainty, rigidity, and ritual observance who struggled to live the excitement and promise of the new era

[3]George M. Anderson, "A Ministry of Presence: An Interview with Jan Van Deenen," *America*, 14 December 1996, 14.

demarcated by Vatican II, which called for an entirely different kind of spirituality and a constantly transforming faith, both of one's self and the world. I was a man who prided himself on walking the tightrope that freelance writing required, but in reality—which I would only admit to God—I was far more faithless than confident about God's place in my life.

The monastic life held, if not answers, at least ways to deal with such things—neither by total suppression or avoidance, nor armed with head-on, twentieth-century prioritizing, analysis, and the superficial emotional honesty currently in fashion. There was a subtlety to the monastic life I had always admired, a certain finesse, at once confrontational and yet detached, at once demanding and compassionate. I would try to achieve that delicate balance. During my monastic sojourns—and now I was happy I had reason to return regularly to Mepkin—I would try to be reflective and honest about myself and my life. I would place myself in the presence of God in the midst of these monks, and ask for his guidance and strength to follow me when I left. I would allow the readings and liturgy in the abbey church, my private reading in my room, my thoughts as I walked about the monastery grounds to speak to me in the circumstances of my life. I might even talk to a monk or two about their lives—and mine.

And, with each visit—yes, this was it!—I would try to take a few thoughts back with me and put them into play in my life. For time spent at a monastery inevitably presents a rich outlay of new possibilities—ideas, insights, tactics. Who doesn't come away with them? There is a certain spiritual overload that novice seekers such as myself experience. Like starving people passing before a table heavy with sumptuous foods, we cannot resist loading ourselves with far more helpings than it is possible or healthy to consume. While I feasted at the monastery table, I was always hungry soon afterwards. This time, I decided, I would not monitor myself while at the table. But when I came to the end of each monastic stay, I promised to look down at my hopelessly heaped-over mental tray to choose one or two thoughts or resolutions for further, focused attention. Then I would try to apply them in my life. In that way, I would be incorporating monasticism into my life, in small, digestible pieces.

I asked a silent forgiveness of Brother Edward for my meal metaphor. Father Christian's elegant and holy profession of such profound love of the enemy, of those who hate you so much they might (and, in his case, did) kill you, was reinforced by the words of St. Benedict: "For we believe that the divine presence is everywhere and the eyes of the Lord gaze upon the good and the bad in every place."[4] Loving my enemies. Resolution one. What a better place to begin my purification? I would not have to face a terrorist ready to slit my throat; but to fully appreciate that divine gaze resting upon both the good and bad, to love those who cared for me and those who do not, *that* was a substantial spiritual undertaking until my next visit.

And Brother Paul: honesty in human relationships, recognizing failings quickly and going on, continuing education in the school of charity. Resolution two. Yes; I had my own "school" to go back to so that I might live out what I had idealized in these monks.

When I phoned home to tell my wife I would be returning the next day, her voice was crackling with irritation. "Stressed" was the word she used. The boys had been acting up. The car was having problems, the dog had fleas. Good, I said under my breath. My "school of charity" awaited me. And besides, the next week we were to go on our first extended vacation as a family. Moses and Antony trekked into the deserts of the Middle East; the Wilkes family, via Delta Airlines and a Hertz rental car, would venture into the desert of the American Southwest. And where might the enemy lurk, so that I might love him?

The day or two after a monastery visit are often like a honeymoon; benevolence and patience, a sense of detachment from immediate cares and irritations, hold me in a gentle embrace. I was conscious of my resolution to live in love and peace within my own community—my family—but it was not really that difficult. Something seemed to filter the decibels of my sons' indignant voices. What were they fighting about, anyhow? That my wife had laced a meal with garlic the night before—the memory of which lingered on—seemed not to warrant comment.

[4] *The Rule of St. Benedict*, ed. Thomas Fry (Collegeville, Minn.: Liturgical Press, 1981), ch. 19, 1.

When I drove to a nearby shopping center and waited for someone to pull out so that I might park, another car darted in front of me. I found another space, and had to walk an additional thirty yards or so. What difference did it make? A woman was hoarding two photocopy machines at Office Depot, using neither of them efficiently. I could see her in a new way, almost as if she were wearing a signboard, with big letters, easy for anyone to read: "I'm pressed for time. I am my own worst enemy. This is not going well. Everything is out of control." Instead of saying something to her in words or with that withering look I can so easily wield, I did nothing. I stood there patiently. Whatever look I did have on my face, she looked back at me—and her anxious frown turned into a weak smile. She gathered her papers from one of the machines and graciously offered it to me. A pile of papers spilled to the floor. I helped her pick them up.

It wasn't that I was approaching these everyday, somewhat banal situations with some pasty smile on my face, the "have a good day," cheap-grace school of teflon spirituality I so intensely dislike. I was considering each an opportunity for grace or undoing. It was—in a strange way—fun. Beneath it all, I'm sure that I longed for these fleeting attempts at holiness to translate into success in my work as a writer. But the blank screen of my computer had no more light than its usual pale gray pall. The phone was quiet; the mailbox held no new requests for my services.

I kept my resolutions before me—honesty and admitting mistakes; loving the enemy. I found myself scanning the horizon for more enemies to love. When two sweaty Seventh Day Adventist boys came to my door to convert me, I invited them in for a glass of ice water and told them that, while a sinner, I had a feeble faith that I was doing my best to pursue. I had brought back some eggs from Mepkin Abbey, and when I took a dozen to my children's Catholic grade school for the secretaries, I brought along another dozen for the principal, with whom I had had some serious disagreements in the past and would surely have more in the future. Again, no terrorists these, but the unwitting boys and principal would have to do until some appeared.

As our family prepared for the much-anticipated vacation, I tried hard not to lapse into the short-tempered behavior that too often characterizes the final hours and last-minute details. But gradually I could feel the inner peace seeping away. All too soon I was no longer allowing my own family to hold up their signs, to let me know what was going on inside them. What was it that my thirteen-year-old Noah did? I cannot even remember. But there I was, standing in the hallway, fists clenched, a blood-curdling howl issuing from deep in my throat.

I was ashamed of my violence, expressed so soon after I had been that fountain of virtue proffering parking places, glasses of ice water, and cartons of eggs. My son looked at me and in his eyes, I read: "Yea, monastery. Great. Just great, dad." What was wrong? What was I missing? But then I remembered that wise and wizened monk in his wheelchair. Be honest. Pick yourself up. Go on. Be honest. "I'm sorry, Noah," I said, looking at him as fellow traveler rather than impatient son. "I shouldn't holler. I'll try to do better."

His justified rage was not to be immediately assuaged, but soon enough we were once again devoted to packing for the trip instead of being engaged in one of those "I had to do this because you did that" volleys I was quite adept at perpetuating. I could fall; I would fall. But I had found a way to quickly get up.

I would like to report that the remainder of this first month saw still more threads of monastic inspiration weaving through my life, but that proved not the case.

As we traveled from the majestic Rockies to Arizona's deserts—and had a pretty wonderful vacation—memories of Mepkin grew dimmer and dimmer. It was not that I wasn't praying; it was not that I wasn't daily reminding myself of my two resolutions—even though enemies upon which to shower my love were even more elusive in the Southwest than in coastal North Carolina. And it wasn't that my reading did not produce moments of understanding and moral brio.

But even so I quickly lapsed back into an all-too-familiar self. A father who could lash out with humiliating verbal tirades, a husband whose patience was paper-thin, a tourist who could be demanding, unreasonable, and generally unlovely. My descent from monastic zenith to vacation nadir seemed to have arrived as we sat in a perfectly wonderful turn-of-the-century hotel in Ouray, Colorado, and I found myself actually weeping at the sheer ingratitude of my sons ("Another mountain; what's the big deal?" "Not turkey subs again!" "There's nothing to do!").

We went to Saturday evening mass at the local church. The priest's words about not waiting for visions and apocalyptic signs, looking instead for the miracles in everyday life, offered a much-needed dose of hope. But like a solar panel turned away from the sun, I was losing the power to regenerate. All my intentionality was ultimately not working. My two-resolution approach to life had no grace about it. I was going about this all wrong. No six-cylinder car runs well on two cylinders, no matter how superbly they were performing. And mine were not performing that well at all.

I knew what I needed.

In Sedona, Arizona, one morning not long after, I arose and headed to the magnificent Chapel of the Holy Cross built into the red rocks on the outskirts of the city. I wanted desperately to pray, to be close to God, to rekindle the fire that I felt so strongly at Mepkin. I reached the top of the winding road that leads to the chapel—and there it stood before me in all its breathtaking beauty, suspended in space and time, glass windows overlooking the valley whose jutting rocks changed colors with each incremental movement of the rising sun. I approached the building. I entered. I knelt. I first took in nature's splendor, then bowed my head. I was ready to reclaim the monastic vision.

A crashing sound at the front of the chapel pierced that hopeful moment. My head jerked up. The custodian was cleaning out the votive-candle holders, roughly tossing the spent glass cups into a cardboard box. It was hardly that noisy, but in the quiet of that place it was nothing less than a din.

Like a man being suddenly pitched overboard, I grabbed for the last bight of line my mind's eye remembered. The Saturday night sermon.

Lord, speak to me in everyday things. Let me see little miracles even as I foolishly want the great. The moments of recognition will occur, whether or not they fit into my neat categories. I am so stupid. Nuance, Lord, give me nuance. Lord, finesse.

I got up, lit one of the fresh votive candles sown by my brother the custodian, went back down the mountain and into my life.

JULY

Faith

The Core of Our Lives

The civilized world fell away quickly as this traveler sped over the Cape Fear Bridge at Wilmington, leaving behind the languorous waterfront and our city's very own battleship, USS *North Carolina*, mighty and ominous though beached in a sheltered inlet and guarded by a benevolent alligator named Charlie. The countryside was black on this moonless night, only to be broken by the gleam of Myrtle Beach, a good-natured Sodom and Gomorrah an hour south. But even here light was muted, neon at rest; no

ʾour to expend much effort to lure the few passersby to
beach toys, video poker games, or Dolly Parton.

ʾer interruptions along this otherwise stark and entirely
_ were the signs extolling the virtues of the many communi-
..nat have risen up out of these stands of scrub pine and tidal swamp-
lands to offer a perfect life. "After this, heaven won't be much of an
adjustment," one promises. Gates to keep away the unwanted, the first tee
nearby, guaranteed picturesque sunsets—what more could a soul desire?

I love this journey, for it is my silent passage to another land. Although
I am traveling on the earth's surface I am almost like a submarine, plunging
below the surface at one point and, except when the mental periscope is
extended, arriving at my destination having traveled in a nether world. I
leave one universe and, after a three-hour drive, arrive in another, completely different.

I drive this route at strange hours, usually dictated by the fitful nights I
spend before I go to Mepkin, or by—as on this morning—a more specific
reason. I didn't exactly know why, but I wanted to be at the monastery
when the monks began their day. After a rather aborted attempt to take
monasticism into my life, I wanted to start afresh. There was no better way
than to align myself with these men in the most basic way. Perhaps that
would help.

During my trip that July morning, I found my mind going back to the
consternation of another pilgrim, who also tried to unlock the mysteries of
a life with God through his monastic experience. His dilemma was expressed in a meditation, one that became so familiar to me over the years
since I first read it that I could almost recite it by heart:

> My Lord God, I have no idea where I am going. I do not see the
> road ahead of me. I cannot know for certain where it will end. Nor
> do I really know myself, and the fact that I think that I am follow-
> ing your will does not mean that I am actually doing so. But I
> believe that the desire to please you does in fact please you. And
> I hope I have that desire in all that I am doing. I hope that I will
> never do anything apart from that desire. And I know that if I do

this you will lead me by the right road, though I may know nothing about it. Therefore I will trust you always though I may seem to be lost and in the shadow of death. I will not fear, for you are ever with me, and you will never leave me to face my perils alone.[1]

Thomas Merton's words always consoled me. If one of the great spiritual masters of our time didn't know where he was going, I felt a bit better about my own difficulties reading divine roadsigns. I had always found great hope in Merton's words: the desire to know and please God was sufficient unto the day. I might not know the way to God, but the desire—yes, I could at least claim the desire to know him and his will for my life.

Could I not call that desire by another name? For this was what I knew I desperately needed as I continued my visits to Mepkin. Was Merton not talking about faith?

In the foggy gloom of a summer's night, Mepkin lay ahead, marked by a simple gate and a stark, somewhat ungainly "M" formed of what looked to be narrow steel girders and bisected by a cross of the same industrial material. Seven miles outside of Moncks (no connection) Corner, South Carolina, I turned off Dr. Evans Road and onto the long boulevard. My headlights provided the only illumination. A half mile later, as I approached the cloistered area, the brightly lit abbey church came into view. That high, circular window, which affords so restricted a view of the world, proved to be but one source for the abundance of radiant light generated from within this place—piercing, defying, the night.

It was almost as if I had held my breath for the entire trip. I could breathe easier now.

The monastic day begins with the community gathering for vigils, the first prayers of the day. At Mepkin this takes place at 3:20 A.M. and, although the hour may vary slightly, the practice is fairly uniform throughout the monastic world. It is an hour when fatigue and docility conspire to open hearts and minds to the murmuring of God and of each person's

[1]Thomas Merton, _Thoughts in Solitude_ (New York: Farrar, Straus & Giroux, 1956), 83.

soul. The bright light of day had not yet dawned; as yet there were no demands. The seemingly timeless dark of night reached out to anyone so bold as to rise and enter it—those bold enough to trust it. Wisely appointed by the monastic fathers and mothers while responding to the psalmist's admonition to arise during the night and give praise to God, it is an hour at which we have not yet fully put on our pretenses and defenses, the mental armor we think this life requires. It is an hour of this desire called faith, as much as anything else. What else could regularly raise humans out of bed in the middle of the night?

In the cloistered area I could see tiny dots form, then emerge from the darkness as the monks slowly made their way to the church. Most were dressed in a hooded white choir robe. It is a curious garment, shaped somewhat like a cross, with long, billowing sleeves extending nearly to the floor, making it impractical for anything but prayer. There is the symbolism of the crucified Christ, of course, but the choir robe also serves as a daily reminder of the monk's own death; in it, he will be buried.

While the *Rule of St. Benedict* admonishes the monks to cultivate silence at all times, at this hour they are additionally enfolded by the monastic "great silence," which actually comprises half their day. It lasts from the end of compline, about 8:00 P.M., until after mass the next morning, about 8:15 A.M. From those who looked up and saw me, there was no word of welcome. They needed not. A nod, a small smile said enough. They knew; I knew.

Once inside the church, the monks bowed low to the altar, blessed themselves with holy water from the font, and proceeded to their usual (though not formally assigned) places. As they waited, some of them stood facing the front of the church, eyes closed or open. Others were seated, hands resting on their laps. Silence reigned and the soft lights in the ceiling cast a warm, amber glow over the assembled monks; a quiet expectancy gently filled the air.

At the sound of the abbot's knuckles rapping once—audibly but not assaultingly—on the paneling of his choir stall, each day and without exception they bow and utter one of the earliest mantras of prayer to be culled from the psalms: "O Lord, open my lips, and my mouth shall declare your praise." It is an unvarnished, urgent plea; even these, pledged to a life of prayer far removed from the swirling tides of the world, need succor and inspiration at the dawning of their day. The first recitation of the psalms begins, those ancient prayer-poems with which monks will punctuate the entire day.

At Mepkin and in many monasteries, the psalms are divided into roughly equal segments—Week "A" and Week "B"—so that every two weeks all 150 psalms are recited. During vigils, at which a greater number of psalms will be prayed than at any of the other hours, some of the psalms are sung responsorially, each choir side alternating verses in plainchant. Other psalms are read by an appointed member of the community. Some psalms are recited while seated, others while standing. Among its many other attributes, monastic life is a study in balance. Bland diet, rigid schedule, limited movement, poverty, chastity, obedience, stability—yes, these are pathways to insight and union with God. Unnecessary tedium is not considered a virtue.

There is a supersensible immanence about the psalms, these prayers of praise and lament, consolation and desolation. I am always struck by the fact that observant Jews throughout the world are reciting them along with Christians—the Orthodox Jew and the monk, both dedicated to their ancient summons, an unwitting alliance that conspires to make the psalms perhaps the most universal prayer of humanity.

Especially as they are prayed by alternate sides of a monastic assembly there is a perception of sending good thoughts and inspiration across the wide aisle, then in silence receiving the same from the brethren opposite you. The plainchant, so austere and unadorned, allows for deep meditation and yet has the airiness of a simple tune, easily learned by even the musically-challenged and adaptable to any grouping of words. The tone is in the middle range, only a slight rise or drop at the end of the line affording its punctuation.

Many people—myself among them—have at times wondered why the psalms are such an integral part of the monastic day. We question whether these words, venerable and poetic though they may be, can aptly address our postmodern, post-Christian, post-doctrinal selves. It is a question, I have discovered, usually answered not by reason, but by time. For as spiritual masters have found and conveyed down through the centuries, the magical power of the psalms finds its way into crevices unreachable by intellects far more deft than mine. Pope Pius X called the psalms the "voice of the church," and the good Anthanasius—theologian and the biographer of the first monk, Antony—aptly summed them up when he wrote, "The psalms seem to me to be like a mirror, in which the person using them can see himself, and the stirrings of his own heart; he can recite them against the background of his own emotions." It is the monks' belief that the psalms ponder and proclaim God's action as both history and their lives unfold.

As the recitation of the psalms began, I looked up to see who besides myself was holding up this mirror. There were some two dozen of them, old men mostly, a good number bent—with age perhaps, or perhaps by the meager diets of pre-Vatican II Trappist life, or simply by so often bowing their heads in prayer and not fully straightening up when they were not. There were a few young men among them—"younger" meaning anyone from thirty to sixty-five—most, by comparison, ramrod straight, of the generation who entered too late to have been burnt by the last tongues of Armand de Rance's scorching flame. The more stooped the posture, the thinking then went, the holier the monk.

Three of the younger men scattered among them wore pale gray half-tunics that marked them as observers. After tasting monastic life for a month or two and making a valuable contribution with their strength and fresh-faced presence, they would be gone.

For those gathered—the permanent and the transient—inclined over the tall books of oversized type before them, this morning marked but one of their hundreds, thousands, perhaps even tens of thousands of such times, coming before God to be succored and prodded by the words of the psalms.

> *Give ear to my prayer, O God;*
> *and hide not thyself from my supplication!*

Attend to me, and answer me;
I am overcome by my trouble . . .

My heart is stricken within me,
death's terror is on me,
trembling and fear fall upon me
and horror overwhelms me . . .

Cast your burden on the Lord
and he will sustain you . . .

The words resounded dully in the abbey church, wafted upon the still air by voices thick with the memory of night. The windows above were black—no outlet there, no hint of inspiration, no blue sky at this hour. The monks were in this together, with only each other, no easy escape, these words, and the ineffable Other.

I could hardly gauge the state of my comrades' emotions that sultry morning, but through the prism of my own, the cry to heaven of the Fifty-Fifth Psalm was at once a whimper of terror and a plea for deliverance from earthly tribulations. It was a summons to have faith—the bedrock of a spiritual life, that most difficult of perspectives. It was an invitation to lay aside plots and plans, to trust in God and to somehow know that, whatever the day held, a divine hand was at work.

We who visit monasteries bring our laundry list of worries. Celibate monks living communally and praying continually turn out to have similar lists. While theirs certainly preclude some of our worldly worries, they too pay electric bills, wait for the results of a thyroid test, and, at Mepkin in these days, wonder whether their proposed new building program, encompassing a new infirmary and library, is God's will or man's folly. But if there is one specific and abiding prayer often in their hearts and occasionally on their lips, it is for new vocations; it is a prayer that the average age of the Mepkin Trappists, now sixty-nine, would rise no more, as it does each day. Someone was watching and would tend to all matters that needed tending, the words of the psalm promised. They—I—needed only have faith.

Faith. It is a theme so ingrained in monastic life—faith that God is with them, that their temporal needs will be met, that they are not fools tucked away in this place for no good reason, that their attempts at goodness are indeed worthy in the eyes of their creator. Faith in faith—that they will not lose that which undergirds everything they do.

So it was faith that was churning around in my mind as, about 4:00 A.M., I began a walk after vigils. Taken as much to prevent me from falling asleep as to invite contemplation, morning walks at Mepkin were often part of my routine during monastic stays. Properly, the monks are to return to their cells for *lectio divina*—to read Scripture, pray, meditate. I found, at this hour, I'd better stay on my feet.

Faith is surely one of the most difficult virtues for us to understand and practice in the world. At least it is for me. Having faith in God somehow implies a certain slackness or weakness, a lack of control, a giving over of that preciously guarded power of our own will, which once we wrested from our parents and which we so firmly assert many times each day just to survive. Faith proscribes a certain free-fall in life, believing that God will indeed guide us to the right people and places, that he will not test us beyond our ability to endure; that God will take care of our needs—and here is the hardest part—in his own time and fashion.

The opposite of faith is control. All of us feel so much more comfortable when we are seemingly in charge of our destiny. The results may not always be pleasing, but simply saying "I am in control" conveys a certain mastery. This I-centered approach to spirituality, physical healing, and mental wellness is very much in vogue today and little surprise. Who would not be tempted by its promises? On talk shows we hear its prophets; we read of miraculous transformations in best-selling books. If only we take charge of ourselves, focus our inner powers, nothing is impossible. Faith in God has a slightly old-fashioned sound to it in today's marketplace of ideas.

Into the black, moonless night I walked slowly and carefully along the asphalt roadway leading from the cloistered buildings to the main road of the old plantation, a broad lane elegantly lined with side buoys of live oaks. As an aid to both visitor and monk alike, tiny lights have been spaced along the roadway and the paths branching off toward the monastery buildings and guest cottages, lest our feet go astray.

But as I tried to make my way, I found the lights disorienting. They formed strange patterns, not a clearly marked path. The glare of the lights—few watts that they were—seemed to blind me, their halos overlapping into luminescent fields. I was having great difficulty making a trip that, in daylight, I had made easily many times before. My step slowed. I became increasingly tentative, worried that I would fall into the ditch that runs along some portions of the road.

Advancing hesitantly, I could see up ahead that the lights soon ended; I would have to find the rest of the way to the main boulevard without their assistance. Now I was even more concerned. As unreliable a guide as they had proved to be—to my eyes at least—they were *something*. At least they had given me the impression that I knew where I was and where I was going.

I reached the last light. My heart was pounding as I took the next few steps. And then a remarkable thing happened.

It was not a moonless night at all. A dull light, coming from an imperceptible source, shone upon the roadway just enough for me to see where my next step should be. I could not see far ahead, nor discern any pattern for a potential path—as I had theoretically been able to do with the tiny, deluding lights moments before. But this omniscient glow, whatever its source, was ample for the moment—provided I asked no more of it than guidance for the next step. And after all, how many steps was I taking at once? One. Then another. And another. I reached the main road and turned right. The light was with me, step by step.

It was an imperfect metaphor for the practice of faith, to be sure, but as that unseen light guided my uncertain way in the middle of the night, so too, I realized, had God surely informed my life. Sometimes I was able to articulate my need for faith, placing myself in the presence of God and asking for guidance—whether it be for help with writing I was working on, a way to deal with a difficult situation or person in my life, or in those days when a hermit madly in love with a woman was simultaneously trying so desperately to fall in love with life as a Trappist monk. But sometimes—more often—faith was little more than the low moan deep within my soul that cried out my aching need to reconnect somehow to the source of goodness and holiness and wisdom—God. In those times, I sensed the need for faith not because I comfortably had it, but because I so thoroughly lacked it.

I could now see it did not matter whether my faith was articulated or not; God was there, undoubtedly smiling at my attempts to control my destiny, taking me places I did not choose to go, seeing my tribulations and showering me with blessings in abundance. I didn't need to review the years of my life to illustrate my various seasons of faith and faithlessness; I only needed to go back over the past few days to see that the roller coaster of human emotions and life events had conspired to make faith's gentle presence assured or absent.

Monday morning prayers at home saw me filled with hope and optimism after encountering the promise of both the Psalmist and the New Testament that God was with those who sought his guidance and protection. Twenty-four hours later—and after one more phone call from a curt editor rejecting my last best idea for a magazine article—I was once again awash in self-pity and apprehension. Wednesday my hope was renewed by a simple act of generosity from Noah, helping his brother Daniel with his homework; by Thursday I was looking upon my children as uncharitable pagans. Friday, like the stock market on a jittery day, my spiritual Dow Jones fluctuated wildly. Pretty ordinary things; pretty bumpy ride. What sad testimony to a life of allegedly unswerving faith.

I have always been a seeker after faith, and throughout my life monasteries have been the setting for this search. But I realized that, at this point in my allotted days on the good but busy earth, I needed the monastery ever more to help me in this pursuit. As a husband and now a father, the stakes had been raised. So much was required of me; I wanted to reach out and lay claim on a sure and certain faith. "Yes! Now I have it. I can go on."

I. I. I. That word; that horribly limiting word.

The times when I least depended on God and most stubbornly looked to myself as the master of my destiny, in things both small and great— these were the hollowest, unhappiest days of my life. I had been through dark nights of the soul, withering depression, hopelessness where even the suggestion of light ahead was little more than a cruel joke. Looking back I could see that even in those times, when I could not even say the word "faith," I needed only to trust that God was present, despite being surrounded by what seemed abundant evidence to the contrary.

The God I'm most familiar with—the God of the Judeo–Christian tradition—is not a fool and is not foolish. He made pacts with his various peoples to help them understand his nature and to invite their response to him. First, he promised the Israelites, "I shall be your God, and you shall be my people"; later, to all tribes and nations came the assurance that "I am with you, even to the end of time." There was the imperative to do God's will, but all this really required was simply to live his ways. Those ways would bring human beings to their ultimate fulfillment, for they would then be in union with God, fully realizing the truth of the divine image in which they had been made. At the very foundation of such a life was faith. Faith was the crucial element, a plea for assistance—but a plea that was guaranteed an answer.

Gone were the days when humankind tried to placate unpleasable, erratic, avenging gods with sacrifice: crops, livestock, precious metals, virgins, sons. God instead revealed himself as compassionate and loving, concerned about the fate of those he brought into existence. He desired sacrifice, not of material, but of spiritual things—sacrifices of praise, of living for something more than self-gratification. Burnt offerings produced ashes, not fuller souls or a better world.

Benedict and Bernard saw this clearly. Their desire had not been to make martyrs, but—though such modern-day jargon would have been incomprehensible to them—self-actualized, happy individuals.

Implicit in God's revelation of his nature was an understanding of the need for mutual trust—that each party would provide what the other required. There was never the promise that life would necessarily be easy or charted, only that it would be rich with meaning. The dance of humans and God would go on harmoniously if God provided the music, while we were free to create our own choreography. For faith in God is at the core of a life of meaning, an openness to guidance, confidence in a power far beyond any that we might conjure up—true freedom. Faith is the understanding that God wants to love and be loved.

Is God not a worthy place for my trust, which is faith by still another name? A trust born of experience? Why is this so hard to say—Yes, Lord, I believe—and to say no more? I have been brought to my knees with this question so many times in my life, coming up short against a basic truth of our spiritual selves: Where else was I to turn, if not to God? Is confidence too arrogant a way to speak of faith? I think not. For confidence in God summons divine power to work in my life. Confidence, trust, faith—these are relational terms. Without them, how is God to begin to work, to guide my life, to be invited to share in my daily existence? For if I do not possess faith, I put God in the role of some sort of erratic shaman, who arbitrarily forces his will upon my own.

It comes to this for all of us: If we believe in God—a God who created us, and who has revealed himself as a God who longs for us to know him, to be happy, to make this world a better place for ourselves and for others—then trusting in his wisdom and desires for us, rather than relying merely on our own abilities and intuitions, makes enormous sense. Faith calls upon us to assume a new, interactive role, that of co-creators of a continuously unfolding universe.

Faith, at once transcendent and yet immediate and practical, is something instinctive to the human condition. Without faith, we realize we are only as strong as our strongest moment, as wise as our wisest judgment. What can redeem us from distress, abandonment, weariness, scorn? Everyone of us has learned many times over how hamstrung we are if we rely only on our limited capacities.

What a dismal life I would have had if I were its sole architect. For without faith, there is no appetite for learning, no thirst for adventure. We all pretend to rule our own destinies; it never happens anyhow. Surely, our native abilities and intuitions, our preferences and desires, have their place, for faith is not spineless or capricious or dull-brained. But without the divine interplay that faith implies, we find ourselves living life with clenched fists rather than open hands.

Years ago a Trappist monk told me that he felt each member of the community should have the words "Faith not feeling" tattooed on his forehead. He thought they all needed a constant reminder that if life with God were ruled or judged by our ever-fluctuating emotional barometers, no one in monastic life would or could survive. Many of us see evidence or "fruits" of faith as we look back and shake our heads, realizing that indeed God was with us through our darkest hours. But beyond—or *before* that—faith is its own reward. Faith imparts a certain assurance, shaky though it may be at times when there is no glow to illuminate our path. Trust in a great power and good friend. And again, adventure. Who knows what God holds in store for us?

I like the straightforward way the Presbyterian pastor Frederick Buechner said it: "Faith is the word that describes the direction our feet start moving when we find we are loved. Faith is stepping out into the unknown with nothing to guide us but a hand just beyond our grasp."[2] Faith pierces the darkness, not only around us, but within us, the darkness in the hidden recesses of our souls that we fear hides things so unlovely they must be kept from view.

I stopped for a moment and let the darkness enfold me. The cool night air seemed so strangely alive, although there were yet no sounds of nature awakening to a new day, no shapes, no shadows. Beyond my immediate vision were deer and beetles and live oaks, real yet unseen. I did not need to move to find them; I simply had to wait there, trusting that the spin of my planet and the face of the sun would reveal them once again.

The darkness afforded its own vision, offered its own fullness. As St.

[2]Frederick Buechner, *The Magnificent Defeat* (New York: Seabury Press, 1966), 99.

Augustine said, "You do not yet see what you long for, but the very act of desiring prepares you, so that when he comes you may see and be utterly satisfied."³ Using an analogy more proper to his time, Augustine speaks of our desire for faith as a wineskin; "By stretching it, therefore, you increase the capacity of the sack. . . . Simply by making us wait he increases our desire, which in turn enlarges the capacity of our soul, making it able to receive what is to be given to us."⁴ Finally, the good bishop of Hippo asks a question to which we all know the answer: "If he wishes to fill you with honey and you are full of sour wine, where is the honey to go?"⁵

The darkness, while revealing nothing, seemed to possess everything. My view was not limited by light or vision; instead it was boundless, free to explore over any horizon, for no horizon limits the darkness. John of the Cross reached out: "Oh, night that guided me. Oh, night more lovely than the dawn. Oh, night that joined beloved with lover. Lover transformed in the Beloved."⁶

Perhaps our greatest barrier to this openness, this availability called faith, is not doubt. It is simply that we think ourselves too ordinary to aspire to such a vaunted virtue. Too ordinary to understand darkness as holiness. We cannot imagine our doubt as its own sacrificial offering, our desire as sufficient. *Faith*—it is a word we think must be spoken in hushed terms, reserved only for the holy, the extraordinary. Certainly it is not for us. So we try to flee from the smallness of our lives, or adorn ourselves in the trappings of our abilities, our state in life, our possessions, or in what differentiates us from others. We put faith aside as unneeded, impractical, too fancy an ideal.

For we are well aware that as faith will teach us, it will also exact its due. Faith asks that each of our souls be stripped bare—as are those of these monks in their daily cycle of prayer, work, and self-reflection—so as

³Augustine of Hippo, Tractates on the First Letter of John, quoted in *The Liturgy of the Hours* (New York: Catholic Book Publishing, 1975), vol. III, 220. All subsequent references to the breviary are taken from this edition, with reference given to volume and page number.
⁴Ibid.
⁵Ibid., 221.
⁶John of the Cross, *Dark Night of the Soul*, trans. E. Allison Peer (Garden City, N.Y.: Doubleday, 1959), 34.

to present ourselves before our God without the trappings or conceits, titles or goods. It asks of us that we present our deepest selves, unprotected by any of the overlays with which the world has camouflaged us.

Try though we might to fight such a stark rendition of our humanity, it is, finally, who we really are. And that deepest self, when we can touch it, is not to be feared—for it is aflame with virtue, overflowing with wonderful talent and ingenuity and with goodness. It is the best of us; after all, it is closest to the place where the God who made us dwells. And, if we think about it for just an instant, if we honestly present that to God, what will he make of us? If we are still, coming forth in faith and with trust and confidence, the answer each of us must eventually hear is pure music. It is truly us. The night shrinks from the power of light.

Might we not turn the question "why have faith?" around and ask instead: "Why not?"

In the company of such noble voyagers as Trappist monks, participating in a prayer regimen as precisely timed as the time checks from Greenwich, it is certainly easier for me to engender a life of faith than it is out in the world. But the very regularity with which the monks raise heart, mind, and self to God underscores that they are not the superhumans we would make them out to be. The midday invocation of the abbot at the short prayers of terce that day—"Keep watch over your heart, for it is the wellspring of your being"—aptly reminded me of this.

We outside the walls may think the monks have some special dispensation from the nagging doubts we all suffer in our spiritual pursuits. But if we look at the structure of the monastic day it is almost embarrassing how often the monks remind themselves of their need of God's presence. In fact, one of the most common bits of monastic wisdom allows that if those who choose monastic life were actually that good in the first place, they wouldn't need such a strict structure. The monks gather to give praise to God at the offices of vigils, lauds, prime, terce, sext, none, vespers, and compline—the canonical "hours" of the monastic day. This is a fulsome acknowledgment of God, unquestionably reverence; but equally it can be looked upon as a sign of their own *lack* of faith. They—even they—need to be reminded of their human weakness, how their best intentions must be constantly reviewed and renewed. For them, seven times a day.

And we wonder why God slips away from us?

Monks don't "get" faith any more than we do, as if it were some kind of implanted pump, once beneath the skin forever releasing its programmed dosage. What is painful for all of us to acknowledge is that the life of faith is a pathetically uneven adventure, with great moments of surety followed by doubt that paralyzes our very ability to think, or hope, or dream. Sometimes, we do wonder if the sun will rise the next day.

If we are to make and keep a divine connection, if we are to strip ourselves bare in faith with the assurance that a sheltering, guiding presence will tend to and shape the essence that is our deepest and best self, we—along with the monks—must continually stake our claim to faith, reaching out when it eludes, embracing it tenderly when it comes near. If our lives are crammed with noise and activity; if our psyches are so well defended and protected; if our reading is mind-numbing, banal, and crass; if our acquaintances chase aspirations rising only to the venal, worldly, and transitory—what can any of us expect?

As the monks do, we must tolerate the ordinary, the unsure, all the while handing over in faith that which we know in our hearts we cannot control. Faith is rarely if ever a peak encounter, the experience of the God we seek. I have never had one of those seismic moments. Monks don't dwell on such things. That experience lies beyond a door. Faith opens that door and allows entry into a place where God lives, where God then is present to us in a peacefulness that does indeed pass all understanding.

Two mornings later, at home, I suddenly sat bolt upright in bed. My mouth was dry; a ring of perspiration bathed my neck, my pajama shirt was soaked. It was 5:00 A.M., well past the hour when monks awake to praise their God, well before the hour most of us arise to face our lives; a preconscious hour of terror, misgiving, panic. Demon time. A time when all of us need faith badly; a time that faith is a hollow word, little more than a foolish promise.

My list of agonies ranged wide. Our house in another state was unsold after three years; my son Daniel needed $4,000 worth of braces for his teeth; the second car, vintage 1986, was sputtering; my chronically balky back was hurting; and what was that new pain in my chest? Writer? Me? The litany went on, like a long list rapidly scrolling by on a computer screen, my mental hand frozen on the mouse.

Faith.

I softly descended the stairs in the darkness and, arriving in the small room I use as an office, flicked on the light. "God, I can't do this. I can't do this alone. Where are you?" The tone of my interior monologue was completely rational, but there was a shriek of terror behind each syllable.

Faith.

I try to begin each day reading from the breviary, the order for daily prayer and reflection of the Catholic Church, but the words of St. Augustine in that morning's offering were distant and clouded; dense thoughts, impossible dreams. From the book of Hosea, a voice mumbled from the pages about thorns and walls and false gods. No help.

Faith.

My eyes keep watch for your saving help.
Awaiting the word that will justify me.

Words from the psalms, words I had heard before in the hushed abbey church. Words staring at me from the page. Flat words. Words without inflection.

Faith.

I looked up at the crucifix over my desk. The torso is carved from a tree limb, thin offshoots forming arms thrust out, grasping for help that appears beyond their reach. It was fashioned by a man I know in what used to be Czechoslovakia, at a time when his own life was in shambles, the government hounding him, his family in danger.

ith.

he noise upstairs was Noah's feet hitting the floor. It was time to
my wife make lunches and get breakfast. Life must go on.

Faith.

I felt no great transfusion of grace that morning; nothing of the sort.
As I desperately searched for words to calm me, to somehow make sense
out of what then appeared to be a life out of control, I realized that the
effort itself was as much an act of faith as I could muster. By muddling
through words that did not at first speak to the circumstances of my life, I
had at least tried to open myself to the psalmist's plea. My hands in North
Carolina had reached heavenward as had his on a desert plain, like the bare
twigs of those crucified arms above my desk.

Did I feel better? Not really. Could I recall my monastic ruminations
on faith? No. Were any of my problems solved? No; in fact that morning's
mail brought a staggering bill I hadn't anticipated. Stabilized was all I
could claim. Calmed. Somewhat. I was not going to fall further. My eyes
would keep watch; I would await a word—that was about all I could say.
But those few lines from the psalmist had mercifully eased my hand off the
mouse; at least there would be no more dizzying scrolling. Perhaps it was a
glimmer of what faith is, as faint—but as real—as the barely perceptible
hint of a soft breeze that whispers off the Cooper River as the sun de-
scends after a day of blistering dominance. No howling wind, no tongues
of fire.

In the days ahead events conspired to teach me more about faith—as
events always do if we are open to them. Oddly enough, the obituary of
a man who had hardly concentrated on the elements of a Christian life
provided a fitting way to see how faith can be understood and then lived.
Viktor Frankl, a Jewish psychiatrist and philosopher who had been a prisoner in a German concentration camp, concluded that everything—save
one thing—could be taken from us. When all choices were denied, all
options closed off, in reality one thing remained: "the ability to choose
one's attitude in any given set of circumstances."[7] Frankl could see that the

[7]*New York Times*, 4 September 1997 (National edition), A15.

horrors and dehumanization and random, senseless murder in a concentration camp caused prisoners to lapse into apathy and a kind of emotional death if they lost that connection with their inner selves. In essence, if they felt all was lost and no human action of theirs made any difference—even if it was something as simple as giving another prisoner a piece of string to hold up a pair of sagging trousers—they no longer could function as human beings themselves.

Frankl was calling faith by another name. For faith is that "attitude," that approach to one's life that flies in the face of the feeling of emptiness or meaninglessness or adversity. Each day, the prisoner chose to have faith or not, calling it by different names, with or without a conscious religious or spiritual framework. Those who held on to this crucial shred of their own beings were searching—as Frankl concluded—for meaning in the midst of that with which life had presented them. Those who lost faith stopped bathing and eating; they would lie about listlessly, awaiting death. Not all who kept faith survived, but each day they lived, they knew they had triumphed in keeping alive that tiny flame within them. The mere act of faith was its own reward. As Frankl eventually concluded, human behavior was driven by the need to find meaning and purpose—regardless of the circumstances.

So it is with faith. Many things can be taken from us, but faith ultimately cannot. Faith is present deep within us and needs only be beckoned to equip us with that certain "attitude" of living. No, most of us have not faced the horrors of a concentration camp, yet each life has circumstances that conspire to shatter our resolve, mock our confidence, cause us to feel at the bottom of a deep pit or within a labyrinth from which there is no escape. It is only through faith that we can see that the smallest of our actions—even the hardly perceptible inclination of our minds—restates our human dignity, and reestablishes our tie with our powerful and loving God.

In order to understand more clearly the benefits of faith all we need do is to look back over our lives, to see that indeed the worst times—those terrible times when all seemed lost and we were tempted to lose faith in God—prepared us for the best, for the moments when those sudden, unsolicited turns in the road exposed us to new vistas that our careful planning would never have presented. It is this attitude—this faith—that remains when all else falls away. It does so in monastic or married or single life, school or business life, when all seems foolish and fruitless and hopelessly wrong. In the dark nights of the soul that any spiritual seeker must endure, faith has no reason and brings no solace. It feels hollow. It feels achingly ordinary. But this is the true moment of the triumph of faith. It is a statement of the mystical dualism of our lives: I am, Thou art. And this bond between I and Thou will never be broken. Neither can really abandon the other and abide.

Viktor Frankl's insights had risen up from the pages of the *New York Times*. Later in the month another searing lesson about the practice of faith was at hand as I walked into a room in our local hospital to face a woman I had visited a number of times before, now here for a fifth round of chemotherapy. A rosary, prayer book, and an inspirational book crowded her bedside table. A tasteful terry-cloth turban covered her balding head, but she was alert, her makeup already applied at this early hour. Surely this was a woman with the right "attitude" of survival; she certainly had faith.

But there was a quality in the expression on her face that haunted me. Something, besides her cancer, was desperately wrong.

She told me of friends who had abandoned her; of a husband of many years from whom she was now estranged, and with whom she was now locked in a legal battle over the division of their possessions. A group of her fellow volunteers here at the hospital had visited and then, out of concern for her well-being, had asked the staff psychiatrist to pay her a call. The cancer had even distanced her from her children. But, oh, no, she defiantly said, none of this would get her down. She would fight the husband to the end; she threw the psychiatrist out of the room. She prayed daily, hourly. She constantly talked to God. She was "strong," she said proudly, and it was this "strength" that was seeing her through a battle with a cancer her doctors had told her could quite possibly be terminal.

I looked at her glowering face, her well-sculpted fingernails tapping out her determination on the tray, the rosary trembling nearby.

Who could help but ache with compassion for this brave woman? But as I sat there listening to her bitter portrayal of all those who had not measured up in her hour of need, I found myself replacing her self-portrayal of "strong" with a word not so dissimilar. Tough.

Here was a woman facing death who was mistaking being tough with being strong. She'd been tough on her friends, her divorcing husband, that well-meaning psychiatrist. Not that she had to buckle under to any of them; but to maintain such steadfast bitterness and resolve as the number of her days decreased was clearly poisoning her, alienating some of the very people who might be able to love her and others with whom she might want to make peace before she died. Her hardened heart could not embrace them—nor, I had a feeling, herself as well. Her prayers were certainly her way of speaking to God, of asking for grace at a most difficult time. And only God knows what exactly was her disposition. But if the "fruits" (as Scripture and modern psychology alike point out) of inner disposition were any indication, her prayers and her spiritual pursuit had brought little relief or peace.

It is this way about faith. Faith must indeed be strong; but if it is tough, we again are not relying so much on God as upon ourselves, our gritty determination. We are still not ready to commend into God's hands our lives, our spirits. We are not ready to trust, to be stripped back to our essence and purified, refined, reformed; we are not able to see anew, to adventure down paths that may appear unmarked or unnavigable. Stretched. Opened. Enlightened.

This woman with cancer is certainly not unique. There are monks of fifty years' standing whose hearts are tough, not strong. They have gone through their monastic days with a steely determination to obey the *Rule*, and yet their hearts have not yet been warmed by the glow of true faith. They have not yet taken the chance that God really is that all-merciful, all-loving, all-patient father. So, too, there are those in the world who would not think of missing a weekly church or synagogue service, who have used the word "faith" to describe their belief, but who as yet have not really had the faith to have faith. What they might have is religion. But religion is not faith.

For faith is not about such staunch resolve. Faith is far more elastic than that. Faith is not a rigid, superhuman, precise adherence to God's laws, but the abandonment to God in all our disorderly humanity. It is not required of us that we have some sort of Special Forces mentality about the practice of faith. We are not made holy by strict obedience to codes or by prodigious personal effort, but rather by a simple and unadorned fidelity to God.

Within the cloister and without, faith is the simple acceptance of a relationship to God, an acknowledgment of our mutual dependence and need for each other. While God cannot be explained or brought into being by our concepts and notions, faith holds a stunning promise: that God can be experienced in our lives. The kingdom of God is here and it is now. St. Benedict built monastic life upon this very premise.

Faith promised that the faint glow guiding my steps that morning at Mepkin would be there as I continued a walk into this year, on a road whose path I could not then see and whose end I could not then imagine. Had I only that tiny mustard seed of faith—even though I might not yet see it, and doubt it would sprout when planted—I would not need to be concerned. I would need simply to walk on.

AUGUST

Conversatio

Incremental Heroism

I don't know much about music, but when I drive through the monastery gates the dull monotone of the lonesome road of life quickly fades. I can almost hear the expectant overture to what promises to be an ever-rising theme, inexorably building, richer and richer, fuller and fuller. Kettle drums roll and French horns introduce a chorus of the hosts of heaven, softly joined in harmony.

It is not that such opulent musical and choral fanfare—albeit imagined—has much to do with the fact that this mere mortal is arriving at

Mepkin. Rather, it is homage and tribute to the place itself. Holy ground is being entered upon. Here is a place where The Great Issues are dealt with, evil forces battled and bested, the numinous God of the ages encountered.

But as I turned off the splendid tree-lined drive that August morning and approached the rather prosaic buildings marking the monastery's forward cloister—low, squat, dun-tinged structures of decidedly 1970s nouveau-tropical design—the music began to subside. Yes, the towering elegance of the church lay beyond, but these buildings immediately before me were those in which monks eat and sleep and work, where they spend most of each day's hours doing what normal people must do to survive. I walked into the kitchen to smell its clean distinctive odor; Brother Boniface's bread rested in a familiar worn box. Outside, umbrellas nested akimbo in racks on the sheltered walkway between the refectory and the administration building; rusty bikes rested on rusty kickstands.

Surely it is the hunger for God and the everpresent need for inner balance that impels people to these places, but there is also a less celestial and quite basic human desire at work in many of us who come to them. Certainly I would have to confess to this. It is our desire to be heroes. Heroines. To have our lives finally play on the main stage, to hear that kind of triumphal music as the backdrop. We are tired (sometimes virtually sick to death) of our ordinariness. We want more of our lives. Perhaps, in a place like this, we shall find that "more."

When I first pulled up to the gates of Gethsemani in search of Thomas Merton so many years before, I wanted something much bigger to live for—and, if asked, to die for; something far beyond the horizons of a high-school senior. When, many years later, I lived as a hermit at the Spencer monastery, no longer an unripe youth but a man by now well buffeted by life's storms, I still wanted to hear the call to live as few could or would.

Students who come to see me at my office at the University of North Carolina at Wilmington, where I teach, often come not to talk about class work or grades, but about life. Often, staring at the floor and into the rest of their lives, they say the same thing, although in many different ways: Give me an impossible challenge. Let me be deafened by the crescendo of some great task. The patients I visit in the hospital on my weekly rounds as a Eucharistic minister often reflect on where life has taken them and where it might have gone. They speak of their various turning points and moments of truth—some with fondness, some with regret.

But most of us will never be summoned to jungle, or cloister, or great calling. Most of us live out our days in life's dun-colored buildings.

It was Benedict's genius that when he emerged from his cave he did not advise similar dreamers to find similar caves and follow his example. The insights he had gained during those damp, dark, but ultimately illuminating years, insights that would eventually form the *Rule of St. Benedict*, pointed to other means that would eventually yield the "more" people sought. I had been reading the *Rule* in small portions during my monastic visits and had by now completed what is a quite modest volume of only some 9,000 words. Learned commentaries considerably fatten most published versions. Certainly, the *Rule* has some sixth-century cobwebs that need to be whisked away in our reading—corporal punishment, procedural pettiness, and ritual exactitude. After all, it was written at a time when barbarians roamed the land, most aspirants to monastic vocations were illiterate, clocks didn't exist, wine was purer than water, and boys entered the monastery as young as twelve. But there is rich wisdom and timeless common sense within those pages. The *Rule* has proved, for good reason, to be one of the towering spiritual documents of both holiness and humanity.

While the early Desert Fathers had stressed the salvation of one's soul through extreme practices and total isolation—even from other seekers—Benedict stressed communal deliverance and salvation. And he was clear that, in essence, heaven could wait; a perfect union was available *now*, on earth. He saw through the conceit that allowed paradise only after life had been tolerated and suffered. God could be touched and experienced on earth, in the company of others, Benedict maintained.

In a prologue and seventy-three clearly written chapters, Benedict constructed the framework for living a model Christian life. But his true brilliance was that he did not design a heavenly ladder for angels; he was more concerned with normal human beings, given to more horizontal lives. It was not necessary to be a hermit; people living in common would be able to achieve this mystical, sweet communion with God. The *Rule* offered challenge enough for the strongest, assistance for the weakest. Goodness and virtue were individual pursuits, to be sure, but ultimately salvation was a group effort. Love was not an abstract concept; it was to be practiced in kitchen and hallway, in cell and church, in field and courtyard.

When Benedict drew up these fundamentals for a life with God, he put aside individual piety and heroic practices and set such an existence in the context of a small group—at that time, usually ten or twelve people, the size of an extended family. He didn't waste much time with poverty and chastity, traits the early church had so readily emphasized as being prefigured in the life of Christ and therefore worthy of emulation. Instead, Benedict summoned others who wanted to share his vision of holiness to band together, and to base their lives in community on three principles that were then a revolutionary amalgam in the spiritual quest.

First, Benedict admonished seekers not to cast about for a place of perfection, but to live in one place and seek God in the company of the others there, whomever they might be. Thus, the monastic vow of *stabilitas*, stability, was instituted as one leg of the three-legged stool upon which Western monasticism would rest.

Benedict had observed the need for leadership and clear guidance, both in religious and ecclesial life, so that the pursuit of God might constantly be set back on track when it went off the rails—as it often did, humans being human. He had seen too many individuals and fledgling communities wither or implode from either too little control or thoughtless, faceless domination. And so Benedict decreed that monks would have to submit to a single, visible, human authority. It would be an authority not appointed or superimposed upon them, but one of their own choosing, a person elected from among them. The monastic vow of *obedientia*, obedience, was the second leg.

Then came the most sweeping yet staggeringly mundane vow of all. In the Latin, it is *conversatio morum suorum*, an idiomatic expression undoubtedly clear to Benedict, but the exact philological mystery of which has confounded scholars for centuries. This much we do know: *conversatio* was the Latin equivalent of the Greek *politea*, which meant citizenship. In other words, it described how a citizen properly lived within the circumstances of that day, a way of life. Translations vary, but in our modern day, *conversatio morum suorum* generally means a conversion of manners, a continuing and unsparing assessment and reassessment of one's self and what is important and valuable in life. In essence, the individual must continually ask: What is worth living for in this place at this time? And having asked, one must then seek to act in accordance with the answer discerned. *Conversatio*'s objective was that each person become the self-constituting, good, holy, responsible person God intended him or her to be—to make their "city," wherever it might be, work.

To many of us the word "conversion" more often means something entirely different—a one-time, apocalyptic moment that forever changes a person. Most of us can only marvel at such a word and such a moment, for we have not experienced it. Benedict, by contrast, saw conversion in an entirely different, and eminently more practical, light. Beneficiary of contemplative years in a cave and a close reader of Scripture, yet a common-sense man who equally well knew the pitfalls that had waylaid other well-intentioned seekers and fiery-eyed holy men of his day. Benedict was an astute observer of human nature. He knew that conversion was not, for most people, marked by dramatic change. In fact he distrusted such spectacular turnabouts, often requiring aspirants burning with divine love to cool their ardor for days at the monastery gate.

In Benedict's time and our own, such conversions—in which the opening of a floodgate of emotion seems surely to validate the experience—can actually sound the death knell for true conversion. Such titanic emotion can easily and irretrievably seal off fruitful stirrings of mind and soul, cementing firmly into place what seemed pressingly evident at that moment, preventing further reflection and introspection about the continuously evolving mystery that is our life. Instead of opening a path to God, it can stand in the way of a continual renewal of self and an openness to the larger community.

I say this out of experience. I have sought such conversion in my life; at times I was absolutely sure it had occurred. My life had been changed; it was the first day of the rest of my life—and it would be a dramatically different life henceforth. But such moments were no more than illusions of permanent change. After the euphoria subsided and the fireworks faded I discovered that no superhuman had come to inhabit my body. It was still only me, standing there on the stage of life, gradually encountering one small revelation after another. It was only after a number of false conversions that I realized only one thing was permanent—change itself. I could either face that truth or continue deluding myself.

Just the week before, my prayer life had seemed an embarrassment of riches. Insights came tumbling from the pages of the psalms, my pulse slowed, my voice took on a calmer tone. I found myself dealing with Daniel's high-pitched wails of indignation and Noah's willful self in an admirably kind and reasoned way. My life truly had changed; surely I was a different man. Then one day both of them stood before their converted father and looked me straight in the eye, even as I mouthed another pious platitude. I felt heat at the back of my neck as they glared at me; my collar seemed aflame. I had not been converted at all. My phony overlay had deluded me, but it had not fooled them. What I spoke was not who I was. *Conversatio* was not yet mine.

Benedict saw conversion as a continuing process, one punctuated with more failures than successes. Yet it was really the *only* way that people, on a daily basis, could pursue both transcendent holiness as well as earthly peace—within themselves, and in common with others.

That day in August, I looked out from the visitor's alcove to the monks seated contemplatively in the main dining area during the noon meal as a book on the history of Islam was being read. I watched as they rode their bikes out to the grading house to pack thousands of eggs for Piggly Wiggly supermarkets throughout South Carolina. I saw Brother William reach for the phone in the office: "Mepkin Abbey; may I help you?" And there was Brother Gregory, pushing Brother Paul's wheelchair, a man of 82 years being assisted by another but five years younger. The dailyness, the plainness of their lives. Yet in each moment—if Benedict is right—the possibility of conversion.

Once the jargon, window dressing, wretched excess, and existential angst are put aside, the spiritual revolution in which we find ourselves these days actually makes complete sense. Where passive virtue, escape from the secular world, and dogged adherence to religious law were once—even recently—viewed as the only safe paths to God (especially within my own Catholic church), we now realize that human beings are capable of far more. For bringing us to this point, let us give thanks to the Enlightenment thinkers, to Dr. Freud, and even to our current crop of human-potential and New Age prophets—misguided in method and averse to God though some of them are. For they are right at least about this: It is "active" virtue that we hunger for, virtue that can animate and inform our lives. Not a Sunday morning experience, but an everyday quality. We are involved in the sea change from piety to holiness. It is a transition fraught with doubt, anxiety, excess, and (for too many) fatigue, confusion and, eventually, a weary abdication. The old sureties are gone, the new ways yet unclear. It is at precisely this point in our human history that the monastery and monastic values stand uniquely ready, once more, to instruct us—to clear our eyes so that we might regain our bearings and strike off toward the mystical horizon once more.

In *Lovers of the Place*, his highly charged, somewhat quixotic, and alarmingly hopeful book, Mepkin's abbot, Francis Kline, is a voice crying—no longer in the wilderness—about how monastic practices can be part of a healthy, happy, spiritual life for those of us beyond the walls. Kline throws open the doors to the monastic treasury and invites us in to blessedly loot what monks have stored away over the centuries, from Benedict's day to our own. He talks of "the possibility of living the monastic charism beyond the cloister," of sharing "something that didn't seem to want to be shared but only joined."[1]

Looking back over the tremendous changes of the past few decades in our approach to God, I can see that my own religious life (to call it a spiritual life or journey in those days would have been presumptuous beyond belief) began in a church that presented precise answers to all life's questions and offered a prescribed list of devotional experiences that were supposed not so much to feed our souls as assure their passage into a blissful eternity. Monasteries in those days were to be visited (or, for a very

[1]Francis Kline, *Lovers of the Place: Monasticism Loose in the Church* (Collegeville, Minn.: Liturgical Press, 1997), viii, vi.

few, joined), but not taken seriously, not allowed into our lives, much less allowed to run "loose." Monastic values were considered only appropriate for monks; the spiritual engines with which we in the world operated had much lower octane needs.

Only recently could I begin to speak of a spiritual life, aspire to a spirituality that reached into every corner and had the potential to infuse every moment, a spirituality with application far outside of any formal religious training or experience. I came to this point not through some intellectual process, or as the result of reading or studying. It was out of sheer need. Poverty. What Blaise Pascal, the French scientist and Christian apologist, had said of all humanity was no less true of me; I had discovered in myself a God-shaped hole that only God could fill.

When each of us puts in perspective our material needs and plumbs the yearnings of our deepest, spiritual selves, we might come up with any number of ways to talk about what we want of our lives. We seek to be at rest, yet awake and alert. To make the most of what we have. To love and be loved. To overcome the poisons that boil up in our minds. To see beyond the inevitable trials that confront us, the frustrations, disappointments, and agonies we suffer. To matter. To make a difference. To be known for something worthwhile. We desire "active" virtues, so that our days might be infused with grace and confidence.

As I pondered the various twisting, rutted roads leading to and from *conversatio* on a walk at the monastery, I found a word constantly appearing at the end of the equation of life. Not so strangely, it was sainthood. Hadn't I been taught in many years of Catholic education that sainthood was the only worthy goal of life? Wasn't it sainthood we were all seeking, if sainthood could be described as that place of ultimate unity with God and with that which is the best in us?

There was an echo on the still wind. This time it was not the voice of an Indian, a slave, or a prominent landowner. It was Father Raymond, an Irish-born Trappist legendary for both his holiness and pragmatism. He was walking, far more steadily, right beside me. And he pronounced a firm "no" on such misplaced piety.

It was a balmy summer day, with the sweet, moist air off the Cooper

River gently caressing my warm face. Suddenly I found myself downwind from the chicken sheds, in which are housed some 35,000 Leghorns whose eggs are the monastery's primary source of income. Nothing like that acrid smell to bring one back to the real world. And Father Raymond said this: "Miracles may show me the saint, they do not show me how he became a saint: and that is what I want to see. It is not the completed process that intrigues me, it is the process itself; for you see, my work is not to be a saint. Tell me what was churning in his soul as he battled his way up from selfishness and the allurements of sin to the great heart of God."[2]

I could just visualize Father Raymond in his crisp white alb and stark, black scapular, standing there squarely before his brothers, zeroing in on the dreamy-eyed *arrivistes*, acquainting them with the realities of life-enduring *process* of conversion. We might aim for goodness, he was advising, but to desire sainthood was to pound on the gates of Heaven, demanding entry; it was to approach God frontally (as Brother Paul had warned against), rather than through the everyday means he has provided for us to seek after our salvation—not only in heaven, but right here on earth. This is what the continually unfolding, mutating, perplexing, rewarding reality of conversion will be for all of us, if we can but choose to take monastic wisdom into our lives. It is a brave choice, for conversion offers a goal we will probably never reach—and in any case might well not recognize if we did.

As I walked further, deeper into that aroma, still another voice sounded on the wind. This one was from deep in church history: Gregory the Great—Roman official, monk, Doctor of the Church, saint, pope, but ultimately a mortal human confessing his inadequacies. "I cannot preach with any competence, and yet insofar as I do succeed, still I myself do not live my life according to my own preaching . . . I am slothful and negligent . . . because I too am weak, I find myself drawn little by little into idle conversations. . . . What I once found tedious I now enjoy. . . . So

---

[2]From the introduction to "The Family That Overtook Christ," Clonmore and Reynolds, Dublin, 1944; quoted in Esther de Waal, *Seeking God: The Way of St. Benedict* (Collegeville, Minn.: Liturgical Press, 1984), 25.

who am I to be a watchman, for I do not stand on the mountain of action but lie down in the valley of weakness?"[3]

It is consoling to know that even those eventually declared saints had the same problems we all do. In his consternation Gregory calls out for his own *conversatio:* "Give me in spite of my weaknesses a higher life and effective speech . . ." Is he not also speaking for us?

Within the monastic tradition conversion is not an end point but a starting point, a challenge encountered again and again. Conversion is both active and passive, being and becoming. Men and women enter monasteries and may call themselves monks, and yet they are constantly becoming monks. Students are not students by virtue of an acceptance letter from a college but by nature of what happens in classroom and library, in conversation, with a book in hand (or, now, an image on a screen). We marry—but can we truly claim to be married on that day? On paper my wife and I were joined at St. Joseph's Church in New York's Greenwich Village on a January afternoon in 1982, but the days ahead would prove whether or not we achieved this sacred union.

We profess our hunger, our need for a spiritual center. While that is a worthy and necessary first step, we must then take the next, often faltering, steps. It is not so much whether those steps take us closer to our imagined goal; it is rather the continuing action and ever-so-incremental transformation of *conversatio* that matter most. Moving this way or that, toward wholeness or disintegration, toward holiness or banality, touching that which is best and deepest within us, or anesthetizing ourselves to what it is that makes us human, whole, and noble—this, of course, is conversion. Or the lack of it. It is an ongoing process, moment by moment, throughout our lives. Despair, refreshment. Dying, being reborn. It is conversion that holds out the true promise of heroism—as well as excitement and danger of the highest order.

Even the briefest consideration makes clear that if we turn our backs to *conversatio,* if we do not periodically go to our deepest selves to find out who we are, the world will surely form us instead. If we do not test ourselves

---

[3]Quoted in *The Liturgy of the Hours,* vol. IV, 1365–66.

daily, in seemingly small ways, our spiritual selves will never build the strength we will need when life's major trials are presented. Our souls will be too small to embrace beauty and goodness when offered to us. Surely, this is why we come to places like a monastery, why we take time to reflect—because we need to strip away our false images of ourselves, the world's grip upon us. We need to look into the mirror and see our true face, comely or unattractive as it may then be.

How painful this is for me when I kneel by my bedside at night for a reflection of usually no more than a minute or two—and realize I have been the impatient, faithless boor that comes too easily and naturally to me. Yet this is all I can do; I can only pray that even my utter failure at conversion in the events of that day might give me a moment's pause in the days to come, so that I might at least see the choices before me.

But one must be careful here. It might seem as though conversion—with its relentless demands—implies some sort of continual groping in the dark, walking about anxiously looking for moments to test us so that we might do exactly the right thing, act in precisely the right way. My church is criticized—sometimes quite justly—for exactly this.

Perhaps you, whether Catholic or not, Christian or not, might have responded like me—in various times of remorse, self-doubt, even self-loathing—by taking on the heavy, ill-fitting robe of self-abnegating moral precision. We will do this, believe that, follow these rules exactly. We use that lifeless, measured tone of voice. What a sure and straight pathway to moral excellence it appears to be; what a dead end, what a horrible killer of the spirit, it actually is. We inevitably come away disheartened after such an attempt. How false a feeling such absolutism has, how bad a taste it leaves in our mouths and souls when we limit ourselves so by staunch resolve and loveless determination.

I cannot stomach the smell of a body powder called Shower to Shower. Not that it isn't a perfectly fine product; but during one stretch of my spiritual journey, when I felt the only way to holiness was to treat my body with utter disdain, I used it because it was an inexpensive underarm deodorant—cheaper than the conventional brands. All this to virtuously save a dollar.

I also have a set of photographic proofs from this same period, taken by a *Newsweek* photographer to accompany a review of one of my books. Around that time I had helped to start a soup kitchen in Brooklyn; I was intent on giving my life to the poor. In those pictures, I am wearing a horribly ugly parka I bought for twelve dollars—the cheapest I could find, I was so proud to say, in my self-conscious approach to voluntary poverty. Yet there on my face is a look of such pathetic sadness; I weep at the sight of myself.

Real conversion is nothing like that at all, I discovered. Conversion is not about being anxious, but rather about being alert to what is happening around us. Conversion is listening to sounds around us, but never straining to hear too far off. Conversion is being able to step back from our ambition, our self-esteem, our willfulness—the fog that clouds our vision. Conversion is humility. Conversion is forgetting about holiness and heroism, accepting instead the grace offered in ordinary things. Conversion is no more than a series of flickering moments, the vast majority of which will be unnoticed by ourselves or others, but the sum total of which continually forms and reforms our very humanity—and dictates whether we will ever come close to finding our spiritual core.

To some, it might seem that conversion would have us going about our lives somewhat limp and ineffectual, a moist handshake and a vague smile our hallmarks—as if we gargled with holy water morning, noon, and night, as Gregorian Chant played constantly in the background. It might appear that the aggressive pursuit of a career or forcefully seeking a goal nullifies the opportunities for conversion. Benedict and Bernard would not have stood for such trivializing and flaccidness—and neither should we. *Conversatio* is far more bold, more dynamic, more exciting than that. Their monasteries preserved Western civilization, teaching both monks and non-monks what it meant to be a good citizen in those days. We have no less an awesome mandate today: the very transformation of our living rooms, the neighborhoods we live in, our places of work. And, of course, ourselves.

Strangely enough, as monks learn—and we can learn from them—conversion is self*ish* as much as it is self*less*.

We know well when we have attempted *conversatio morum suorum*, for our spirit soars with the first small effort to transcend our venality. Not adding our words to the character assassination underway at a coffee break; a deep inhale instead of a shout at some irritation; morning spiritual reading after a late night out. Simple things. We know as sure as anything we can know when we have attempted to convert some part of ourselves, for the feeling has a majesty and sense of mastery we want to experience ever more deeply.

Depending on where they have room and how many guests are present during my monastery stays, I am sometimes given one of the cells designated for a monk, within the cloister, and thus by proximity somewhat more privy to Mepkin's inner life. On those occasions, I am able to sit in on chapter. Chapter is a monastic staple, the periodic gathering of the community, either to discuss business, issues, or difficulties at hand, to hear spiritual, historical, or theological discourses from one of their own or a visiting expert, or most commonly simply to hear the abbot's reflections. Abbot Francis Kline is still a young man, only 48, but a man of manifold talents: an extraordinary musician; wise spiritual director; excellent writer; talented retreat master; discerning community leader; inspired liturgist; and if it may be said (intending incorporeal, not secular standards), a rising star in the Trappist firmament. But as I sat among the Mepkin monks on that August day in the high-ceilinged room just off the sanctuary, his words were devoted instead to the short-tempered, impatient man beneath all that the world sees him to be.

After trying various other emissaries, the bishop of Charleston had dispatched Abbot Kline to talk to a man who had written letter after letter of bitter protest—to the bishop, the papal representative in Washington, and finally to Pope John Paul II himself. The man's objection was that the perpetual adoration of the Blessed Sacrament in his parish church was being denigrated by masses held there. For the non-Catholic—as well for most Catholics—it was, to be sure, an arcane protest. Adoration of the Blessed Sacrament, in which a consecrated host is revered in a monstrance—an ornate receptacle, often with gilded metal radiating from the glass compartment enclosing the host—is more a product of pre-Vatican II piety than post-Vatican II thought. Vatican II taught that the Eucharist was to be looked upon as God in our midst—a presence to be taken into the world, rather than worshipped only within the confines of a church. Perpetual adoration of the Blessed Sacrament, by contrast, meant that the monstrance was exposed twenty-four hours a day. Ordinary mass, for the man the abbot was to visit, was little more than an interruption to the veneration.

The visitation required that the abbot drive halfway across the state of South Carolina to try to talk sense to a man whose view of the church and of Eucharistic theology were hardly Francis' own, and whose abrasive manner guaranteed still more irritation. The monastery's building program, terribly underfinanced, had reached a crucial point; there were no novices on the horizon; Brother William had been diagnosed with congestive heart failure; there were retreats to prepare. Francis had no time for such intramural foolishness. The abbot related how he seethed with anger as he got into the car, promising himself for the first hundred miles that he would deliver this agitator exactly the dressing down he so richly deserved.

"But then I realized," the abbot told the community, "once my rage simmered down below the boiling point—this is *exactly* what we have to do for the stubborn among us. And we will all be stubborn and stupid at one time or another. This stubborn man may not be changed by anything I might say—and, indeed, he was not—but loving transforms the lover even though the person toward whom we extend our love may refuse it. No one knows who or what such an act converts, but it is our inner disposition that continues to convert us."

As I walked the Mepkin grounds, sat in church, and read in my room, *conversatio* continued to swirl about in my mind. And into that cacophony of cries, whispers, and shouts of "enough" that characterizes our mind's state when confronted with something so seemingly impossible yet so clearly necessary for our true inner well-being came a voice of the ages. It came during a period of *lectio divina*, when I simply picked up the Bible, opened it to a random page, and began to read.

And there it was—*conversatio* so clearly delineated, in the story of John the Baptist. John, an ascetic of the first order, saintly for sure, girded in an animal skin and living on a diet of locusts and wild honey. The poor, disenfranchised, oppressed, and sick gathered around him could readily see the promise in a new way of living a life. John embraced them with his words and presence; but he also looked beyond them, to those in the shadows at the edge of the crowd. There stood the publicans, already wealthy, who purchased the right to collect Rome's tax and then went about their business with ruthless efficiency. And there were the soldiers, brute occupiers whose might gave them power to do as they willed. They were two of the most hated groups in Palestine. But John summoned them closer; they were not excluded. Conversion was not beyond their reach. No, finding another line of work was not the prerequisite, he told them. For now, just to do their work fairly was enough conversion: extracting no more tax than was just, keeping order without being bullies. Conversion could begin today, *within* their life's circumstances.

As this simple example so vividly pointed out, conversion is distinctly individual for each of us. There is no bar all must reach, no grand plan of spiritual homogenization. Rather, conversion is daily, incremental. Balanced. Personal. Doing the possible, not the impossible.

Conversion came—and comes—in many forms. Benedict and Bernard did not seek to produce cookie-cutter monks—for they quickly saw that each monk had a different spirit, different contributions to make, different demons to fight. It was continuing conversion, not apocalyptic acts, that these monastic fathers understood would have far greater impact in recreating man and woman in the image of God, in building harmonious communities in which happy, virtuous lives might flourish. Conversion obviously has a practical, apparent effect: such actions set an example. They are contagious. And they can be replicated by normal people. The monastery and its monks could be a beacon for the world, a light unto the nations—while being an inspiration to each other.

It was the additional genius of Bernard, Benedict's spiritual son and the wellspring of what has come down to us as Trappist tradition, to go back to the strong, bold foundation of monastic life, and to build upon Bene-

dict's concept of conversion. The Trappist writer Hugh McCaffery, probing the basics of monastic living, examines what the spiritual father of his
order considered "the deepest existential reality in each of us." McCaffery
concludes, "Bernard would hold that it is that each of us loves oneself.
True, it is a kind of weakness and defect, but at its best and deepest it is a
throbbing, thriving gift of God."[4]

We can begin to see more clearly that while conversion at first appears
to be completely outer-directed and selfless, its motivation is actually self-
love and our desire for self-healing. We feel better when we are good. We
are more in touch with that which is holiest, whole, and best in us. Quite
frankly, we need a payout, reinforcement. I know this well, for when
conversatio is not a forced, but a natural outgrowth of inner desires—regardless of how difficult the choice or task—I have a feeling of invigoration and
replenishment.

Conversatio is at the heart of monastic life, its very dynamism. Comple-
menting the necessary but more static vows of stability and obedience, it
creates the spirit so apparent in monastic communities. Why is it that we
feel such a personal welcome in these places from monks who see hundreds
of visitors a year? Why does the fresh bouquet or elegant arrangement of
dry flowers on the altar bespeak something beyond good taste? How could
Merton continue to write as he did? What of this sense of peace and joy
that seems to infuse monasteries? Yes, of course, God's presence. But are
these also not the manifestations of a group of people continually facing
life's realities and their own human limitations in the crucible of conversion's daily demands?

Does not *conversatio*—or its lack—have a ripple effect, in monasteries
and in our lives? It is not so difficult to love and live with perfect people,
but there are few of them in monasteries or in our homes. Yet loving
ordinary people, while recognizing both their humanity and our own, is
what allows the spirit to soar—and lives to change.

Conversion is something monasticism offers equally to the heroic and
those who, sufficiently battered by misplaced hopes, want to live life to the

---

[4]Hugh McCaffery, "The Basics of Monastic Living in St. Bernard," *Cistercian Studies Quarterly* 90(3),
158.

fullest. It offers an opportunity to become, in St. Frances de Chantal's words, one of the "great-souled individuals." It presents the option for a new and all-encompassing kind of obedience: the demands of goodness.

When I walked the *Via Dolorosa*, the Way of Cross, which winds its way through the streets of Jerusalem I found myself oddly unaffected by the sites I was viewing. They may or may not be the actual places commemorating the places where Christ suffered and, finally, died. Instead, I was thinking, in the large cities and tiny villages in which we live, we all have our own *Via Dolorosa*, our own crosses to bear; we are all scourged, all humiliated. There is horrible heartbreak. Unlike Jesus Christ, much of what we suffer is often not inflicted by strangers, but by ourselves. Usually it is because we are unwilling to change our ways, even though those ways are detrimental to us.

I remember vividly a painful scene from my own life that illustrates the cost of this stubbornness all too well. The setting was unlikely, simply exotic—a seeming dream come true. I was in Negril, Jamaica, for a week's vacation in a fashionable resort. Credit cards and cash in my pocket, a swimming pool just steps outside my private room, the warm, inviting Caribbean but a few yards further, fabulous food available at any time of day or night. There I was, a single man, free to partake of this tropical paradise.

But one night in that pleasure dome is forever seared into my memory. I found myself on my hands and knees, sobbing uncontrollably. My nostrils were not filled with the scent of blossoms that floated on the night air, but rather with the damp, musty carpet as I pressed my face, sobbing, to the floor of my room. I thought I was looking after myself so well in those days; I was doing nothing of the sort. By a life of reckless selfishness and lack of commitment to anything beyond what might provide instant gratification, I had thrown myself into the dark abyss that looms for those who refuse to employ—in some manner or another, and call it by this name or another—what the monks call *conversatio*.

Only by continually taking stock of ourselves, agreeing to a difficult alliance of our minds and wills, can we ever know the beauty and depth of *conversatio*. We will never find what is best and purest in us if we do not constantly summon the grace our souls thirst after. Life is not a romp through a field, plucking passing pleasure and avoiding pain. We know the stakes—and rewards—are so much higher.

While the years on my own faith journey have made me neither pure spirit nor any sort of exemplary being, I know that my attempts at continuing conversion chart the only path that will ultimately make me happy, that gives me any chance of allowing me to be the person that God created me to be. I am easily confounded by the contortions of my mind, by the unpredictable events of my life. Sometimes faith feels so strong and God so near—and in the blink of an eye, I am buffeted by the cold winds of despair. I struggle for balance all the time. To be decent, fair, kind; to live up to whatever small gifts I have been given.

I have found that I can begin to address those lofty goals only if I am humble enough to continually examine what I do and who I am, wise enough to be honest with myself, and strong enough to act as a man, not a mindless beast being sucked down by the vortex that is moral indolence and counterfeit self-absorption. I need to keep before me some simple guidelines if I am going to attempt to live the monastic wisdom of *conversatio.*

Foremost, I constantly remind myself that real and total conversion is impossible. What *is* possible is the single act before me right now; that frame of mind, this word, another held back. I pray the breviary and read a page or two from an inspirational book each morning, kneel by my bedside at night, and utter prayers during the day. Realistically, this takes about twenty minutes all told. I find that I pray for alertness, insight, patience, courage—and, much of the time, help. I am not consciously aware of those prayers even moments later, but God knows that I have at least tried to put myself in his presence.

I try to remember certain people and words that speak of this ongoing, impossible, but absolutely essential quest of conversion. I find myself reciting those comforting words of Scripture: "I ask for mercy not justice, a loving heart more than sacrifice." I remember that conversation with Brother Paul, who said God wants no more than that we be honest with him when we have failed, and asks no more than that we simply get up and go on. I recall the perception of God that brought Thomas Merton to Gethsemani and infused life for his twenty-seven years there: "Mercy within mercy within mercy." I remember that the goal of monastic discipline is not to punish the body but to liberate the soul. I remember Cardinal Joseph Bernardin telling me always to be kind in the face of oppression, even as he was at that moment being falsely accused of molesting a seminarian. I recall Dorothy Day's sure voice above the din of the Catholic Worker soup kitchen in New York, calling for more clean bowls so that everyone might be fed. I remember Noah Wilkes making an unsolicited cup of hot chocolate for his brother Daniel after a fight.

I try to look for who I am in the harsh light of reality: an impetuous creature not readily asking for permission for what I do in life, but often needing to seek forgiveness for my foolishness. I cannot reshape my personality; I can only govern how I will use that personality in whatever circumstances I am faced with. And in many ways, though I attempt *conversatio* daily, I may not measurably change—at least in the eyes of the world. But if I do not at least make the effort, I will regress even deeper into my old ways. Only I will know that I have or have not tried and, at times, tried valiantly. After all, if any of us were truly converted, we would become saints. Most of us do not.

I remind myself that my attempts at conversion—say, a better and more open attitude to my children or patience with a co-worker I really don't like very much—may well do nothing to change the situation or person. Of course, most of us would like to produce exactly that with our little acts of goodness. We know it is manipulation, but nonetheless we want it to be so.

I recall Leonard Boudin, a great (and atheist) civil-liberties lawyer I once wrote about, a man who took on cases representing great injustices, many of which he knew he would likely lose. "If I don't stand up, the other side wins by default, regardless of how wrong they are," he said. Our attempts may touch people; they may be greeted with derision, rejection, or failure. The end result is not what matters. What matters is what is in our heart.

I also need to remind myself that whatever moments of conversion I may experience during my day equally may not make my life any easier or better—there may be no "pay out" elsewhere. Stubbornly, though, I find myself rationalizing that if I do this good act, I should get some sort of reward. But conversion is not a matter of bartering. We cheapen and short circuit our relationship with God by such witless attempts.

Equally, as I struggle for conversion, I must not be stupid about it. There is a mental health principle that one should not continually go to places for affirmation or redress (say, to an impossible boss or parent) where there has never been any; the situation is not likely to change. It is no different in monastic life, or our life. Yes, faith can move mountains, but most of us cannot summon that sort of faith. The old practice in religious life, exercising a kind of distributive love—where one attempted to act the same toward everyone—has produced more mental illness, disconnectedness, and dysfunctional behavior than any of us would care to know about. Some people are not to be "converted" or changed, and it is not our mission in life to attempt continually to do so. I was reminded of this by an unsmiling and rather rude post-office worker whom I tried to cheer up with some idle chit-chat. My good will was promptly stuffed right back down my throat. In fact, she may be quite satisfied with what I might consider unpleasantness. She has a right to be as she is, and I have no obligation to change that.

Sadly, I have a brother from whom I am estranged. I don't really know why, but my attempts even to talk with him are constantly rebuffed. He wants no relationship with me. What have I done? I send him books and he returns them. I can only pray about this, and hope someday it will change. And this past Christmas, when a card arrived bearing nothing more than his signature, I cherished it above any other greeting I received.

I realize that as *conversatio* is central to monastic life, it is also at the very basis of any sort of human life worth living. The proof is all around us. Modern psychology, holding up serenity, calmness, and simplicity as goals—these, certainly, the fruits of conversion—attest to this. The new concept of emotional intelligence is built upon a life of continual introspection. My wife, a social worker, tries to help troubled children see that while some circumstances are beyond their control, they have power over their behavior and actions. She advises them, in streetwise language, to think and act for themselves and "not to catch somebody else's stupids." Benedict, Bernard, Abraham Maslow, Daniel Goleman, and Tracy Wilkes—wise teachers all—are saying the same thing.

And I know that while I may not always act on a desire to be converted, that desire itself is an extraordinarily important first step. As the monk Thich Nhat Hanh, Thomas Merton's Buddhist alter ego, writes, "Pronouncing words does have an effect. When you say, 'I am determined to study medicine,' that already has an impact on your life, even before you apply to medical school. . . . When you become aware of something, you begin to have enlightenment."[5]

I realize there is no greater opportunity than now to begin the conversion process, or to get it back on track after it has, once again, been derailed. Whenever acedia—moral fatigue—sets in, whenever I find myself asking, "why me?" or "why now?" I may not have a good answer. But I realize, with Thomas Merton, that "[c]auses have effects, and if we lie to ourselves and to others, then we cannot expect to find truth and reality whenever we happen to want them."[6]

It is in the ordinariness of our lives that, looking back, we will usually find we have been most heroic. It is those ordinary moments that, stone by stone, comprise our very foundation. Actually I will be living a life of *conversatio* when I least know it or expect it or feel it. It is life's leaven, so small an ingredient, yet absolutely essential.

And lastly, as I see over and over again—in my life, in the life of the monks at Mepkin, in the monastic wisdom that has come down through the centuries—regardless of what happens as a result of our attempts, to close ourselves off from *conversatio* is to close ourselves off from growth. It is to rob ourselves of any hope of regaining those virtues that were sown in our innocence when we were created by God, to prevent ourselves from being continually refreshed and renewed. We have no choice if we truly want to live.

[5]Thich Nhat Hanh, *Living Buddha, Living Christ* (New York: Riverhead, 1995), 116.
[6]Thomas Merton, *New Seeds of Contemplation* (New York: New Directions, 1972), 32.

When I returned from the monastery, careful not to allow that sappy tone of voice to emerge, I told Tracy some of my thoughts about *conversatio*. She looked at me with that totally honest gaze that only children and wives are allowed.

"It doesn't come easily for you, does it?"

She was right. It doesn't.

Stability

A Sense of Where You Are

On the refectory wall was a splendid new group picture of the Mepkin monks taken no more than six months before, a mere blink of time's eye in a religious order of such longevity. The black-and-white photograph was far more than a collection of crisp, flat images, for each monk's face seemed to beam out its own much fuller message, almost like so many computer chips—tiny dots of emulsion brimming with so much vibrant information. No arms were thrown over another's shoulder, no other outward signs of esprit de corps were shown. But what profound togetherness emanated from that picture. What great testimony of lives well lived radiated in those faces. Hundreds upon hundreds of years of Trappist life were represented. A team of stalwarts, one many of us would be happy to join.

As Brother Edward and I scanned those faces on a late September morning—exchanging anecdotes, quirks, and funny stories about the various monks, Edward supplying identification to faces I knew, but not all by name—his voice dropped at the mention of certain of them. A momentary melancholy passed over this characteristically upbeat man. For in this place where stability was not merely a hope but a vow, transience hovered as an everpresent possibility. Three of the twenty-odd monks in the photo were no longer there. One, in fact, had left in the middle of the day, saying not a word to anyone.

While outsiders—myself included—might try to accord monasteries otherworldly status, these are, alas, places where ordinary humans dwell, and where those humans, like all others, have to deal with that weighty word—commitment. For Trappist monks, starkly, it means a commitment to remain in one place for the rest of their lives.

Stability. Not much excitement in that word, is there? In our mobile world, teeming with the possibility of what tomorrow might bring or what could lay just beyond our horizons, stability might seem one of the least desirable of monastic traits to try to practice in our lives. After all, who doesn't want to drink fully of people, pleasures, and places?

I, for one, fought stability almost from the moment I realized there was a world outside our modest house on the East Side of Cleveland. I fought to loose what I perceived as the chains of my tightly-knit ethnic neighborhood, going to a high school far away and then to a college I had never so much as visited, knowing only that it was not close to home. I bridled at restraints; I moved again and again. There was always something more out there I wasn't finding. I spent much of my life one step away from—well, from something. From what, I did not know.

One of the monastic guests during these days in early fall was Father Eugene Zoeller, a professor at Bellarmine College in Louisville, which, among other things, happens to be the repository of the Thomas Merton archives. We began to talk about church life, and I found myself telling him—he seemed open enough—of my misgivings upon returning from a recent talk I had given at a parish within a good-sized Catholic diocese. There was a strange feeling about the diocese, something immediately palpable from the moment the parish priest and his director of religious education picked me up at the airport. They were uneasy with any serious talk about what was happening within the church today, almost as if they feared we were being taped or *Big Brother* was watching on closed-circuit television. Deflective, breezy conversation was our meager conversational fare for the forty-five minute ride.

It was soon apparent that this was a diocese whose bishop exerted strong—and, I would find, intimidating—control. He had made it clear he did not want to be embarrassed by innovations or mistakes; he wanted Rome to know that he was a loyal son, adhering to the letter of church law and practice. Communication with his priests was limited to admonishments and veiled threats, disarmingly conveyed in what were inevitably called "helpful" letters and phone calls. There was little reason for the bishop to talk honestly and openly with or hear from his coworkers in fields of the Lord, for he was looking beyond them.

Although he certainly would never have openly said such a thing, it was common knowledge in the diocese that the bishop had his eyes on higher church office, perhaps a Vatican appointment. He longed for a cardinal's scarlet *zucchetto* to rest upon his head, to someday sit in the Sistine Chapel as a new pope was chosen, to be reverently called a "prince of the church." He had learned well how imaginative and pastoral bishops could be passed over, how loyal ecclesiastical bureaucrats fared better. The Catholic Church's corridors of power are littered with the shattered careers and broken lives of such men, clerics who ventured too far outside the accepted path—who seemed to pay undue attention to their troops, not enough obeisance to the generals.

Months before this visit to the monastery I had unconsciously begun to reflect on stability, and the cost inflicted when its truth is refused. Here was a diocese of priests and people who lived in fear of alienating their bishop—in fact, it had become their primary and overriding concern—because he was a man who had not incorporated the practice of stability into his life. He was a man not fully invested in his diocese, because it was not yet where he thought he should be. Perhaps, he might even have presumed to himself, it was not yet where God had truly called him to be; it was not his *true* vocation. It was not a home, but a stepping stone, and he had to make sure the surface stayed clear of the slippery moss of controversy. His priests could not be trusted to be themselves, trying to reach their disparate flocks through their individual approaches. They were to live by a sanitized, safe, common denominator. They were to maintain tight ranks, constantly passing in review so that his superiors would see good—if uninspired and intimidated—order.

Of course, this middle-management cleric with his eye on the next rung—not one of those whom Abbot Francis wrote about as a "lover of the place"—is not alone. He has his colleagues in corporation executives who are constantly looking beyond the people and task at hand to that prestigious post they imagine will ultimately satisfy their insatiable drive. They can also be found in the so-called helping professions, leaders who sacrifice the good of their subordinates and those they are supposed to help in their failure to see that it is not the title they hold or the power they wield, but what they do *today*, to *this one person*, that ultimately matters. They are the factory workers or fast-food counter jockeys or security guards who dream of a supervisory job or another stripe on their sleeve. Relationships that seek to exploit rather than enhance the other person, men and women constantly in pursuit of that perfect partner whose only function would be to satisfy all desires—and reflect favorably upon oneself.

In both carefully hidden and all-too-apparent ways, it is not difficult to see that lives are the poorer for not being at home in the moment, not being able to accept the present circumstances. When stability is not practiced, each moment, each deed, each thought becomes only a step to something else, rather than having inherent worth and dignity in itself. And the pursuit of that something more perfect becomes a master never satisfied. Such an unstable (and now that word takes on new meaning) person can never be at rest. There is always going to be something or some place better, some person who will please them more.

If this bishop does reach his goal, when the door is closed and he is alone in his Vatican apartment, his heart may swell for a moment. And then—perhaps immediately, perhaps after a little while—he may feel a hollowness so numbing he may think he is going to die. He will then begin, of course, to plot his next move.

It is not that a sense of stability is somehow one of life's neutral valences that we can merely will to be irrelevant to our well-being. It is far more than that. It profoundly affects everything we do. I think of an acquaintance who married an extraordinarily rich man and was forever on the move between a number of luxurious homes, each of which was constantly being redecorated, moved into and out of. She seemed to be managing homes, not really living in them. I visited one of these places to find a frenetic ballet of sorts going on—chauffeur, handyman, gardeners, valet, maid, nanny. There was even a dog psychologist in residence to deal with an unhousebroken pet. My acquaintance looked frantic and despondent, and she had every right to be—for she was living in a self-designed hell that afforded no rest, peace, or satisfaction.

Michael Casey, an Australian Trappist, has pondered "The Value of Stability," asking questions that we, if lacking his precision, could easily find on our minds about now: "What monastic value is enshrined in the vow?" Or, getting closer to home, "Is stability a value that may worthily be embodied in any serious Christian life?"[1]

While I found myself resonating to Casey's wise observations, I recalled, during a walk through a fall drizzle at Mepkin one afternoon, that a far less well-known theologian had perhaps told us in simple words exactly what stability was about. This is one Bill Bradley, basketball player, Rhodes Scholar, and later United States Senator. To Bradley, basic to playing good basketball—and, by extension, living the kind of considered life for which he is so respected—is "a sense of where you are." For Bradley deduced that if he knew where he was (and of course, stability on a basketball court is a movable feast), and *was* where he was, then whatever the task was—a pass, a vote, or simply the daily decisions in his personal life—became that much easier. He knew where he stood. He perceived his constantly changing

[1]Michael Casey, "The Value of Stability," *Cistercian Studies Quarterly* 31(3) (1996), 287.

relationship to the other nine men on the court, and to the events in his life. Bradley was not talking only of the physical space that he occupied or a position he took, but of investing his presence there with a certain intensity, intentionality, a centering in each place that he found himself. It was as much metaphysical as physical, at once abstract and concrete.

We need not look too far into our disjointed lives and fragmented society to realize that "a sense of where you are" is missing from too many lives.

When Benedict bid his followers to make a vow of stability, he wisely did not attach it to something as abstract as an institution, namely the religious order that would eventually carry his name. Benedict saw that holiness would be found not so much by searching for a perfect haven to inhabit or having the right religious affiliation, but in the giving of oneself fully to a specific place: to its transformation and to one's own. Benedict was sure that God could be found in all places—in his simple monasteries of a dozen men, in grand churches—just as God could be found and experienced by those who actually walked with Jesus Christ. Or, as we might expand it to encompass—stability being something of a universal principle at the heart of all the great religious traditions—by those who listened at the feet of the Buddha, Moses, Muhammad.

What was needed, Benedict taught, was maddeningly simple. It was a commitment to trust in God's goodness—that he was indeed there, in that very place; and that holiness, happiness, and human fulfillment were to be found, not tomorrow or over the hill, but today—here.

Monastic values are mystical values, and mystical values are profoundly human values for all those who seek a relationship with God. Not surprisingly, then, stability can be spoken about in many ways. Ram Dass, the former Harvard professor once known as Richard Alpert who became a New Age guru, crystallized his teachings in the phrase "Be here now." Is this not a call to stability? Thich Nhat Hanh returns again and again to the principle of "mindfulness," the practice of being present in each moment, in each place, with both a calmness and intensity. Is this not a restatement, in Buddhist terms, of the stability of the cloister?

As we look upon our world, it is not difficult to see what our quest for the new, the different, the latest has produced. Movement is today a popularly accepted narcotic. Change has become an end in itself, serving its own ends, making us subservient to its process. With our cellular phone nearby, the "ideal" vacation spot just beyond our budget, the "perfect" mate offered in a personals ad, the right house just coming on the market, we are hardly ever satisfied. Constantly in touch, yet unconnected. From place to place we search for fulfillment, from spirituality to spirituality, relationship to relationship, skimming the surface, never going deeper. We seem ever hungry, seldom fed. Instead of being satisfied, the human spirit is deadened. Fatigue, dullness, and a loss of consciousness set in. We cry out "more!" fully realizing that *more* begets a desire for *still more*—while what we truly need is a resting place for our weary selves.

An understanding of stability offers that resting place. But, equally, understanding what stability is *not* is just as important. For if we practiced stability slavishly we would never leave our home, job, relationship. I would still be in Cleveland, Ohio, wearing corduroy knickers, delivering phantom newspapers for a daily that no longer exists. Such paralysis does no justice to the grace of God, the excitement of this fantastic journey called life, the opportunities that will present themselves, our individual and changing tastes, hopes, and desires. Stability is woven of the ability to stay put and yet never lose the explorer's desire for new experiences. It is not merely a leaden weight meant to anchor us so securely that we might never go astray. To advocate for stability does not imply that we must make monotony somehow "work for us" or learn to abide by other unhelpful moral bromides.

Rather, stability's goal is that we might see the inner truth of who we are and what we are doing. That we might be still enough long enough to be joined intimately to the God who dwells within, in that center of ourselves alive with goodness and grace. It is difficult—no, it is impossible—to find and maintain that center if our waking hours are a blur of mindless activity, without the presence and practice of stability in our lives. Unlike the monks of Mepkin, we will never be called to vow ourselves to stability. But stability's power and wisdom can provide a framework for surviving, even mastering, our frantic world that will never fail us.

If we remain open and alert, we will see how stability is to be applied—when we are to stay, when we are to go on our way. Both are different faces of stability; the principle remains. This discipline of looking honestly at the events, circumstances, and people in our lives is called discernment, another monastic staple. Corrosive, dead, sinful situations— situations that take us farther from our sense of connectedness with God— are not to be held on to (although our frightened selves may do just that). Conversely, there will be dark and troubling times through which we will pass in all parts of our lives, but just because they are difficult does not mean that we are meant to move on. Prayer, solitude, quiet, being available to the murmurings of God—all will help to point the way, penetrating the mystery of what we are going through. Peacefulness, happiness, that sense of patience and kindness that naturally results in a generosity of spirit— these traits are some of stability's litmus tests. Our bodies tell us; the very look on our face is a sign.

While the monastery presents a model, even monks living decades of the most circumscribed life imaginable sometimes never find the true meaning of stability. For if while their bodies are inside the walls their minds are outside, yearning to be with souls more alert, more perfect, more sensitive—this is not stability at all. (Is it any different in married life or work life or family life?) Stability is not accomplished by merely signing in. Its value can only fully be realized when it has led us to bring ourselves into a stable structure of life so that we may truly be able to live fully. To have rest and experience activity in appropriate balance.

What is more important than walls and signs forbidding entry—those typical markers of stability in monasteries—is the interior cloister. For this is the place where God truly dwells, where we dwell in unity with him, even though we may fight such terrifying intimacy. Finding a perfect geographical space is often not possible. But inner space ever awaits our bidding. The interior cloister sets our soul on solid ground so that we need not (indeed, cannot) frantically thrash about, diffusing our energies, failing to see the graces that abound for the soul wholly present. Such graces are often obscure. But in the interior cloister, that place of solitude and silence, we may enter into this holiest of holy places when God awaits us.

With all this talk of monastic stability and the interior cloister, we might think that Trappists live an isolated life. Actually, they are perfectly aware of what is going on in the world outside. Yet in order to have any impact on that world, they must be centered, present, active, involved—not the world's life, but in *their* life. I think of that each time I come to Mepkin. This place offers its healing and magic not because it is home to great intellectuals or influential leaders, but because it is a place where people simply attempt to do the work at hand as well as they are able. They pray regularly, forgive each other's offenses, get up when they fall down, bake bread and package eggs with affection, and rise before dawn with humility and hope, beseeching God to open their lips so that they might praise him—with word and work, thought and action.

Are our lives so different from theirs? We do not rise before dawn and wear medieval white tunics and black scapulars; but like them, we can only take one breath at a time, be in one place, perform one action. If we treat ourselves as constantly transplanted young saplings, our starved, attenuated leaves and spindly branches will never bask in the warmth of the sun, even when it shines upon us. We will bear no fruit. And when the winds of life howl we shall blow down, for our roots have never had a chance to find their home.

But if we choose our ground carefully, and allow our roots to continue undisturbed their search for the nutrients we need—even when another plot of land looks momentarily sweeter or sunnier—we will have achieved a degree of stability. Stability is commitment, and that commitment, so lacking in our relativistic, drip-dry, disposable, replaceable world, is what makes us whole—and in turn helps others to find their bearings. The monastery is a perfect example, where ordinary men become extraordinary and in turn—not by preaching to us or expounding their views on talk shows or prescribing "Ten Steps to Holiness," but simply by their *presence*— invite us to the fullness of life.

Monastic wisdom does not teach us to practice stability exactly as monks do, but to live its essence. For stability has less to do with place than with a state of mind. Monastic wisdom can show us that stability does not mean limitation, attenuation, and deadening routine, but actually ultimate freedom and the ability to derive deep satisfaction, holiness, from every situation in our lives. Yes, I know that seems an impossible dream; but it is at the heart of monastic life. And it is something we want for our lives as well.

When a monk vows stability—or when we begin to practice it—the whole cosmic drama of life is transferred to the place and circumstances in which we find ourselves. For monasticism ordains that there is a depth to everything. Life, so often spread out to the far horizons but lacking any real depth, takes on a vertical dimension. We are rewarded with sustained contact with people, places, things.

For the Mepkin monk, there is no escape, no tomorrow; only the reality of this meal, this time of prayer, this loading of eggs for market, this going to bed, this rising, this room. Present opportunities are taken seriously because nothing much is going to change. The drama of religious conversion or blinding apocalyptic insight is irrelevant; a new clarity emerges from sustained contact. Time is at once willingly submitted to—and transcended.

For us in the world, stability prevents daydreaming about "what if . . . ." and inserts us totally into what we are doing, causing us to live with a new intensity. It breathes new life into commitment and reawakens the awesome gift of fidelity, revealing a new kind of truth revealed only to those who are brave enough to stay in one place long enough. It asks God to be present constantly in our midst.

Marriage, work, our spiritual journey—all take on a new dimension. We are present, fully present to the people around us, the tasks at hand, the inspirations that used to pass unnoticed before our eyes, because before our focus was ever *there* and never *here.* We are able to infuse new meaning into that hackneyed term "quality time," which is often no more than an excuse to spend less time with children, spouse, or friends. For the person who embraces the concept of monastic stability, all time is quality time.

What is crucially different between those who strive for stability and those who worship activity is that stability-seekers are rarely disoriented—not by failure, not by success, not by the changing circumstances that the day may bring. They have a center, that interior cloister that is at once rock solid yet mobile. Worshiping activity means that the activity must ultimately produce something, yield something. We must win, conquer, wring something out of it. With stability, presence is its own perfect gift—and outcome.

Of course, marriages fail; we change jobs; there are damaging situations we must leave. Stability does not mean that we simply plant ourselves someplace and tough it out regardless. If we are at once present to the moment and able to present ourselves patiently to God, we will be able to see the signs. There is a period of dying, of disaffection, of gradual withdrawal when the crucial elements of devotion, satisfaction, human need, or vocation are no longer present. Stability is not like turning an electrical switch on and off. It involves continual reassessment and dying, conviction and new birth.

Stability's possibilities rang clearer during a short conversation with Brother Joseph one afternoon on this September visit. Brother Joseph joined the Trappists at the age of sixteen some fifty-four years ago. He has an impish smile and a rapier-like nose, and his waist is girded by one of the most telling and beautiful belts I have ever seen. Given to him while a novice it is cracked and worn, held together by but a sinew of leather. But he wears it with both confidence and pride—a modest pride, to be sure. He is a Trappist through and through. It is his brown badge of courage.

As we stood in the brilliant sunlight just inside the cloister enclosure our conversation turned to the ocean, just ten minutes from my house and a place I often visit. "Oh, there were porpoises leaping out of the water and crashing and the waves were pounding on the beach," he said excitedly. "And blue; I mean it was BLUE. The sand was warm. I just watched those porpoises, they were so close I could almost touch them. I love the ocean." His eyes sparkled; he was a mere boy once more.

That this fifteen-minute experience had occurred during a happenstance detour on a trip seven years ago to another monastery, and marked only the second time in his more than half-century as a monk that he had seen the ocean, made little difference. The ocean was far more present to him than it was to me, who had seen it one more time in the past week than Brother Joseph had in his entire life.

Stability yields the gift of rapture.

Brother Joseph told me of being in the choir at Gethsemani, the monastery he had joined. As they chanted their Latin psalms one day, a baby's cry gently echoed through the vast church. In those days, the monks were kept strictly out of public view, a high screen separating them from the occasional visitor. They knew they would never see the source. Nonetheless, huge smiles spread across the faces of these men even in the midst of their serious and sacred task of praising God, men who had not heard such sound for years, even decades. Brother Joseph recalled looking across the choir—tears were streaming down the face of one of the most stern, ascetic monks in the monastery.

Stability releases the gift of tears—and of sheer joy.

Brother Joseph remembers fondly the days at Gethsemani when the practice of silence was strictly observed. "But you could tell everything about a monk without talking," he says. "The way he walked down a hallway, the look on his face—it told you what was happening inside him. Words would have been superfluous. But, oh, monks knew how to laugh. They didn't laugh all the time, but when they did, it was from the heart, it was like music."

Stability engenders the gift of true laughter.

So, it becomes apparent that the stability of monastic life hones, not dulls, the senses. There is a preciousness of appreciation for the beauties of this world, a depth of emotion from which we might find ourselves immunized by casual familiarity. These men who remain in one place are hardly throwing away life untasted; they are living it to the full.

"I never chose this place for myself, it was chosen for me."[2] Thomas Merton's words take on even more poignancy when we realize that, while he loved Gethsemani, he was constantly tempted to leave it, paradoxically both for more solitude and to see first hand what he only knew from books and letters. His dilemma was never solved, really, for Merton always felt

---

[2]Thomas Merton, *Conjectures of a Guilty Bystander* (Garden City, N.Y.: Doubleday Image, 1968), 257.

himself a wanderer on the face of the earth. His wide range of interests and hundreds of correspondents both enriched and vexed him. Yet something deep within Merton urged him to stay at Gethsemani, to seek both holiness and stimulation there.

The window high up in the monastery church, which affords that stunning but limited glimpse of the sky, is another way to look at stability. We see more rather than less by having our lives, in a sense, "framed" by the intensity of stability.

All of us have our own stories about flight and stability, of finding ourselves restricted to places we would have never chosen, yet sensing in them something that, with all our misgivings, was ultimately right for us. When I look back to my own midlife crisis days of ultimate freedom, my frenetic but desperately unhappy existence, I realize that I stubbornly fought the very thing that would ultimately bring me peace. I looked upon married life and children as punishingly restrictive, and certainly not a path to holiness or heroism. After my devoted attempt to be a man of the world, I swerved onto other paths, believing I needed to live with the poor, then to be a monk, do some work of great value to humankind. Something out of the ordinary. But, it was marriage that chose me—as surely as I chose it.

I cannot fully explain what happened; but looking back, my marriage has made complete sense. With two sons embarking on their teenage years and a working wife, my freedom of movement is severely restricted, my own desires secondary at best. Yet I experience some of the richest days of my life. I have the sense—with all the problems and limitations—that I am where I am supposed to be. Now, my conversion of manners is set first and firmly in the tiny community of my family. I do not have to trouble myself to sort out what I should do each day. It is quite easy to see what needs to be done, where I am failing, what I must do to live this life more completely and well.

I thought about this during one trip to Mepkin with my family when my younger son Daniel and I traveled over to Charleston for a reunion of my shipmates from the USS *Power* (DD-839), a destroyer on which I had served for three years in the early 1960s. In *Trappist*, a recent film about the monastery, Father Aelred notes that he would never have chosen his fellow monks to live with.[3] I would have surely agreed about my shipmates, young boys at the time, some of them troubled and many of them difficult. But seeing these men, now shaped and worn by the years—as was I—I felt an affection so deep I found myself embarrassingly on the verge of tears as I talked to them. Yes, we were thrown together by the grace of the government, and we had a specific job to do. But it was more than that. By transcending our differences, sanding the edges of our respective egos and backgrounds and personal tastes, our enforced stability had accomplished something that went far beyond the Cuban missile crisis we helped defuse, beyond the Russian submarines we kept at bay, beyond the astronauts we stood ready to rescue. Our time together afforded us the opportunity to see beyond skin color or accent, beyond talent or shortcomings. We grew to love and care about each other. We saw each other's fragility and each other's majesty. Our enforced stability nurtured transcendence daily; we became better people than any of us thought we might hope to be, in a situation few of us would have chosen. Although we never would speak in such pieties, we saw the face of God in each other.

Is the "job," the hope, of living a full, decent, and centered life any less worthy a goal? Is love and care only restricted to military and marriage? Could it be that the casual groupings in which we find ourselves equally hold the seeds of our redemption and happiness?

So much of our energy goes into *conquering* time and space—be it with cell phones and beepers, e-mail or attempts at more efficient management of time, moving into a bigger house or apartment or the corner office with windows on two sides—that it is no wonder we feel disoriented by a sense of placelessness. We yearn for a home so our soul might be at peace, and yet we do everything to keep ourselves spiritually homeless.

Mepkin monks have only an eight-by-twelve-foot cell to themselves; their time is rigidly controlled. But they have acres of beauty surrounding them and enough time to apportion between prayer and work, eating and sleeping. They take time for composed silence, doing nothing. They need

---

[3] *Trappist*, videotape (Mahwah, N.J.: Paulist Media Works, 1997).

not conquer time for it is their friend; their abode, if small, is a place of simplicity, utility, and peace.

Yes, the monastery is a holy and wonderful place for me—and many people have their special sanctuaries—but they are but tiny islands on a vast, boiling ocean. If monasteries were the only places one could find peace and holiness, it would be a peculiar God indeed who had concocted such a skewed plan of earthly existence.

Sometimes we fail to see—or to seek—the sanctity in the places and people in our own lives. We might visit a grandmother's farm where we once spent youthful summers and run our hand along a familiar pump handle, or walk the hallways of a school we attended. While we may have not chosen them, these are places that formed us and centered us; they are often precious in our memory. Ordinary gestures, done with simplicity and purity of heart, take on new meaning. The place is sanctified by our memories, by the rituals we performed there. When we honor the consistency in our lives we can better see the direction of our path and discover the potential for the future.

That farm, that school, were not places that offered great revelations or Delphic oracles; rather, it is simply because we were there and invested ourselves in them they are holy to us. Simple habits—pumping clear, cool water; playing in a schoolyard at day's end—became rituals, invested not so much with rational thought as sacred meaning unknown to us at the time. Similarly holy events happen each day, yet we often let them pass by unnoticed. As Merton said, "Here is the unspeakable secret: paradise is all around us and we do not understand it."

Understand it. Or just see it. At a minimum, be open to this unspeakable secret. This is the key to living the mystery of stability. When we present ourselves, whole and aware, to the places where we find ourselves in life—both those consciously chosen and those chosen for us, those we find pleasant and those we find difficult—we may not initially see them as felicitously as Merton. But with time we will slowly begin to understand each moment as a moment in the presence of our Creator, Father, and friend.

Thoreau celebrating the ordinariness of Walden Pond. Merton in his hermitage, saying, "What I do up here is breathe." A desert father advising a seeker, "Go, sit in your cell, and your cell will teach you everything."[4] Esther de Waal, a British woman of our own day, concluding, "Only after we have given up the desire to be different and admit that we deserve no special attention is there space to encounter God, and to discover that although we are unique and that God calls us each by name, that is completely compatible with the unspectacular, possibly the monotony, of life in the place in which we find ourselves."[5]

Each of these writers acknowledged the space they inhabited, the place where they found themselves, had the potential to form and shape them, if only they allowed it to. Instead of "cell," we can substitute dinner table or conference table, church pew or theater seat, windswept pasture or Times Square, basketball court or meditation bench. Then, with these great teachers, we will understand that being here, now, is as perfect an act as one can hope to perform.

Thoreau, Merton, the desert father, de Waal, the Mepkin monks—these, profoundly shaped by their daily life, responding to and honoring their surroundings; not escaping for something other or different or new, continuing to invest their energy in the present, believing in the omniscient presence of God and the sanctity of their place and moment in life. They discover that stability is actually learning to love a place—and both physically and mentally remaining in place so that love can be experienced deeply.

Is this not possible for all of us if we also honor where we are?

This is no passive endeavor. As monks are formed, they form. As we are formed, we too form. If monks have this calming presence upon us, we can bring it to others. If we have an interior cloister, it will show. Our very manner can be the beginnings of reclaiming the interior cloister for our friends, family, children, coworkers. Words inspired by this sort of stability resound from the spiritual classic *The Imitation of Christ*: "Above all things, keep peace within yourself, then you will be able to create peace among others. It is better to be peaceful than learned."[6] Our presence, our

---

[4]Thomas Merton, *Wisdom of the Desert* (New York: New Directions, 1960), 30.
[5]Esther de Waal, *Seeking God: The Way of St. Benedict* (Collegeville, Minn.: Liturgical Press, 1984), 61.
[6]Quoted in *The Liturgy of the Hours*, vol. I, 280.

stability, provides that still point for others going through difficult times. If our hearts have been set free by stability, then we are available in a new and deep way. No, we don't have answers and can't solve complex problems, but by our calm presence we provide something even more useful. Who cannot remember patient friends who offered nothing but themselves—when that was exactly what was needed?

On the job, in the neighborhood, in a crowded shopping mall: the presence of a person who embraces stability brings solace and peace. Stability does not ask, it gives. It does not judge, it accepts. It instills a deep confidence. It is God's presence manifested in the world. For if God is not in these places, with us, reflected by us, then where is he?

Thomas Merton was a budding writer before he joined the Trappists. He had written some poems, a not-very-good coming of age novel, reviews, and occasional pieces. When he died twenty-seven years later, he had produced a body of work impressive not only in terms of content but sheer size—some forty books, hundreds of poems and articles, a voluminous correspondence, and a journal that was eventually compressed into five volumes. Many Gethsemani monks wondered who this Thomas Merton was. The Father Louis they knew was a monk who participated fully in the monastery's life, for many years performing all the functions of a Trappist monk, long hours in choir, physical labor, teaching, kitchen and housekeeping chores. Where did he get time to do all that writing?

Merton's stability at Gethsemani might shed some light on our lives. I certainly think about him as I look back on my own. When I had the least restrictions, the most seeming freedom, I experienced the least productive period of my life. My mind flitted from going to cover some far-off war (any war!) to being a talk-show host, from living in sybaritic Mill Valley, California to laboring with Mother Theresa in Calcutta's slums. Any place, any work, was better than what I was doing right now, I convinced myself. I grasped and grasped, but never reached.

Only in that hermit year did I begin to change, painfully, slowly—and actually unknowingly—preparing my life for stability. For although I was seemingly living the most contemplative, quiet, and certainly stable of lives, I was not yet at home with myself. Only when I married and had children did I grow up, and begin to be truly grounded. Now my life, woven among three others, has found its way. I am still a restless pilgrim, an imperfect husband and father, faithful or abysmally faithless before God depending on the day and mood. But I am solidly *here.* That much I can say. I have no time for so many things I used to believe I simply had to do; yet I have more time for everything that is integral to this life, be it prayer or my younger son's basketball practice, my own writing or working on a chromosome chart for my older son's science class, baking bread, swimming, or reading over a draft of my wife's work. Yes, it is a life of some sacrifice and compromise, but equally of far deeper satisfactions. This is where I am; no other place. I must attend to the real, not evading the uncomfortable, meanwhile experiencing the good, the grace-filled, the wondrous. A healthy mix of advice comes for all of us from an unlikely pair of sources: the words of St. Matthew's gospel, where Jesus admonishes his disciples, "Therefore do not be anxious about tomorrow, for tomorrow will be anxious about itself"[7]; and the Latin poet, Horace, who blurted out, *"Carpe diem"*—"Seize the day!"

In monastic, married, or single life—and really all walks of life—it is all too common to come to the sad realization that some of us are simply going through the motions in the place or vocation where we spend so many hours of each day. Often, a cheaply acquired stability has offered itself, its primary attribute being emotional detachment, which may even masquerade as a certain kind of spiritual erudition. It is not necessarily that we are performing poorly; it is just that what we do is somehow flat, moribund, lifeless. While physically present we are emotionally absent, carried along by inertia, not desire. Any sense of vitality or adventure is precluded; the spirit sleeps. It is an all too common ailment of our wounded world, vividly teaching us that stability is not merely a case of so much protoplasm being in one place. In fact, if that is all there is, stability is unhealthy—mentally, physically, spiritually. It then becomes a certain kind of tacit agreement to allow a part of us to die.

Which of us hasn't been tempted to give up emotionally when pre-

[7]Matthew 6:34.

sented by an unpleasant, irrational child, parent, relative, or friend, or an impossible situation? How often as a father have I silently vowed to do the minimum required of me? I would no longer invest myself; it was more than I can take! I would await the return of reason or changed circumstances.

Believe it or not, this also happens regularly in monasteries. Difficult turns in their spiritual path, the time of their life, demons, or countless other extenuating circumstances make certain monks unbearable. Community life—for them, and certainly with them—becomes not a paradise but a hell. The moral fatigue of acedia melts one day into another. At such times, thoughtless and uncaring behavior or chronic flouting of Benedict's *Rule* are sure evidence of the lack of a true vocation. Masking itself as a call to purity of vision, the temptation to withdraw into one's own world becomes overwhelming. Rather than deal with the others, let them dangle.

But the monastic way demands involvement. Contemplation, transcendence, and communication with God are desirable and wonderful—but they are optional. Emotional involvement in the life of the community, not just as an abstract idea but as individual brothers, is mandated. The same is true for us, wherever our stability finds us, if we hope to be both human and holy.

Early one evening, before compline, I walked through the sun's scarlet and orange rays, shimmering off the Cooper River through the huge live oaks along its banks. Their brooding presence pays proper tribute to that dazzling couple who once laughed and chatted in this formal garden, now their graveyard. Down the slight incline from the Luces' graves, a lone alligator slipped into the water, his daily sunning complete. Egrets, like well-placed statuary, stood motionless among the tidal grasses. Earth and flowers and river concoct a heady aroma, so rich it bids one to inhale deeper, deeper. This is a sacred, timeless land, unaware of what our frenetic world is up to. It is a land that seems entirely sure of itself. Green all year round, adorned by azalea and camellia, seemingly unaware of real dying. Stability reigns.

As I turned and walked along further, the dazzling rays of the setting sun, filtered by the live-oak branches and the gently swaying Spanish moss, danced on the dull brick of the pump shed and the egg-sorting house. Behind, tucked amid a group of shorter trees, were two unfamiliar and equally strange vehicles: a stubby panel truck and a small, somewhat rusty mobile home. I could not resist investigating.

Inside the truck, I would find, was an altar, a tabernacle containing the reserved sacrament of the Eucharist, and shelves stocked with books. The mobile home was, in essence, a traveling convent. Sister Jo and Sister Priscilla, whose family names had been discarded as so much excess baggage, were Little Sisters of Jesus—and they were circus workers. Sister Jo was a ticket-taker and concessionaire, usually of cold drinks. Sister Priscilla, an expert seamstress, worked in wardrobe and makeup. Their tiny contemplative order follows the example of Charles de Foucauld, a one-time French soldier who at the turn of the nineteenth century found the Trappists not austere enough and too far from true poverty. Brother Charles, as he was called despite being a priest, spent his life in the Algerian desert living with those he felt were outcasts. Like Brother Charles before them, the Little Sisters do not openly attempt to evangelize or convert, but just be present to those on the margins of society. In their case, a small traveling circus.

When we talked at a tiny table in their mobile home, they told me how Charles had first constructed a stone wall around his desert hut in the Hoggar Mountains to maintain a cloister, but then saw that it prevented him from reaching the nomadic Tuareg he had come to serve. So he went out among the people, eventually being killed by the very tribe he served.

Stability? They laughed. They felt great stability with the rhythms of a circus that might play a new town every other night. The big top was hoisted up and brought down; animals were fed, costumes mended, supplies procured. Instead of rising before dawn and praying in a conventional church, they would rise before dawn and read the Divine Office in their truck before traveling to the next town. They seldom could get to daily mass, so they would hold a service in the truck when the schedule allowed, which it did not always do. It was when they weren't on the road, when they were stopped for awhile, that they felt unstable. So, here they were, parked on holy monastery ground, feeling not nearly as stable as when on some weed-covered vacant lot on the edge of another forgettable town.

I arose the next morning and after vigils began my trip north, toward home. My companion on this 4:00 A.M. journey, meant to keep me at least awake if not alert, was a tape of Leo Tolstoy's *Anna Karenina*. Anna, beautiful, desirable Anna, blaming everyone for her unhappiness, moving feverishly from Moscow to St. Petersburg to a remote *dacha* in search of peace of mind for her tortured self. As if a change of venue could allow her to avoid a change of heart.

That evening I helped Noah as he attempted to recite by heart one of President Theodore Roosevelt's most memorable speeches. The words, reached for, coming in short, thoughtful phrases, seemed to hang in the air. It was not unlike the monks chanting the psalms: words, ideas, presented for observation, and possibly application.

It is not the critic who counts . . .

. . . or where the doer of deeds could have done them better . . .

. . . credit belongs to the man who is actually in the arena, whose face is marred with dust and sweat and blood . . .

. . . comes up short again and again because there is no effort without error and shortcoming . . .

. . . who spends himself in a worthy cause . . .

. . . and . . .

. . . if he fails while daring greatly, knows his place shall never be with those timid and cold souls who know neither victory nor defeat.

"Dad! Dad! Are you listening?" he asked.

"Stability," I said, looking at him as if I had just made a great scientific breakthrough. "It's all about stability."

"What's stability?"

"It's . . . it's being someplace and doing the best you can," I found myself saying.

"Oh."

Benedict and Merton and the circus nuns would say it other ways, more elegantly I'm sure. But this would do for now for a thirteen-year-old and his somewhat obtuse father.

Detachment

Freedom of the Heart

It was but a moment—perhaps a few seconds, no more—on my otherwise peaceful ride through the black Carolina night. I was not as alert as I had convinced myself I was driving past Georgetown, South Carolina, whose steam-belching electric generating plant and pungent paper mill always marked the halfway point on my journey to Mepkin. The reader on the audiotape of Jack London's *Sea Wolf* playing on my cassette deck had lulled me with a soporific monotone. *Midnight in the Garden of Good and Evil*, the other tape I'd brought along, had proved an ill-chosen companion, simply too racy as a prelude to monastery days. So I had been riding for over an hour in silence.

Then came that momentary lapse. My eyes flickered closed. Cinders pinged at the fenders. A guardrail's reflective strip flashed by, then another, closer, larger. My eyes bulged open. I jerked the wheel to the left. A thump shuddered the front end as I came back onto the road. I slowed to a crawl.

These rides to the monastery often provide fertile ground for contemplation, sometimes intended, sometimes not. As I collected myself in the nervous seconds that followed, I found myself suddenly and vividly remembering the two occasions, some thirty years apart, when I could easily have died behind the wheel of a car. The object of my somewhat dreary contemplation certainly reflected an inner disposition. Death is not usually on my mind. Except at times like these.

I was trying to put on the best face as I approached this fifth monastic sojourn—some sort of Knute Rockne–like effort—but I was obviously having difficulty being my own spiritual cheerleader. My friend Father Joseph Greer, when faced with anything from ennui to cancer, had been fond of saying, "Just lace up the sneakers and get out on the court." That is not always so easy for me. Things were not going at all well in my professional life, and it was hard to pretend otherwise. Another string of rejections for ideas that seemed so good. A quick call to the bank on how much money was in my overdraft account. Some of our modest savings would have to be used to meet daily needs. Spiritually, my prayer life was dogged, but uninspired.

I am not a person given to prolonged or clinical depression, at least not to an extent any professional has pinpointed. But I do know a dark night of the soul when one comes, and such a night had descended upon me. At times like this all effort seems foolish, all plans misguided; self-worth is a cruel joke from which everyone—except me—would enjoy a good laugh. Death stalks the wayward soul. Having been through these nights before, I equally knew that when the temptation came to find some quick and easy way to pierce that darkness, to grab hold of anything that ever so slightly appeared to offer solace or comfort or cure from the soul's malaise, this pilgrim had to be careful. Rather than grab or reach out, it was usually a time to let go further, painful and unnatural though this might be. To be patient, not act impulsively. To try to see deeper than the roiling, unsettled surface. A much misunderstood monastic disposition, I had found, needed to be employed.

It is called detachment. And, especially when things are not going well in our lives, it is the most difficult to practice.

Over the past few weeks, an image had been recurring to me. I was building a bridge. It was a sturdy and certainly well-intentioned bridge, with crossbeams and uprights, girders and thick cables. But it was a bridge toward a far shore shrouded in a thick, impenetrable mist. A bridge, it seemed, to nowhere. How much easier it would be to toss a line, or extend a single, thin plank over to the other side, and then—fragile though it might be—build upon it. Or simply go back to firm ground. But the spiritual life is not so disposed, and I knew it.

Even when I arrived at my holy sanctuary an hour later, everything seemed to conspire against me. Not that this required any great sacrifice, but this time I was not assigned to a cell within the embrace of the cloister, where I could feel and see the presence of the monks. Instead I was cast out from their midst to a doublewide prefabricated home, set in the woods about an eighth of a mile away. It seemed an entirely unmonastic way to spend my days at Mepkin. It smelled new and decidedly secular. The walls were thin and bathed in a covering so unremittingly beige I found myself lulled once again, this time into a senseless vertigo when I walked into my room. Detachment—detachment from the cloister community was my first offering, whether I wanted to make it or not.

Instead of a welcoming smile, what I received as a rather unpleasant, somewhat dismissive look (interpretation: "Oh, *you* again!") flashed across the abbot's face when I first saw him after mass that day. Perhaps this was just another sign of my ability to put entirely too much store by such ordinary disappointments, proof of my inability to disregard or go beyond externals to the essence of what was at hand. Such qualities are at the heart of detachment to be sure. After all, did it matter where I lay my head at the monastery that night, or what the abbot was thinking?

It did. That was the problem.

From the moment a new monk arrives, turns in every item he has brought from the world, and is issued new clothes from a common storeroom, detachment is at hand in earnest. He eats the food placed on the refectory serving table; observes the hours of prayer, work, and sleep; often is given a job assignment unlike anything he has ever done before. His will, equally, is handed over; while he may speak his mind, he is to obey the abbot in all things. If a warm pair of slippers arrives that might warm cold toes on wintry mornings, he must not claim them for his own, wearing them only with the abbot's permission. Books, tapes, candy—all are common property as soon as they arrive at the monastery; the name on the address label is irrelevant. Detachment from things simple and great is but a symbolic offering of the monk's total self, so that God might have an opportunity to shape him. The idea is not so much to break a man, but to separate him from the nonessentials of life, so that he might seek the essential—God. Detachment is meant to create in him an ever-growing and evolving state of *being*, not a process of *having*. Certainly at odds with the world, detachment is nonetheless at the heart of monastic life.

Not too long after Thomas Merton arrived at Gethsemani, the young monk triumphantly proclaimed his unquestioning fervor for the life he was then undertaking: "The best way to keep the spirit of the *Rule* is to keep the letter as perfectly as possible."[1] Merton had willingly left the world and its goods behind in order to create in himself a new being. Detachment, he sensed, was a key element of his monastic formation, crucial to his spiritual growth. Fasting from food, abstinence from sex, the subrogation of his will; all this emptying of natural desires would help him find the intimate relationship with God he so ardently sought.

I had arrived at Mepkin on the feast of All Hallows and the monks—showing that, though men of God, they hadn't yet lost their boyish sense of humor—had fashioned a particularly poignant jack o' lantern. A bold cross, with radiant streams shooting out to the edges of a huge pumpkin, greeted them during their rounds of prayer in the church.

---

[1] Thomas Merton, "St. Robert: Founder of Cîteaux," *Cistercian Studies Quarterly*, 33(1) (1998), 12.

I found myself watching the monks closely that day; in their uniform attire in choir, in their only slightly more distinctive work clothes as, like a small, low-flying flock, they streaked toward the egg-grading house on their rusty bikes. I watched as they ate, both at a relatively sumptuous lunch of amazingly good kale pie within a whole wheat crust made by Sister Louise, a visiting Cistercian nun, and at the routinized evening meal of sliced cheese, bread, and a huge bowl of the ubiquitous fruit cocktail, cubes and shapes of decidedly unnatural hues and suspiciously uniform consistency. All of the externals of their life constantly reminded the monks that they had nothing of their own.

Yet, if Benedict and Bernard and Merton are to be believed—if monastic life is a road to holiness and inner peace—they had everything they needed.

I so badly wanted to be like them. But I could not. I live an entirely different kind of life, one that would not abide such communal abandon. But I knew that their sense of detachment was crucially important if my imaginary bridge were to course on toward that misty bluff. The dark night might not allow for construction right now, but I could not simply stop. I had to go on, letting go of solid ground with one hand, not yet being able to touch the other side.

For most of us detachment is another of those much-too-fancy words in spirituality's lexicon. It bespeaks a state of ethereal indifference. At turns wispy, dreary or plain, impractical, detachment is an impossible-to-attain ideal not grounded in real life, real experience, real need. Detachment is often regarded purely in terms of having or not having—things, status, love, powers. We imagine that the poor and otherwise wanting practice detachment somewhat naturally, almost by default, having little to hold on to or hope for. Conversely, we smugly assume that those well endowed with the riches of this world are less likely to practice detachment; their possessions and accouterments seem to signal their desire to acquire and retain.

In my own life, at least, it hasn't worked that way. I have never been rich, but there have been times in my life when I lacked for nothing—could have gotten on a plane and gone anywhere, anytime; bought any article of clothing; eaten regularly at the best restaurants. Nothing tied me down or prevented me from having virtually whatever I wanted.

This period saw some of the unhappiest days of my life. My soul ached within me even as my body was well-clothed and fed. My appointment calendar brimmed with possibilities. I was invited to the best New York literary parties; I knew many famous people. Pictures show Kurt Vonnegut and Betty Friedan in my living room at one of my birthday parties. I cannot even remember it. All too often, riding an elevator to a penthouse suite or walking up the stairs to an elegant townhouse or a Hamptons' summer cottage, I felt so wretchedly destitute I was ready to weep. My well-cut French blazer could not hide a naked man. I can still remember the excruciating hesitation before ringing a doorbell—when what I wanted to do was jam my hand back in my pocket and run away.

I had everything a young writer in New York could have wanted and yet I cared little about any of it. Was this, after all—although I wasn't aware of it—a sort of detachment? I think not. True detachment is born not of rejecting or hating things, but of an inner disposition I would only later begin to discover.

At another time in my life, moving from pole to pole, I lived a life of voluntary poverty. I shed all pretense of having anything at all. I gave up my townhouse, its furnishings, my car. At a soup kitchen I helped to start in Brooklyn, I served the poor and homeless, addicts and alcoholics, ex-prisoners and the mentally ill. I advocated for them, visited them, consoled them. I lived with three mentally disturbed men (and one true saint, Jacques Travers) in a dank, cockroach-infested apartment marooned in a bad neighborhood. I considered any personal need nothing less than a temptation I had to resist, a barrier to pleasing my God. I wore cast-off clothing; I ate cast-off food. At least externally I was living what might be considered a model Christian life. But I don't know if it brought me closer to God. Something was sorely missing and wrong. This kind of detachment had not liberated my spirit at all. Those were painfully unhappy days, dissonant days, angry days, self-pitying days. I wept at my poverty, for it was a poverty of spirit.

I still did not understand detachment.

Having or not having things has very little to do with true detachment—at least little to do with the kind of detachment that runs through all the great religious traditions. It is the sort of detachment that challenges spiritual seekers to see exactly what matters in this life and what does not, what are real needs and what is excess baggage—carefully packed, transported, and protected, but ultimately unneeded. On our journey through life we all have our various knapsacks and steamer trunks crammed with what garments and goods we have convinced ourselves that various situations of the spirit and climates of the soul might require. Yet all too often when we arrive at strange destinations, we realize we have overpacked—or brought the wrong things.

As I spent these fall days at Mepkin, I found myself again fascinated with the ingenious—and oftentimes maddeningly, if indirectly, prescient—church calendar. Through the various liturgical seasons, the Common of Saints recalling lives of noble, holy voyagers from the first two thousand years of Christianity, and the many feast days celebrating mysteries of the faith, the calendar provides a continuously changing backdrop for the consideration of our lives. Especially at this time of year, when the earth has lost its summer vigor and night steals more and more of each day, the calendar appropriately deals with death and the mystery of what lies beyond death. This, combined with the concentration of prayers and readings that punctuate the monastic day, present anyone seeking wisdom with many images of detachment.

On All Saints, celebrated the first day of November, I was starkly confronted with death, that of martyrs (at one time, you had to be a martyr to be a saint). The next day, All Souls, celebrates the lesser acknowledged but equally exemplary in our own lives who are to be prayed to and, especially, for, so that (in Catholic teaching) they might not linger in purgatory. But as is often the case when one doggedly searches specific places or times for solace and The Answer on a particular, narrow point— as I had learned so well in June—the opposite as easily might occur. As I read and thought and walked, detachment was delivered in a paralyzing concentration, a kind of double or triple whammy. It was still another reminder of the fine nuance of the spiritual life: the pilgrim may be asked even to be detached from detachment.

For the voices that initially rose up from the pages I found myself reading were those of perfervid martyrs who simply couldn't wait to suffer and die. "Let it be known that I will gladly die for God if only you do not stand in my way," thundered St. Ignatius of Antioch from the second century, bound for martyrdom in Rome. "Let me be food for the wild beasts . . . the animals will be the means of making me a sacrificial victim for God. . . . If I am condemned to suffer, I will take it that you wish me well. If my case is postponed, I can only think that you wish me harm."[2] And why did my eyes fall upon this passage in the First Letter of John: "Do not love the world or the things in the world. If any one loves the world, love for the Father is not in him. For all that is in the world, the lust of the flesh and the lust of the eyes and the pride of life, is not of the Father but of the world."[3]

Death was considered the ultimate form of detachment in the early church; life itself offered up in martyrdom, the ultimate statement, a release. And after all, as the first Christians believed the end of the world could come any day, of what worth was it to bother with such a trivial pursuit as life on earth?

My own Catholic church has done too good a job perpetuating this approach, extolling a life of self-abnegation. It is little wonder we have a skewed view of detachment. Bleeding martyrs, eyes cast heavenward, are an indelible memory of my religious education. Virginity was presented as the highest calling, withdrawal from the world the only safe path to heaven. *The Imitation of Christ*, a spiritual classic otherwise rich with memorable gems, advises, "How wise and fortunate is he who now strives to be in life as he would wish to be found in death! That which gives sure hope of a happy death is utter contempt for the world. . . . Learn now to spurn all earthly things . . . Chastise your body now by penance, so that then your soul may be filled with unshaken confidence."[4]

[2] Quoted in *The Liturgy of the Hours*, vol. IV, 1491–92.
[3] I John 2:15, 16
[4] *The Imitation of Christ*, bk. 1:23, quoted in John M. Ballweg, "Christian Detachment: From the Imitation of Christ to Teilhard," *Review for Religious* 33 (1974), 1315.

Within the Cistercian world, the vision of holiness that Armand de Rance forged at La Trappe in the seventeenth century brought appreciation of detachment to new heights. If it was enjoyable, forgo it. If it was of the world, eschew it. If it caused suffering to the flesh, pursue it. If it made life easier, resist it.

Gethsemani in Merton's time, while certainly a place of holiness and happiness for many, was unspeakably unsanitary and unhealthy. Monks slept in their working robes, and showered weekly at most. When a flu epidemic hit, the conditions of life in the community invariably allowed it to become a grim reaper. Monks wore hair shirts, whipped themselves, and often fasted far beyond what a body could bear. At times they were very much attached to a sort of competitive zeal to be the first up, the last to eat, the most devout in prayer. It was as if holiness could be attained through hard work, denial, will power. The means *were* the end. The Trappists had a reputation like the Marines—these monks were the shock troops of holiness. No pain, no gain. God's grace stood off stage, in the shadows.

Literal detachment had been very much in vogue throughout much of my church's history, practiced with ferocity in American monasteries until the Second Vatican Council bid all Catholic religious orders to look back to their roots, rather than to the gnarled branches they had sprouted.

While he did indeed make great demands of those who would follow him, a look back to the roots of monasticism and the essence of Benedict's wisdom shows that he turned his back on the romantic notion of martyrdom, instead plunging his monks into seeking full and blessed lives, not merely early and holy deaths. Monastic life was a means, not an end. It was never by their actions alone or strict adherence even to his own *Rule* that monks would make their lives pleasing to God, but rather, Benedict taught, through an inner disposition, an availability to God that would be *fostered* through the demands of monastic life.

Benedict's view of detachment also indicated a healthy component of attachment, for he wanted his monks to consider all things holy. They were to handle a knife in the refectory kitchen or a sickle in the fields as reverently as the chalice that held the blood of Christ. Work in the barn was as potentially edifying as hours spent in church. Both glorified God— work by providing the means for the body to be sustained, prayer so God might be honored and touched.

Modern monastic life has radically changed since the early part of this century, coming to a far more balanced and realistic view, and reclaiming— certainly with a contemporary overlay—the real purpose of Benedict's way. At Mepkin, there is no push to live some sort of primitive existence just so the monks can claim no need of such a demon as technology. To plow their fields with a horse-drawn plow would be poetic, but not practical. In fact, they rent out most of their tillable ground, as it is economically unfeasible for the monks to work it. This is an aging community; and it must necessarily use whatever appropriate labor-saving devices may be found. In order to provide a steady stream of eggs to a supermarket chain, they need computers and telephones, not a feather quill on parchment and good intentions. They are not about to give away their land, the timber in their forests, their vehicles—for, such are necessary instruments for their sur-vival. They must pay attention to the ways of the world outside the monastery gates, and to the abilities of their members to contribute to the work of the community—or they will not be able to provide, as Benedict demands, for their daily needs.

As I scoured the monastery library and drew back the curtain of memory, I found many ways to look at detachment and what might be expected if it is practiced. There were the words of John Henry Newman— a man of the century before the Second Vatican Council, but whose wis-dom surely shaped those deliberations. Newman reflected on the links between detachment and the courage to live in uncertainty:

> [O]ur duty lies in risking upon Christ's word what we have or what we have not; and doing so in a noble, generous way, not indeed rashly or lightly, still without knowing accurately what we are do-ing, not knowing either what we give up, nor again, what we shall gain; uncertain about our reward, uncertain about our extent of sacrifice, in all respects leaning, waiting upon him, trusting in him

to enable us to fulfill our own vows, and so in all respects proceeding without carefulness or anxiety about the future.[5]

I also found Pierre Teilhard de Chardin, a Jesuit of our own century, brilliantly drawing the connection between his field of paleontology and theology, showing that as humans evolved so had spirituality. Addressing the classic versus modern approaches to detachment, he pronounced supernatural-natural dualism dead:

> Which is better for the Christian: activity or passivity? Life or death? Growth or diminishment? Development or curtailment? Possession or renunciation? The general answer is this: Why separate and contrast the two natural phases of a single effort? Your essential duty and desire is to be united with God. But in order to be united, you must first of all be—be yourself as completely as possible. And so you must develop yourself and take possession of the world in order to be.[6]

And I found Raimundo Panikkar, an Indian monastic theologian, who observed at a conference convened to study monastic life a few years ago that

> [H]aving can exert a deadly weight on being. To lighten being in order that it may truly be is the task of monastic spirituality. . . . Having is all the accessories that serve some purpose at first, but further down the line leave us entangled in the means without allowing us to reach our true goals. . . . [H]aving is the many fabricated interests that impede . . . truly purifying action. . . .[7]

If these were voices from afar, right here at Mepkin was Abbot Francis—he of the harsh look just hours before. In *Lovers of the Place: Monasticism*

[5]John Henry Newman, "The Ventures of Faith," *Parochial and Plain Sermons* (London: Longmans & Co., 1900), IV, 299.
[6]Pierre Teilhard de Chardin, *The Divine Milieu* (New York: Harper and Row, 1960), 69–70.
[7]Raimundo Panikkar, *Blessed Simplicity: The Monk as Universal Archetype* (New York: Seabury Press, 1982), 47.

in the Church, he calls upon people who desire a sanctified life, inside or
~~de~~ the cloister, to resign themselves to a certain kind of marginality,
~~g~~ in the world but not being absorbed by it. "At first tentatively, and
then more frequently," the abbot writes, the individual is "more engaged
with the truth of things, persons, situations. Less and less self-referenced,
minimally concerned about what any particular action will mean for him,
how he will look, and what others will think, he is captivated by the
workings of God in all events."[8] The abundance or poverty of one's possessions has no intrinsic moral value. It is our proper *use* of what we have
that makes holy or profane those things, persons, situations—as well as
ourselves.

So it is that detachment—healthy detachment—comes usually not as a
moment of sudden and complete conviction, but rather as a tentative,
incremental realization of God's working within our lives, swirling in the
world around us, appearing in disappointments as well as triumphs.

Detachment is involved with the ordinary, with littleness, with balance,
with wholeness, true integration; the physical world recognized, material
things accepted. Monks don't wear rags to worship in church—their choir
robes are made from a quite good wrinkle-resistant gabardine; it falls in
poetic folds to a well-polished floor. They burn good incense and the
eucharistic wine is a very palatable tokay. Abbot Francis plays on a very
good Zimmer organ; Father Aelred an expensive Martin guitar. Detachment rebels against cheapness, the poorly made, the craven, the spirit-
denying.

By the time Thomas Merton was Gethsemani's master of novices, his
attitude had changed considerably. He countered the then-prevailing attitude, telling young monks not to blot out but to bring all their senses to
monastic life. "The body is good," he told them; "listen to what it tells
you."[9]

It is not difficult to see that detachment has wide-ranging implications
for many of the various expressions of our spiritual selves. If we take on the

[8] *Lovers of the Place,* 110.
[9] Thomas Merton, *A Hidden Wholeness: The Visual World of Thomas Merton,* ed. John Howard Griffin (Boston: Houghton Mifflin, 1970), 10.

attitude that we must use well but not covet, appreciate but not manipulate or exploit, then we have embarked upon a new and fresh approach to life. Faith is fed by detachment, allowing God to work in our lives, putting our wills at his service. Chastity looks to detachment for guidance; only in this way can the precious offering of celibacy be assured of being used to enhance, not denigrate. Choosing and pursuing a vocation need detachment so that transitory success or failure, acclaim or rejection will not blur our vision of how we wish to use the gifts, attitudes, attributes—and even shortcomings—that we possess.

And there is still more depth to this well. Detachment prevents us from being dragged down by the undertow of situations we cannot change, by the failures of other human beings who have disappointed us, or by our own imperfections. Merton struggled with detachment all his monastic life. In his journals are almost daily entries of his attempts to abandon himself to God. Yet by their frequency it is evident that he had failed each time he promised. In general, he wanted to do God's will: the specifics were much harder. But as he matured, having at first nearly idolized Trappist life and Trappist monks, he came to a realization of "the faults, imperfections and weaknesses of people who are supposed to be holy! . . . How sweet it is to forget all that stuff and to realize that it is none of my business to worry about the apparent faults of others . . . How many burdens there are that you don't really have to carry! In fact you sin by carrying them."[10] In essence, Merton had to detach himself from the idol of monastic life in order to enter it deeply and truly live it. We can easily see in his words that he found in detachment grace, liberation, and the truth of things.

Even in the continually evolving, and ofttimes morally and emotionally murky circumstances we find ourselves, the practice of detachment, like most spiritual disciplines, is actually quite simple—that is, if we have the courage to face it head on. For what we are talking about is rudimentary stewardship—no, not the stewardship of fundraising, but the stewardship by which we remain accountable for the good use of all things entrusted to

[10]Thomas Merton, *Entering the Silence: Becoming a Monk and Writer, 1941–1952*, vol. 2 of *The Journals of Thomas Merton*, ed. Jonathan Montaldo (New York: HarperCollins, 1996), journal entry for May 13, 1947.

us. Do my possessions and the people I relate to, the decisions that I make, my very thoughts and desires and plans—all of these, do they make me a better person and closer to God, or not? Do I hold on with clenched fists and covet those things for which I am little more than a temporary steward? Do I demand that objects and people produce for me, or do I simply allow them to be what and who they are, firm in their own nature? The questions are obvious and clear; our answers tend to be mumbles and murmurs as we try to avoid this kind of honesty.

While detachment might be easier to practice where nobody has anything anyhow—say, in a monastery, or in a homeless shelter—neither the contemplative nor the active life, nor any combination of the two (which is where most spiritual seekers find themselves) are perfect in themselves. Each can be the means to holiness and inner peace. If this is so—and certainly I am not alone in maintaining it is—then a monk is not inherently holier than a realtor, a banker, or a bartender, provided each uses what is in their life for good and detaches themselves from anything that gets in the way of that goodness. It seems idealistic, I know; but if monastic wisdom is true, it must be so.

What does this all mean to those of us in the secular world, living lives in which the needs of job, marriage, children, or friendships seem to mitigate against the "lightening" that Raimundo Panikkar speaks of? The answer might come, oddly enough, from a view of detachment offered by St. John of the Cross. He called it a freedom of the heart. It is too difficult and a bit too pious to ask ourselves: What is it that prevents me from being closer to God? For myself, while it is undoubtedly a question I need to address, such an approach to detachment is more than my paltry soul can muster. Rather, why not say: What is it that I really need in life? What price do I pay to acquire and hold on to whatever it is that I own in the material world? When I have acquired something, do I somehow attach more meaning to it than I should? The same goes for dealing with failure and disappointment. Am I a better or worse person because my plans didn't work out, I didn't get the promotion or raise I felt I earned? Does God love me less or more?

I think back to the musical *Jesus Christ, Superstar* I saw on Broadway many years ago. In one scene, Jesus appears impossibly attired in layer upon layer of robes, each of more luxuriant fabric. He wobbles on platform shoes. The itinerant preacher who had once walked among them with a simple garment of homespun cloth and rough sandals has changed. The world has praised and acknowledged him; he has allowed himself to be covered with their well-intentioned adoration, to be raised above them. He can hardly move.

With our advancing knowledge of how the mind works, together with our increasing awareness of the many demands and tempting opportunities we face each day, detachment takes on added importance for all those who seek their spiritual center. As Eileen P. O'Hea, a psychotherapist, spiritual director, and Catholic nun writes, "A cluttered and preoccupied psyche has its energies so constrained that it cannot experience a deeper reality. . . . A cluttered psyche can imprison us. We begin to treat its contents as the only reality of our lives. . . . In a human person composed of body, mind, and spirit, what is left out of this picture is the spirit." We "look outside of ourselves for what we think is missing. We pursue relation-ships, tasks, accomplishments with the hope that they will fill in what is missing."[11]

Is this not exactly what we experience today—burdening ourselves with so many demands, regarding as necessities what were not so long ago unheard of luxuries? My father had no car at all when he moved six children and wife from the Depression-era coal mines of Pennsylvania to Cleveland where he hoped to find work. I have two cars. Absolutely essen-tial. Shirts, curtains, honors, a fully stocked refrigerator, hair-cutting ap-pointments, orthodontists, a swim-club membership. We virtually demand our marriages, relationships, and work to be always fruitful, open, nurtur-ing, fun. How can we *not* be disillusioned?

Without a sense of detachment in our lives we will be weighed down by the possessions and approbations we so assiduously work for (and perhaps even deserve), as well as by the expectations our cybermedia world continually tells us we should expect, even demand. We waddle our way

[11]Eileen P. O'Hea, "Detachment in Our Psychological Age," *Review for Religious*, July–August 1992, 541–42.

through life, huffing and puffing under the heavy load of what we think we must have, what should be the qualities of our love life, work life, family life. Ironically, in the midst of all our getting and spending, we call out for the simple life, for life to become less complicated, to slow down. We long to devote less of our energies to getting, and the consequent complications of preserving and protecting. On vacations we seek out primitive surroundings, without normal creature comforts. Yet when we return to what the world calls "normalcy," our eyes pass over the catalogue of delights searching for one more thing, somehow hoping its pleasures will satisfy the void in our souls. But it does not. And we choose again and again, only to be unhappy, unfulfilled, unsatisfied.

My visit was nearing an end. Learning from monastic example and from the wise teachers I had encountered, I was coming to realize, was one thing; putting detachment into practice was certainly another. I wondered what the days ahead would continue to teach me as I sought to keep this question of detachment in my sights. My bags already in the car, I spent my last moments in the church with the Mepkin monks.

My mind must have been floating up among the windows high overhead, but the words of the fifty-first Psalm, spoken with little drama or intonation, pierced that mental haze. Once again, the voice from the ages was ready to speak to this very day, to this man and his muddled mind. The words that had so struck me were from a familiar passage in which God, speaking through the psalmist's poetry, states clearly that he wants his followers to break firmly with the past—from pagan, even from early Israelite forms of worship. He does not desire burnt sacrifices of animals. After all, does he need this flesh to eat, this blood to drink? Does he not already own all the animals of the earth? The sacrifice God desires is a broken and contrite heart, a heart detached from foolish thoughts, words, and desires, a heart broken open to him so that he might enter and live there.

Offer yourself to me in love, be open to me—that is what God was asking. Not burnt offerings. Not death. This is a covenant of love, one requiring that we detach ourselves from ourselves, our selfishness, our calculating, our plans, and that we realize we are not alone in this adventure called life. With detachment comes the promise of attachment—to God.

As the monks filed out, Abbot Francis presented me with a broad smile. Farther along on the path, he hesitated so that I might catch up with him. He asked about my wife and children as sweetly as a concerned uncle. And how was I? Did I have a good visit? Leaving so soon?

There is probably no better place to be educated about detachment than in a hospital room, specifically one of the cubicles in an intensive care unit. I had been through the upper floors of New Hanover Regional Medical Center, taking the Eucharist to an unusually large number of people—one recovering from back surgery; several new, beaming mothers; a woman with a recalcitrant gall bladder, another with pneumonia, and a man with a good soul but a heart in need of catheterization. But here, in intensive care, are patients of a distinct category. They are at once detached—from hope, from self-sufficiency—and attached—to the array of tubes bringing nourishment, oxygen, medication, or taking away toxic fluids their bodies cannot expel.

There in cubicle six lay James Bresnahan. I stood beside his wife Velma, both of us in gown, mask, and gloves lest we bring any more infection to his fevered body. His arms, lying still on the newly changed sheets, were festooned with the souvenirs of many of the places and moods a Marine of thirty years might have visited and experienced. But the tattoos, no longer stretched taut by his muscular biceps and forearms, looked like the printing on a deflated balloon. His skin was slack and dry, his eyes closed; a ventilator kept him alive. World War II, Korea, and Vietnam, as well as thousands of recruits at Paris Island—the Marines' own time-honored novitiate—had witnessed his devotion to his country and the Corps, his strength, his vigor. Now, this man who had risen to the rank of sergeant major was entirely dependent for something as basic as each breath he took.

I found my voice cracking as I prayed a prayer I hoped he would hear. We had joked and laughed when we first met about a month before. Having served in the Navy, I kidded that we had always considered the Marine Corps our ladies' auxiliary. His confident look put me in my place. I liked him immediately. One surgery to correct an aneurysm, and then another—and he went downhill all too fast. I stood there, the screens on the monitors telling their sad story, and I thought about detachment. Not a profound thought, at all. Simply that everything we have will someday be taken away. Everything—health, breath, status, love, children, parents, objects—is on loan. A loan that can be called in at any time.

Or perhaps there is no better place to learn about detachment than sitting in a conference room of a potential funder. There, two unsmiling men grilled me about an idea that I had come to them with, asking for their support. I mentioned another writer. They "owned" him, one said, because of all the money they had given him for his work.

I stared at them. They didn't own him at all. The money they had the power to disperse wasn't even theirs. Without this job, they would find themselves quite ordinary indeed. And that could happen any day, any time. But, here and now they had tremendous power—which they obviously believed in, without realizing they were but temporary stewards. They thought detachment had to do simply with being unsmiling, neutral, and unenthusiastic. Of course, they must say no to many people. But need it be like this?

There is an art to detachment, of intensity yet unconnectedness and unconcern. In essence, yes and no must have the same weight—for this yes may be a no and that no may be a yes. A closed door only means that we must turn and look for another. Detachment allows the true meaning of the situation to emerge, as I found when a broad smile broke onto my face as I rode back to the airport from my conference-room encounter. Rejected, humiliated—and strangely at peace, centered. Detachment allows our ego to be properly situated—not beaten into the ground, not elevated beyond reach or seeing—but to take on its own buoyancy, to float with the tide of life, to keep us afloat. So much of life is out of our control. Why attach so much to achievement?

When I got home, I took the file on that project to its final resting place in my attic. There, it joined drawers filled with file folders of other projects I was once passionate about, but which never came to be. As I scanned them later, I knew that the vast majority of them never should have been done. Thank God. I stood there, a bare bulb illuminating boxes and file cabinets that in some ways were the history of my writing life. Was I a different person because of being rejected and, on occasion, accepted? Bad or good, worthless or worthwhile, because of someone's appraisal? How foolish to think so—as I all too often did.

The actor Robert Duvall was rejected by Hollywood studios for fifteen years as he presented them with his idea for a movie about a Southern preacher and the power of the Holy Spirit. He was thankful they had turned him down; "It turned out that I probably made a better film because no one would touch it back then."[12] The seed sprouted not when he wanted it to, but instead at the best time. He was never detached from the idea of his film, but had to be detached from the continuing rejection he experienced. And now he can be proud of the resulting film, *The Apostle*. It is his.

There were still more lessons about detachment lurking in the attic that day. There was a downrigger, a present lovingly bought by my wife a Christmas ago, a piece of fishing equipment which no longer has a boat onto which it (and to which I) might be attached. I once had a boat, and I loved it. But when the expenses of supporting a family superseded what was coming in, the boat had to go. It's an oft-told adage that the two happiest days in a man's life are the day he buys a boat and the day he sells it. When my boat's new owner took it away I realized how true that was. Yes, I missed my twenty-foot Wellcraft; but I felt a huge burden lift the day the deal was done. Now I have to cadge a ride on others' boats when I want to bring home some of the king mackerel that range off the Carolina coast. Maybe I liked the idea of a boat more than actually owning one.

Or, what about detachment from my will and desires, in the form of that luscious, fat *New York Times* sitting next to a cup of freshly made coffee

[12]*Newsweek*, 13 April 1998, 60.

and a comfortable chair on a sun-drenched patio on a Sunday morning after mass. And then there are two sons, who want to play a game of Risk with a father who has been spouting off about keeping the sabbath holy, doing family activities, practicing detachment from trips to the mall and supermarket. "Hey, I'm writing about monastic life; you mean I have to practice it?" Silence. Risk played. Conversation had. *Times* read later.

I don't want to put facing death on a par with selling a boat, or monastic detachment with board games. But there are whispers within many of life's situations that speak ever so softly to us. As we struggle to practice the kind of detachment that is sensible, life-enhancing, and spiritually sound, we must begin by rubbing away the cobwebs of ego, greed, revenge. Detachment allows the true meaning to emerge, moments of grace to appear where we once saw desolation and disappointment. So much of our life is out of our control; why do we struggle so hard to impose our will in our way? Is not God with us? Will he not help us, as Merton prayed, to read the road signs and navigate our way through life?

For me, detachment asks that I not be imperious in the classroom before my students, not stupidly powerful before my children, not arrogant as I drive a car that might be better than the one in front of me, not superior as I solve a problem another kind of mind might approach in another way, not prideful that I have whatever strength I have. For while all these are in my keeping, they are no more than that. I "own" none of them. Any could be gone in an instant.

It is not our option as spiritual pilgrims to loftily criticize others for what they have; it may mask what is little more than envy in our hearts. Rather we must look deeply at what frees us and what chains us. This isn't as simple as it sounds. Take the things that make your life easier. Are you too attached to your washing machine? Well, then, you could give it away. But more likely, to give away a washing machine would be foolish; how would you wash your clothes? By hand? At the Laundromat? Yes, those might further purify you; in the hand-washing you might find a Gandhian meditative medium, or in the laundromat you might find God. But probably you'll end up spending more time getting your clothes clean or trying to figure out how to. ~~Simply ridding ourselves of things is not what detachment is about.~~

Detachment helps us to hold things at a distance—and then have the freedom to embrace, cast away, or use in a new way. Using a friend's oceanfront cottage but not owning it; a good meal on occasion, but not a weekly delight, a job, or status, or even a loved one. Conscious, willful, willing detachment from things can penetrate our essence with a new kind of wisdom and appreciation for this moment, the now—and prepares us for the days when, unwillingly, we will be detached from those things most precious to us. Our choices will some day be restricted; we will be forced to obey strange masters; we will be denied. But we need not be numbed and blinded by all the possibilities we once thought would bring us satisfaction. Instead, we will have peace.

Brother David Steindl-Rast, a Benedictine monk, looks at detachment this way:

> The economics of affluence demand that things that were special for us last year must now be taken for granted; so the container gets bigger, and the joy of overflowing, gratefulness, is taken away from us. But if we make the vessel smaller and smaller by reducing our needs, then the overflowing comes sooner and with it the joy of gratefulness. . . . The less you have, the more you appreciate what you've got. With the extraneous stripped away, you begin to realize how you are graced by life's gifts. . . . Monks experience the overflow sooner; poor people experience it sooner than wealthy ones.[13]

The novelist Ignazio Silone wrote it this simply: "You have only what you give."[14] Freedom of the heart.

But we must be careful, and continually prayerful, about detachment.

[13]David Steindl-Rast with Sharon Lebell, *The Music of Silence: Entering the Sacred Space of Monastic Experience* (San Francisco: HarperSanFrancisco, 1995), 30.
[14]Quoted in Robert Ellsberg, *All Saints: Daily Reflections on Saints, Prophets, and Witnesses for Our Time* (New York: Crossroad, 1997), 361.

Abused, we can mistake it as a license for being emotionally absent from a spouse, loved one, or child. No, detachment is seeing them neither as possession or burden, but ours in this moment to share with, care for, be fed by. Detachment is but a form of attachment—attachment with trust in God, true love, and respect for the person, place, thing, situation.

There are simple litmus tests for true detachment; monks have looked to them for centuries. True detachment should make us happy, not sad or wanting—even though we think we may truly need something we have given up or have been forced to give up. Even with loss, there is a sense of liberation, that we are free—not from want or grief, but from our insatiable selves. Detachment promises that there is enough for all to share, if we are not so blind in our greed and so lacking in faith. When one monk gets a box of fine chocolates, all the monks get fine chocolates.

And if we allow it, detachment opens us up to this abundance.

Detachment is *abandonment* that closes off one option, but then opens up a multitude of other possibilities we had never dreamed of.

Detachment is *patience*, realizing that now may not be the right time, that perhaps there will never be a right time, for us to have something. But it is realizing, too, that God is with us. He will never leave us; he listens to our needs and provides in due season.

Detachment is *purification*, a reminder that by emptying ourselves of our dependences on the things of this world we are cleansed from what makes us unholy—to God, to ourselves, and to each other.

Detachment is *humility*, the simple realization that I often don't know what is best for me, even though I desire something with all my being.

Detachment is *symbolism*, pointing beyond the immediate and real action at hand to a much deeper desire for unity with God.

Detachment is *transcendence*, loosening the chains that bind us, rising above the immediate, the sure, to that mysterious something that is the mind of God. "When you touch the reality of non-self," writes Thich Nhat Hanh, "you touch at the same time nirvana, the ultimate dimension of being, and become free from fear, attachment, illusion and craving."[15]

---

[15]Thich Nhat Hanh, *Living Buddha, Living Christ*, 185.

Detachment is *a monk's face*—all you have to do is look into those eyes to know that the person with the fewest needs is the richest of all.

Detachment is *not death*, only the death of the self-centered and self-sufficient me. It is being born again.

Detachment is *dormancy*, the neglect of winter so that spring might bring new life, a new life resting securely in God's hands.

NOVEMBER

Discernment

Charting Life's Path

It was over the rising dough of a prospective batch of pizzas that discernment looked me straight in the eye—and persisted, unblinking, as tiny balls of peanut-butter cookie batter received their characteristic cross-hatched fork imprints.

The quest to discern the tao for his life was written all over the face of Brother Dale. It was a handsome face indeed—squared-off jaw, strawberry-blond hair, penetrating dark eyes; he was the young man many a young woman would dream of bringing home to her parents, who would, in turn, be delighted at her good fortune. But the tautness of the skin over his face signaled the tension deep beneath. He smiled vaguely at my best efforts to lighten our hours together in the refectory kitchen, but they were smiles that came neither from his head nor heart; rather they seemed like reflexive responses to the commands of a muscle-control center sending out signals of acknowledgment at random intervals.

It had been well over a decade ago that Dale had come to the gates of the abbey at Gethsemani. He was still a teenager, as I had been on my first visit there, and he had been told quickly and firmly that the day had long since passed when such sincere but unripe youth were accepted. Undaunted, unlike me, he came back at twenty-three and stayed for six years. After a period when he returned to the world, Dale had come to Mepkin and stayed two years. I first met him then, just as he was about to leave to study with a Buddhist teacher, in whose company he hoped finally to find the true path for his life. All he had ever wanted, he had decided while still a boy, was to be a monk. This had not worked out for him, as a Christian or a Buddhist. Now he was back for a second time at Mepkin—his final effort, he said, to discern whether his desire to be a Trappist was God's desire as well.

He is not alone. Beneath its seemingly timeless, calm surface, discernment is afoot throughout this venerable order. At just the hour we were busying ourselves in the refectory, Father Bernardo Olivera, the young abbot general of the Trappists in Rome, was completing a letter that would be sent on the occasion of the 900th anniversary of the order's founding at Cîteaux. The letter spoke frankly of a world, a church, and the Trappist order set in "a culture of change," of "a search for new gods, a thirst for the true God." Old answers and pieties would no longer be enough. What was demanded was "creative fidelity to our own identity."[1]

As one of the communities within the Trappist commonwealth Father Olivera was addressing, Mepkin was attempting this "creative fidelity" on a local scale, dealing with its own pressing issues. Should they be more open to the public now that a picture book and video on them have been

[1]Letter from Abbot General Bernardo Olivera, January 26, 1998.

released? Do they need to tighten the strictures on the cloister to maintain their monastic life style? How are they to preserve silence in the cloister? (Oddly enough, it is the newest Mepkin monks who are calling for the strictest rules.) What should be done about the Trappistine nun who wants to stay for an extended visit in this traditionally and decidedly male preserve? Should that proposed satellite group in Charleston go forward with plans to create an ersatz lay monastic community within the city? The $5 million building project now underway—what might be done to raise that enormous amount of money? And what about vocations? What could be done to encourage more men, young men, to embrace Trappist life here—a little-known, aging community in an out-of-the-way place?

Then there was the continuing personal discernment of the men already at Mepkin, posing searching questions to determine whether Trappist life was their life's calling. Men working throughout the monastery grounds—in egg-grading house and feed bin, dispensary and office, pump room and library—as Brother Dale and I stretched and plied the dough onto fourteen waiting circular pans. Men who have taken vows, some in perpetuity, some for shorter periods of time. Men who have seen many others come to join in their noble pursuit—only to watch virtually all of them leave. Men who have seen their order go through unprecedented change. Men who ask, as do most of us, the most elemental questions. What am I to do with my life? Is this where I am supposed to be? What kind of "citizen"? And what—for those who dare ask—is God's will for my life?

The winds of change that have blown across the world have buffeted their lives as well, even those who have been Trappists for forty or fifty years. This is not Benedict's or Bernard's or even Merton's day. Monks are trying to chart their path, peer into the future, assess their daily actions— as are we. They, like us, sometimes look back longingly on a less complicated time, yearning for simplicity and stability. But they know those days will never return. And they realize that if monasticism is going to respond to the renewed interest in its wisdom, if it is to reclaim its place as society's example and leaven, a living presence as well as the vehicle for their own holiness, it must continually adapt to the world in which it is set. It is the dilemma faced by spiritual seekers in all times and cultures: to be in the world yet not controlled or subsumed by it. A delicate balance. To strike the balance, it is to discernment—a noble word and an exacting process—that they must turn, time and time again. Whether or not it is the word we would use, whether we face it or run from it, discernment is part of our lives as well.

"Discernment may be defined as a conscious experience of God's grace drawing one to a course of action or exposing the influence that a projected course of action will have on one's relationship with God," is the way the Irish Jesuit Brian O'Leary frames it. "It is not," he clarifies, "some kind of generalized awareness of God or of his presence, but an insertion into a process—the process of finding and owning the will of God or, in other words, of Christian decision making." It is an expression of trying "to respond to God's love and to serve his kingdom."[2] Another Jesuit, Thomas Green, notes that discernment involves "recognizing what God is asking of us . . . what he would like us to do with our lives, how he wishes us to respond to the concrete life-situations which we encounter."[3]

In certain ways discernment is really another aspect of detachment, which I had pondered the previous month. Detachment asks us to consider things at a critical distance; discernment takes the next step. What we are talking about is judgment, but judgment with a divine component. Discernment is judgment that trusts in and expects God's presence—not only in major decisions, but in every aspect of our daily existence.

Later that day—after a round of silent but nonetheless enthusiastic nods from the monks for the pizza extravaganza presented by Brother Dale and his assistant—I went over to the monastery's small administration building to photocopy some articles. I looked across the hallway to Abbot Francis's door, which was closed. Taped to the door jamb was a cascade of messages from his monks—seeking his counsel, hoping to catch his eye as he entered or left. It reminded me of the supplications pilgrims stick between the huge stones of the Wailing Wall in Jerusalem, or of the questions that seekers would pass through a chink in the walls of a holy

---

[2]Brian O'Leary, "Discernment and Decision Making," *Review for Religious*, 51 (1992), 56.
[3]Thomas H. Green, *Darkness in the Marketplace* (Notre Dame, Ind.: Ave Maria Press, 1981), 69.

man's hermitage in the desert. Each sought answers to their pressing problems. Insights. Discernment.

In the early days of Christianity, seekers came to the mud huts and caves of the ones they called "abba" for the advice of these who had sailed the seas of life and had known both tradewind and squall. In those days, steeped in pagan Greek and Roman mythologies and traditions, the truths of venerable Judaism, and the claims of the varieties of emergent Christianity, life was considered a constant and bitter battle between bad and good spirits, tempestuous demons and comforting angels, each whispering their message and influencing events so as to lure souls to their side. These holy ones of the desert were the first spiritual directors, listening to the cry of the afflicted and confused, trying to discern which was the voice of God and which was that of the Evil One.

As monasticism spread throughout the Western world, discernment was at the very heart of this new spiritual expression. "Is this God's will, part of God's plan?" Such was the ultimate litmus test for their decisions. Monks made some dreadfully wrong decisions, but discernment offered a continuing and evolving assessment of their lives. Discernment provided a page upon which words might be written guided by God's hand.

Ultimately, as modern psychology revealed to us in terms of science what the best of the ancient monks already knew instinctively, the goal of discernment is actually self knowledge. Simply put, it hopes to know truthfully and deeply who I am, today—in this particular time in history, given the circumstances in which I find myself, in the presence and with the help of God—and then to act accordingly. In our exceedingly self-referential age, we have skewed the meaning of discernment as we have brushed aside the various elements that discernment asks us to consider. We have elevated personal feelings to the status of irrefutable evidence of truth. "I feel, therefore I judge," isn't exactly what the desert fathers and mothers had in mind. Discernment's call is far more subtle and deep than that. The so-called new spiritualities that focus exclusively on the individual's needs and abilities can never be rivers of grace flowing through us into the world. When God is forgone, divine wisdom is left untapped.

We imagine our age to be uniquely difficult, but of course all eras have their own challenges. If you are reading this book, chances are you don't have to cope with war or plague. It is the dizzying array of decisions and choices that we wrestle with; we are a people torn apart, tortured by the many judgments we must make. Abhorring any restrictions on our range of choice, we ironically find ourselves equally confused by boundless personal freedom.

It is into this confusion that the practice of discernment offers itself.

Looking back on my own efforts to practice discernment—unaware for many years that it was what I was trying to do—I realize I had misunderstood it completely. Discernment for me as a young man meant I had to decode a complicated message in order to do exactly what God had planned for me. It was almost as if God had his hand over my page in the Book of Life, and I had to guess what was written there—or I would be consigned to unhappiness and probably eternal damnation. Later in life, I found myself numbed by too many options. Somehow, I believed discernment was purely an intellectual exercise, "figuring out" what to do. It also seemed to me that discernment always implied action. I prayed to God—but I blazed right by as he stood there offering answers.

In grade school and high school I tried to subdue my hormones and convince myself to enter celibate religious life, which my church told me was the highest calling. In college and during my time in the Navy, I looked out in total bewilderment to the vastness that lay beyond my small experience of life. After my first marriage I turned my back on anything material or comfortable in an effort once again to find the most meritorious path. The years of wondering and wandering in a self-made hell of pleasure-seeking followed, when my senses were dulled despite (or perhaps because of) living in the most sensual of worlds. After meeting Tracy, I spent years in a daze, deeply in love but unable to commit myself to something so seemingly ordinary and unspiritual as marriage and children.

Even as I looked back to the first of my regular visits to Mepkin, now a half-year distant, I realized that rather than allowing the mercy of God and the stark beauty of this place to work their miracles I had piled on a set of demands and goals. Only in the unfolding of my Mepkin days had I just begun to understand the alchemy, the mystery, the mysticism of this thing called discernment.

During all those years, my fancy rationalizing and calculating, my lists of options, my endless weighing of pros and cons—these had not been entirely wrong; just woefully incomplete. As I walked the familiar Mepkin lanes and paths in the cooling air, or stood mutely once more before the Luces' graves, or watched the alligator lay in the sun, or listened to the monks chant in the middle of the night, discernment danced at the edges of my consciousness. Complex? Yes—but as with all of monastic spirituality, quite simple. Indeed, unnervingly simple. Despite my desire to say "yes, this is it; now I have it," it seemed never quite within my grasp.

Discernment, as best I could understand it, came down to two basic truths.

The first is that God is with us. He is there as we try to see through the fog and find our way through life. This is a crucial first step, one all of us must take to put discernment into practice. It's something like falling backward into the arms of a friend we cannot see, but who has told us they will be there to catch us. The second is that there are ways—real and accessible ways, as both ancient and modern monks attest—to know the will of God for our lives. I wanted to understand these ways better during my Mepkin days. First, I had to understand God's role.

Too many of us have been raised with an image of God as some sort of celestial bookkeeper, tallying up our many bad deeds and recording the few good ones. Or we see God as some kind of absentee landlord, sending our souls down to take up residence in a body, letting us swing in the wind for a certain number of years, and then swooping back down to reclaim what is his.

It takes no great theologian or biblical scholar to realize how misleading our images of God can be. God is with us throughout our lives, an active partner. This is spoken of in the Psalms, assured in the gospels, confirmed in the writing of great mystics, and continually reflected in the lives of people we have known and admired for their steadfast confidence in a power greater than their own. How could we have thought differently? In modern Catholic thought, Vatican II speaks of a new partnership: "[I]t is the task of the entire People of God . . . to hear, distinguish and interpret the many voices of our age, and to judge them in light of the divine Word. In this way, revealed truth can always be more deeply penetrated, better understood, and set forth to great advantage."[4]

Our God is no longer the God of ancient Israel who could only be addressed or revered at one temple in one city. For Christians, God entered the human condition through his son, vowing that he would remain with his created ones until the end of time. Hindus, Moslems, even some in Buddhist tradition—however they may conceptualize that higher power that we call God, whatever practices they employ—attempt equally to express the nothingness and everythingness, the transcendence and the immanence, that is God.

Paul Tillich, the eminent twentieth-century Protestant theologian, wrote of God's love for us as a love not blind, but seeing, knowing.[5] In other words, by means of that love, that searching concern for us, God is continually working in the world—through our lives. Where we sleep, and where we live; at stoplights, in shopping malls, on the beach—there is God. It is not so much a series of apparitions, pillars of fire, or voices; God is far more omniscient and subtle than that. He respects our freedom too much to evoke a preordained response from us. We have a God-given free will; what sort of God would then interfere with the free will that was his gift? God is not a puppeteer, coyly out of sight but manipulating it all by means of strings.

Some of the most powerful stories of God's assistance in discernment come in the gospel stories. A favorite of mine is the story of the adulterous woman. As the scribes and Pharisees gathered around, loudly condemning her, ready to stone her, Jesus pensively wrote in the sand. That, to me, is Jesus' moment of communication with his father, his moment of discernment. He opened himself to the wisdom of his father in order to discern what he should do. And out of his mouth came the words: "Let anyone among you who is without sin cast the first stone." Exactly right for the

[4]"Gaudium et Spes," in The Documents of Vatican II (New York: Herder and Herder, 1966), 24.
[5]Paul Tillich, The Shaking of the Foundations (New York: Charles Scribner's Sons, 1948), 110.

moment, releasing the woman and calling everyone present to a moment of reflection. Thus the will of God is lived out.

The will of God. Those words have such a thunderous, presumptuous sound. And they are so misunderstood by so many of us—me first of all. I have mouthed "the will of God"—the goal of discernment—countless times in my life. I have both ardently sought its power and, I'm sure, done my best to thwart its pull. No better time than these cooling days of November to see whether I might, at last (or at least), come to know something of what those words actually meant.

Monks appear to have some distinct advantages as they seek the will of God for their lives—an abbot and a spiritual director to help them sort the enduring from the ephemeral, the spiritually nurturing from the soul-killing. They have a community of people with similar goals, a common vocabulary, a disciplined life conducive to such controlled introspection. Most of us have none of these. We consider ourselves more or less alone in our spiritual quest, hesitant to talk about such matters with either loved ones or more casual acquaintances for fear of alarming them with the depth of our uncertainty and the intensity of our hunger. We have no great spiritual guide to turn to for counsel.

But the underpinnings, the basic principles of monastic life, I was discovering, are not so detached from the things we seek in our life—if what we seek is a life of the spirit, a life close to God, fulfilling, happy, balanced, human, authentic. After all, Benedict forged his approach to monasticism from human experience, and applied it successfully to a very broad cross-section of ordinary lay people. The principles the abbot and monks employ are not so mysterious, not a secret and exclusive method. Their path to wholeness and holiness, I believe, is also open to us—altered, surely, by the circumstances of their lives and our own.

Yet while monastic wisdom is woven of simple threads, I had also learned from these monastic visits that it is not without complexity. Excessively intentional and insufficiently faithful, I was still tempted to construct for myself a careful blueprint for discernment. I drew back. Instead, I found myself coming up with a rather eclectic and somewhat quixotic list of roadsigns to consider.

To begin, listening is the important first step to knowing. When the ancient abba listened in his cave, when Abbot Francis listened behind his note-adorned door, their first action was a non-action; it was openness. Listening is not merely hearing words spoken. It is seeing, feeling, sensing. Did not Brother Dale's face tell us as much as his words? Did not my own contorted body, chest pains, atonal pitch, and furtive eyes portray what was going on during the difficult periods in my life?

So, for one thing, we must develop a habit of listening—especially to ourselves. What is our internal tone of voice? What is our body saying? What is it that we seem to be praying or asking advice for—and what is it that we cannot yet put into thoughts or words that is truly troubling or confounding us?

Many voices will call out to us—friends and parents, the culture we live within, our personal history and previous experiences. Supposed insights and revelations will command our attention and action; our conflicting and constantly changing impulses will confound us. We must listen for true voices among them. Which is the decent, fair, life-enhancing, genuine voice, that which summons our best? There, quite simply, is the voice of God.

It is true that God seems closest to us when we are silent. It is not so much that God is speaking more clearly; it is rather that, having turned off the static of our lives, we are just listening better. So it is in silence that we should listen. Silence needs no list for us to scan anxiously. Silence needs only itself, a great gift indeed. Is it any surprise that my best thoughts come while I am swimming or showering or driving (and occasionally while sitting in church)? It is at times like these that I seem most able to resolve issues and see open paths.

When we listen, it needs to be a listening not only with openness, but with deep affection—with love. For unless there is love—for ourselves, or for others, if we are trying to help them discern—there is no life force flowing through these moments. We may have an abundance of reason, but it is love that disposes a person to care deeply. Not that there is a "right" answer (or even an answer at all), but rather that listening in love allows us to be ourselves with ourselves—and therefore in union with God.

In our listening, we must lead with the heart, not the head. Discernment is not an exercise in mental acuity; it is not reserved for the smartest among us. It is available to those who are able to open their hearts to God. Our minds can sort out the details later, but without this opening, the power of the Holy Spirit—no less than the spirit of God in our midst—cannot enter our lives.

If the answers to life's questions are to come from within us, we must listen to our emotions, those supposedly non-rational voices. Our fears, pleasures, desires, and sorrows tell us profound secrets about who we are, and we must listen to them. We are not excluded from our own history; our memories are in themselves sources of wisdom and insight. If we have placed ourselves in the presence of God, we need not fear that these feelings and remembrances will send us off to our destruction. They are, indeed, part of our salvation, as much a part of us as our physical selves. Monks don't become solitaries; they were solitaries before they entered, even though they might have been members of a large family or worked for a huge corporation. "[T]heir hearts tell them what God desires," writes Jean Pierre de Caussade, a Jesuit of the eighteenth century. "They have only to listen to the promptings of their hearts to interpret his will in the existing circumstances. God's plans, disguised as they are, reveal themselves to us through intuition rather than through our reason."[6]

In a non-monastic way, my marriage to Tracy is a perfect example—in the end—of how this can work. In those New York years I met many other women, but none like her. My heart was always there; my head was too many steps behind. I analyzed and weighed and schemed. Did our temperaments match? What about the difference in age, some fourteen years? Her maturity? My own? The future? Her desire to have children? All this was information, mental chaff. I really needed to listen, and listen deeply, to my heart.

The real challenge in discernment is to let obedience, not willfulness, be our guide. But though seemingly simple, here again the matter is not quite as it seems. "[O]bedience in the monastic context does not mean just

[6]Jean Pierre de Caussade, *Abandonment to Divine Providence* (New York: Doubleday Image, 1975), 105.

doing what you are told, the sort of obedience a dog learns in obedience school," writes Brother David Steindl-Rast. "It means . . . listening to the Word of God that comes to us moment by moment, listening to the message of the angel that comes to us hour by hour."[7] So the monks' vow of obedience is a vow we all can, and should, take. As Brother Steindl-Rast advises, it is not rigid and unthinking obedience to a set of rules, but obedience to the messages that come to us in the people and circumstances in our lives—messages that urge us to do things that are alive, filled with hope and optimism. It means obedience to our best impulses, following them wherever they lead.

Spiritual vigor depends on our uncalculating, spontaneous response to all that is good and beautiful and right in the world. Our very character, our karmic self, is being formed every day by our obedience to the impulses that we feel in so many small ways. Graces flow constantly. We magnify them or we allow them to die. All that needs to be done is to align our acts and thoughts with our best intentions. Now. In this situation. After all, that is all we have the capacity to do. Obedience asks not for perfection, but for the desire to do what is right. And, when the moment comes for a great discernment, it will not be so difficult. It will be the same natural response.

And, all the while, we must resist the "tyranny of the should." Karen Horney, a psychotherapist profoundly influenced by Carl Jung, wrote a book by this title that resounded deep within me when I read it many years ago. This woman knew the storms of my mind exactly, and the distractions that had played far too great a role in my attempts at discernment. The "tyranny of the should" basically short-circuits the process of discernment. Finally, it offers only one answer, for when we are ruled by "shoulds" (I should say this, act this way, go into this line of work, marry this kind of person) we cannot respond to the murmurings of our souls. Rather, we respond to some artificial projection of what we think a person is. It is a stale and unachievable ideal. It is not that we ought to flee from anything we think we "should" do. Obligations do matter; sensible behavior is hardly

---

[7]Steindl-Rast with Lebell, *The Music of Silence*, 55–56.

wrong. But when we allow "should" to be the dominating force in our lives, God's power is overruled. It is irrelevant, for the goal has already been set—only the achieving of that particular goal then matters.

It is the "tyranny of the should" that cripples and eventually kills the spirit of even the best-intentioned and most prayerful monks. When they hold up ideals or idols of what the monastic life should be and refuse to face their own and their brothers' humanity, they are doomed to fail. When they make a decision to join a monastery in romantic elation expecting permanent bliss—or in a depressed state that they imagine will be alleviated if they only do *this* for God—they will inevitably be disappointed.

We are no different. In our career choices, our married lives, our relationships, and our everyday actions—in all our choices we can give life or deny it—discernment asks that we constantly be open, both to God's gentle nudges and to the many opportunities for grace that are constantly being presented.

Allow both faith and pragmatism their place. While faith in God plays an enormous role in the art of discernment, it is not a substitute for common sense and reality. Our spiritual and physical selves are not at war, but are complementary. The art of discernment is to understand this integration and to act both filled with the spirit and grounded in the possible.

From time to time in my life I have dreamed of going to medical school so that I might help heal people. An idealized vision, I know, and probably a tyrannical "should" at work, too. But the reality of having absolutely no aptitude in biology, chemistry, and physics strongly indicates this is not going to be my calling.

I thought about this on one of my monastery walks after vespers as my mind went back to my hospital rounds of the week before. I had visited about twenty people and given the Eucharist to all who wanted it—a man whose leg had been amputated that morning; a mother at the bedside of her paraplegic daughter, cruelly injured by a car while she was jogging; cancer patients, patients with blood diseases and intestinal disorders. I had done nothing tangible for their physical healing, but if the look on their faces was any indication, or the soft sigh that I heard from that woman as she received the host—a woman who had just been told her ovarian cancer was no longer in remission—something had happened.

I came to this hospital work through a kind of discernment, many years in the making. Early on I had also wanted to be a priest, which would have given me the opportunity to help in another kind of healing. But as my life moved along, I became husband, father, and writer, and thought that my chances for fulfilling this doctor/priest role would never be.

Then one Sunday I saw a note in the parish bulletin saying there was a need for lay people to take the Eucharist to shut-ins. I thought I might get an elderly person or two; instead I was given what turned out to be an unbelievable opportunity to enter hundreds of lives in ways both spiritual and human. I will neither be accepted to medical school nor will ever be ordained, but for three hours each week I am, in a strange way, doing something that fulfills the desire I had for so many years. I may not have the title of doctor or priest, but in a very small way I am doing the work of both.

I will also never be a Trappist monk, yet I am able to come to Mepkin on a regular basis and share in this life I find gratifying and rich. Our deepest desires will be fulfilled, discernment promises, though not always in our time or in ways that we would choose or even imagine. God hears our prayers, knows our yearning. He is at work in the world. We need faith and we need patience, but he will fill the heart that is open to him.

Discernment offers insights into our actions and suggests new avenues to grace. It is not usually a blinding flash, and it cannot be switched off and on whenever we might wish. Discernment is a growing light, a growing awareness, a growing confidence both in God and ourselves. Not so much a series of peak experiences, it is more a background presence.

As we go through our day, we are not consciously aware that we are living a contemplative life. We rarely say, "I am discerning this now." But if we allow it, that growing light will begin to shine into the murky corners of our lives. Something we read or see or hear will strike us in an entirely new and profound way. The guidance we need will be there. If we intend to live a life open to grace, we will live such a life. Those graces may sometimes bring us pain; difficult judgments may need to be made, relying on radical trust in God's care for us. The spirit of God may be giving us ambiguous messages. We may not have all the pieces for a decision; our discernment may be no more than to continue to put up with uncertainty. But we can be assured that true discernment leads to truth, and truth brings us to freedom.

At vigils on the morning I left Mepkin, I watched as Brother Dale stiffly bowed at the altar and hurriedly blessed himself with holy water from the font whose soft bubbling was the only sound within the church. I did not know where he was in his discernment process, but his was the face of a tortured man. This was his last chance, he had been told. Even a loving community such as Mepkin can only withstand so much coming and going from one to whom they become attached. Moreover, they wanted what was best for this fine young man, whether he stayed or left.

Discernment demanded a price, that of utter honesty. Brother Dale was paying that price, one that many of us might not be so ready to ante up. I prayed for him with little more than a glance in his direction, one I'm sure he did not see. It was all I could do, for I had no wise words for him. I could only hope that God was also affirming Brother Dale's goodness, that God would lead him to that place where his soul could soar, his world blossom—the place where he was supposed to be.

I returned home like a man with a new tool, eager to find something on which to use it. What would I need to discern in the days ahead?

I was rather disappointed in myself for the first few days. It did not seem as though there were any judgments to be made whether of great significance or small. I must have been daydreaming—about discernment or about my Mepkin days thus far—when my eyes came into focus on an elongated folded card on top of my desk. I had received it from Brother Patrick Hart, a monk of Gethsemani who had been Merton's secretary. It contained pictures of faces and the six Trappists who had been killed by Algerian terrorists in 1996, and a short biographical note about each.

They were no longer names, but real men now. Father Christian, who had written those powerful words of love to the man who would kill him had a warm, boyish smile. Father Christophe wore a beard adorning Holly-wood-caliber good looks. Brother Luc's soft eyes, Father Celestin's mischievous grin, Brothers Michel and Paul, Father Bruno—all in white cowl, but each so different. Men with light in their eyes, a certain centeredness that a photo conveyed *sans doute*. When asked to discern their future commitment to a harsh place, a place where they were beloved by those who knew them and hated in that generic way that ideologues hate any who disagree with their perceptions, they did nothing more than stay put at Our Lady of Atlas. They remained open, available, going about their daily work.

Once unknown to the outside world (and even to most Trappists), they have now taken their place among the saints of our day. We look and they are there, far more real to us than they ever were in life. They went on with their lives, as best they knew how, in the place to which they had not so much been romantically "called," but where they pragmatically and existentially *were*.

Discernment.

I thought of the Atlas Trappists as I stood over a looseleaf notebook in the tiny chapel at the New Hanover Regional Medical Center in Wilmington that week. I often stop here before my Eucharistic rounds, but instead of sitting for a moment or going to the bible open on the small wooden table at the front, for some reason I went to this notebook provided so that prayers might be written, both as a personal statement and as an inspiration for those who come here for solace. As the Atlas Trappists stayed in place, even though the place was fraught with peril, so had the writer of these words—a woman, I presumed by the handwriting.

I need help, she called out clearly to her God. I need to let go of hidden resentments toward coworkers. Help me cope. Help me make good decisions. I need your help to do what is right. The next six to eight hours are crucial. I will be tested.

The specificity of the request underscored its utter sincerity. Had the Atlas Trappists prayed each day for anything more than this? More eloquently? As simply? As wonderfully?

Discernment.

Steve, one of the regulars at the local YMCA, was out of the shower when I arrived with my son Noah at 6:15 for our morning swim. A muscular guy in his mid-thirties, he's usually still in the weight room at this time. When I asked, he told me he had a 6:30 meeting. At work? At church, he replied, quietly.

This is the place of biceps and sports scores, not religious dialogue. I hesitated. But my heart was at work quicker than my head, and the words were coming out of my mouth before I could catch them. What I said I can't remember, but I made it clear I wanted to hear more.

A Methodist, Steve had been on a "Road to Emmaus" weekend that had obviously affected him profoundly. He said it was based on the Cursillo movement, of which I knew—and which had performed the minor miracle of making more practicing Christians out of practicing Catholics than any religious program of the past fifty years. Another fellow dressing asked when the next Emmaus weekend would be held. Yet another came forward and said he was a member of Steve's church; they shook hands, comparing what service each went to and why they hadn't met before. Talk in the locker room—not for long, but for those few minutes—revolved around churches and faith commitments and the necessity of group support. Moments of grace in an unlikely place.

Discernment?

Meanwhile, an acquaintance of mine was having continuing trouble at work. He was a hard worker, but his brusque ways didn't always serve him well. I talked with his wife and in so many words suggested that his manner was not helping him. Might he not "sand the edges" a bit to make things go more smoothly? There was not the slightest flutter of recognition, but that didn't matter; I realized, as I was speaking to her, that I was talking as much to myself. My own soul's groaning with its own poverty of spirit, my own impatience and lack of kindness, needed its own remedy.

Discernment?

I needed to hear words about discernment once more and to turn them over in my mind.

. . . a conscious experience of God's grace drawing one to a course
of action or exposing the influence that a projected course of action
will have on one's relationship with God . . .

. . . recognizing what God is asking of us . . . what he would like us to do with our lives, how he wishes us to respond to the concrete life-situations which we encounter.

It was about a week later, still pondering discernment, when I happened to pick a novel off my shelf. I turned to a section I knew well. I should have; I wrote it. The passage told of an earnest but conflicted man who has spent months in prayer and fasting at his hermitage near a monastery, trying to discern whether or not he should become a monk. After so many women in his life, he has met *a* woman. She is vibrant and marvelous; now all his careful discernments are being thrown to the winds. In this section, he talks of "seeking the face of God"; she tells him instead to look into her face. I seek the will of God, he bellows in his agony. I want to do what God has planned for me. She places her hands on his cheeks and looks deeply into his frightened eyes.

"God wants what you want," she answers.

I put the book back on the shelf.

Discernment?

As for now, there was nothing more to do than continue building the bridge, even though I could not yet discern how, or even whether, it would reach the other side.

DECEMBER

Mysticism

Eternity Now

When a pre-monastery night of fitful sleep puts me on the road early, my first morning at Mepkin is usually spent in an exhausted haze. If I were more saintly this time would find me fertile for guileless contemplation; but being only human, instead it must often be punctuated by a nap or two. After vigils at 3:20, some reading, a short nap, lauds at 5:30, and a breakfast of softly scrambled, always fresh eggs and a few slices of Brother Boniface's whole wheat bread, I thought I was launched for the day. I was wrong.

As I sat reading in my cell, my eyes fixed on a familiar line just before they flickered closed. "This is the day which the Lord has made; let us rejoice and be glad in it." The quote from the Psalms was contained in a sermon of St. Gregory of Nyssa, a fourth-century bishop and theologian whose subtlety and spirituality have only recently been properly recognized.[1] Gregory had used those words from Psalm 118 to underscore the continuing possibility of new birth, new life, for those who unite themselves to God. I was repeating the words to myself as I dozed off, knowing their literal meaning but trying to unlock their secret for me, in this day— in the time-honored monastic practice of *lectio divina*. I found the words were still on my lips as I awoke. There was a certain blissful quality about them, an expansive horizon before me, a limitless sea to sail.

A little later that morning, another psalm conveyed a different idea.

At terce, a short, ten-minute time of prayer after mass and just before the morning work period begins, the stern admonishment of Psalm 90 pierced my personal fog to speak with alarming urgency. Consider, mortal being, the psalm forewarned—how many years do you have on this earth? Seventy? Eighty for the strong? The sea that I was sailing was not so boundless after all. Tracy and I had met twenty years before, beginning this period of my life—the best time, I believed. Twenty more years—if that many—and this sailor likely would be beyond the horizon.

It wasn't that I had a feeling of panic or imminent decline as I stood among the monks that morning holding our well-thumbed choir books. As my mind wrestled with the words from these two psalms, my eyes rose up from the pages to search out that small window in the cupola. Wide sky, limited view. That window and my life. How to find God as we squint through our peephole on the universe, attempting—as we all do—to make something wonderful, holy, and happy of our days on earth?

God is everywhere, everpresent. Yes, I could say those words. I have said them many times, in fact. But I did not *live* them.

A voice was sounding in the church, yet another of the ingredients for the supernatural stew that come relentlessly and unbidden at a place like

---

[1]From a sermon by Gregory of Nyssa, quoted in *The Liturgy of the Hours*, vol. II, 825.

Mepkin, adding new flavor, thickening or thinning, speeding or slowing the boiling point. It was a simple enough invocation floating through the air, one that I had read and heard many times before: "I want a loving heart more than sacrifice, knowledge of my ways more than holocausts." But today it hung there before me, no longer a series of words, but a demand to be answered.

Offering over the usual joys of human existence for life in a monastery was certainly a holocaust—of desires, of will, of movement. Family, friends, career, an exclusive companion—all these are sacrificed, the smoke wafting heavenward. Trying to live a secular life inspired by the principles of monastic life was different in substance, but not intent—it also brings us to the fire. There were restrictions and deliberations in excess in both lives. But the emphasis in the words I had just heard was not on self-immolation and deprivation. It was on knowing—and by inference, practicing and living—God's ways. And it was on having a loving, generous, and open heart.

My visits to Mepkin had laid a certain kind of foundation, one on which I now hoped to build. My initial intensity had (fortunately) been blunted in the first visit. I had then seen it was faith, not intentionality alone, that marked the real first step toward a relationship both with God and with one's true self. *Conversatio* promised continuing spiritual, psychological, and emotional regeneration and growth, if one did not tire of its persistent demands. Informed by monastic wisdom and practice, stability, detachment, and discernment provided the framework for a spiritual life.

But I needed to change in a more fundamental way. Quite frankly, I was pretty good about sacrifice. I was lacking in the loving heart category. I could wear a hair shirt of penance; the mantle of happiness fit less well on my shoulders. It is not that I am some sort of morbid soul; most people think of me as a rather upbeat, happy person. But I was better at motivating guilt in myself—and my wife and children—than I was in fostering a loving heart within and encouraging it in others.

For there is more, far more, beyond such quantitative terms as "growth" and "regeneration" in the spiritual life. To simply be glad in the day. To experience the sublime reward of life with God, while yet on earth.

After all, this was the promise of a life of the spirit, a life ". . . t′
to the monk in each of us, to our soul, which longs for peace a
tion to an ultimate source of meaning and value."[2]

Although I was at a Trappist monastery, the longing to fulfill suc
a promise as this occurs to us all—on subway trains and on freeways, in a
line at a supermarket, on the sidelines of a soccer game, in the darkness of
our bedrooms. We are struck as if an absolutely new and profound concept
has mysteriously been presented. We ponder the number of our days. We
look about us. "Is this all there is to life?" we ask. "There must be more!"
We may not know how to say it, but we seek that divine connection that
will make us whole, that will transcend our failures and successes, that will
never leave us to face our lives alone.

When at Mepkin such thoughts usually propel me to one of two
places. I had just been to the church, so I headed for the second. Mepkin's
library is housed in the basement of a low structure built into a small
embankment that overlooks the Cooper River and has ten monks' cells, two
offices, and a sitting room used for meetings of the novices. The library has
the feel of a catacomb, bunker, and proper Cistercian scriptorium all at
once. Humidity is a constant problem in low country South Carolina, so—
God willing and the funds forthcoming—ground would be broken for a
new library in a month.

Though isolated here in Berkeley County, far from any major popula-
tion centers or universities, Mepkin's library arguably has the best spiritual
and theological collection in this part of the country. Priceless manu-
scripts and incunabula—notably some of the sermons of St. Bernard and
exquisite early editions—would amaze even the casual browser. Now in the
process of being bar-coded and computer-cataloged (two retired women
librarians have volunteered their services to bring order to the chaos of fifty
years of a little too much monastic detachment and Abbot Francis's propensity to return from his travels with entire small libraries), the collection
is now indexed and cross-referenced as never before.

But what is the questing soul to do with such brave new order? "This is

[2]Steindl-Rast with Lebell, *The Music of Silence*, 5.

the day the Lord has made. . . ." is not exactly an acceptable search term. Computers have no patience with the confusion in the human heart. Worse, standing before these shelves was like a starving man being confronted with a smorgasbord of tasty delights; choosing just one among them would be impossible. At times like this, it is often best to be somewhat monastic and yield to obedience, obedience to whatever finds its way into an outstretched hand. I closed my eyes and extended my arm. My hand came to rest on the spine of a book.

It was about 8:30 when I emerged from the library, waved to Brother Edward—dressed in his signature dark-green coveralls in preparation for his morning work—and walked through the cloister quadrangle. It was an uncommonly warm day for this time of year and threatening rain. It seemed as though winter had been beaten back by the sun's sheer power, even though shrouded by a heavy overcast of clouds. The temperature would easily reach seventy degrees, perhaps higher. The humidity was that of July or August. Red and white camellias were displayed in embarrassing profusion, their waxy leaves glistening in the refracted light.

I must have been daydreaming, for the intersection a quarter of a mile distant presented itself suddenly. There before me was a finely sculpted statue of Jesus with arms outstretched. As I drew closer, it was readily apparent that these arms offered clear choices. There was the option to turn back toward the world and escape swiftly along the smooth pavement of Dr. Evans Road; or to turn along a rougher, dirt-and-gravel road leading deeper into the monastic enclave. Loving but stone arms offered no promise of the embrace one might wish for in a moment of indecision. There might be momentary rest in the statue's shadow, but then you have to move on. This was not yet heaven; this was life. I turned down the dirt road.

As I slowly made my way further along the rutted and winding roadway, I raised the book I had chosen and let it fall open to the page gravity would choose. On my left were the remains of a once handsome stand of feed corn; on my right a field of beets where the footprints of Brother Callistus (who had sowed and hoped to reap) and his brother deer (who left the sowing entirely to Brother Callistus) intermingled in peaceful coexistence. A familiar smell lay upon the gentle wind.

The book I had chosen, *The Practice of Faith: A Handbook of Contemporary Spirituality*, turned out to be a collection of Karl Rahner's shorter articles. Rahner, perhaps the greatest Catholic theologian of the twentieth century, was a pioneer who had the audacity to explore that fertile yet swampy delta formed where scholastic teaching and modern thought converged. Condemned and censored, a disinherited son before Vatican II, he would prove to be one of its true fathers. I liked him for reasons other than his checkered career. He was transparently human. At a time when unstinting loyalty to dogma was considered the highest virtue for Catholic seminarians, he was a relentless questioner. He looked to Scripture, history, and philosophy as theological sources. A Jesuit sworn to celibacy, he nonetheless ardently loved a woman, Luise Rinser, and though his love was chaste, he was not ashamed of committing his emotions about her to paper. Constrained by the vow of poverty, he was an inveterate window-shopper who delighted in beautiful things. Rahner was not one to be bound by the letter of the law. In his life, the spirit always triumphed.

The article fate presented to my eyes that morning, "The Simplicity of Faith," was nothing less than a blessed bombshell, detonating the "picture of God . . . being too transcendental, too absolute, too incomprehensible."[3] Rahner instead called for a religious belief that was "seen to be divinely simple and self-explanatory." It was classic Rahner, dealing with a favorite topic: the self-communication of God. Rahner always maintained that God was revealed in human actions and natural events. In these short musings, he set aside institutional Christianity and erudite theological distinctions to hold out a less encumbered path to God. Mysticism—or the communion with God that so many seek—was not an end stage, Rahner maintained. And, it was not only achieved by the holy or cloistered. It was available to all, now.

The threatening skies delivered on their promise of rain and I took shelter under a huge quonset-hut-shaped enclosure built to protect Mepkin's newest product from the elements. As monks down through the centuries have aspired to make the ordinary beautiful and useful, the Mepkin

---

[3]Karl Rahner, *The Practice of Faith: A Handbook of Contemporary Spirituality* (New York: Crossroad, 1983), 39.

Trappists looked at the chicken manure piling up from their 35,000 Leghorns and saw not animal waste but "Earth Healer." Properly composted, this concoction was encased in bright green bags and made ready for shipping. Across the way was another quonset hut, this one with the pungent scent of a yet unseasoned product closer to its original source material. It was a smell that I found strangely comforting that December day, a redolent and centering reminder of exactly where I was.

I continued to read Rahner's words as the gentle rain turned into a downpour, beating ever louder and more insistently on the mylar roof—as if trying to break through the thick husk of my own obtuseness. "God's universal saving power is always and everywhere at work, the grace of ineffable, silent access to the mystery of God communicating himself in love and forgiveness. And this experience of grace, this indefinable 'mysticism' of everyday life, will be seen to be the essence of Christianity."[4] Rahner, able to lay down dense theological German with the best of them (he had, after all, studied under the existentialist thinker Martin Heidegger), was but a boy in wonder at the continuing presence of God in the world. It was that obvious, that profound: "God's self-communication is given . . . in grace and accepted in freedom whenever (a person) believes, hopes, and loves."[5]

The "mysticism of everyday life." What a wonderful way to say it, Professor Rahner. But after all, wasn't this a keystone of monastic life, a promise implicit in Benedict's *Rule*? Without glimpsing the presence of God in everyday actions, moments, and interchanges, as well as in their many hours in prayer, how could monks go on? Even while on a spiritual quest that those of us in the world would not attempt, they too needed grace and inspiration to be reminded of God's presence among them. We might use a more familiar term: positive feedback.

These mystical moments seem so readily apparent in a place like Mepkin. I could—anyone could—fill up notebooks with examples. One of the other guests, Anita Burroughs-Price—a young, brilliant harpist from the North Carolina Symphony—playing "Ode to Joy" in the infirmary,

[4]Ibid, 41.
[5]Ibid, 70.

while lay brother Bill McGrath's hands so tastefully conducted the rest of an invisible orchestra. Father Benjamin, who sits so many hours with a vacant look on his face, suddenly brought to life—and grace—by the melodic strings. The eager eyes of Brother Edward as the abbot returns to the monastery after his trip to South America. Incense swirling about the altar during vespers, stirred by the wings of the Holy Spirit (also known as the air-conditioning system).

I have felt very close to God many times in these holy places, monasteries—alone, in the silence of an abbey church; reading in my cell when the words on the page took on breathtakingly new and profound meaning; walking in the dark or in the light of day; sitting on a bench. Yet only once could I say that I had something close to a mystical experience.

It was at the Trappist monastery outside Spencer, Massachusetts, during my hermit's year. Walking back to my pew after receiving the Eucharist, I became aware of a blue light glistening on the polished marble floor before me. As I moved toward the light, it retreated. I walked slower; it slowed. It summoned to me, urging me on to reach it, touch it, enter it. I walked faster and faster and appeared to be catching up with the light. But just as I was ready to step onto its soft blue halo, it disappeared.

It was God, beckoning to me. That much I knew. I also realized that had I touched him, I would be no more. It was not yet my time. It was a first, and very possibly last, moment of incredible lucidity, though to others—even others in a monastery—it might have seemed rather odd; a seeker chasing around a glow on the floor.

In the world, I have found, I am less able to see God present. Yes, I have had transcendent surges of energy and calmness while walking among the California redwoods, or stepping onto the creaky front steps of my boyhood home in Cleveland, or looking out onto the placid surface of the Indian Ocean at sunset off the coast of Pakistan. But as for "everyday mysticism"—no.

"I want a loving heart more than sacrifice, knowledge of my ways more than holocausts." Here, of course, was the pathway to mysticism; pointed to in the psalms, codified by Benedict, no less fresh or relevant in our day. Don't torment yourself thinking that only grand gestures will please God or satisfy the soul's deepest yearnings. Rather, attempt to search out those "ways" of God—those paths toward God's nature—and try to follow them. Was it really no more than that? I didn't want to be some sort of spiritual Luddite or a postmodern reductionist; but there were the words. I wanted for them to be written on my heart, not merely in my memory or on a page.

The wind was still. Then, softly, a lone cool gust washed across my face.

Ever the doubting Thomas, I looked about me, performing an existentialist's litmus test. The very spot where I sat, a dusty table and simple formica stool—doubtless somebody's tag-sale castoffs—set me in a place of unaccountable peace in the midst of a torrential downpour, in the company of well-tended chicken manure and a good book. An abundant crop of Brother Callistus's spinach and lettuce stood at the ready in the garden, should I need them for sustenance. I scanned the table. Could it be? A salt shaker! I had food to eat, shelter in a storm, the companionship of these rich, warm mounds, and many pages of Rahner to feast upon.

I closed the book and walked out into the warm rain. I gathered some lush, full leaves of spinach and lettuce, washed clean by a diminishing rain so gentle and utilitarian it could have been the spray in the kitchen sink. I sprinkled salt upon the leaves. What flavor and goodness, crisp and clean, unfettered, unadulterated, purity itself.

Why is it that we—I—too often find such ordinary beauty so hard to recognize and savor in the dailiness of life? Are our eyes so blinkered to these bursts of grace? Are we so stubborn to refuse to acknowledge God's presence in the world, in our individual lives? Do we not realize that our appreciation for such things as these will be returned by them a hundred-fold, in the fullness, beauty, and integrity of their own natures? That our love for people, in their magnificence and their brokenness, is the tidal power that animates the rivers and streams and oceans, propels the planets, lights the sun?

While they may see beauty in God's creation, mystics are hardly sensing the presence of God every moment. Monks don't really talk that much about experiencing God; the mystical life, it turns out, doesn't work that way. The holiest monks I know talk about experiencing each other, daily events, the rewards and harmony of what some might regard a terribly routinized life—but in which they have found freedom. Monks are often called "child-like," and they are. Behind their ready smiles, gentle voices, and easy, unhurried stride, what they have is something philosopher Paul Ricoeur calls a "second naivete."[6] It is not simple-minded sentimentality but an enthusiastic innocence seamlessly annealed to the wisdom that comes with experience. They are believers in the sacrament, the holiness, of the present moment. They look, without anxiety, for the message in each circumstance in which they find themselves—for, in the divine plan, there is one. Monks' senses are disciplined—not denied—so that every dimension of existence is greeted with a heightened sensitivity. They hear more clearly, see more deeply, taste more fully. The result of the ascetic life, removing the unnecessary, is a keen awareness, one that makes God real in the ordinary and expected.

Monks with wan, glazed looks are often those whose faith is based on the expectation of divine theatrical productions. When the show folds, so do they. I know a monk who spent many years in two monasteries, whose fingers constantly played over a well-worn and over-sized strand of prayer beads—yet who could not make a connection to the men around him. He sought God in pious acts, missing the fact that God was right there before him in ordinariness.

But I should not be so sure in judgment. After some forty years of experiencing monastic life in dozens of monasteries, I am still myself far from understanding—or practicing—Rahner's call to look for mysticism in everyday life. I still try to freeze dry the precious moments of insight or inspiration at monasteries, as if they were the only places I could expect such moments to occur. I then go out into the supposedly arid, unspiritual wasteland of the rest of my life—where, of course, transcendence could not be expected.

Many people who have experienced spiritual awakenings in such holy places as monasteries recall with great vividness a wondrous moment or a

---

[6]Quoted in Steindl-Rast with Lebell, *The Music of Silence*, 41.

wise teacher. These are certainly good and precious. But are they enough to sustain us in the rest of our lives? I have found they are not. The danger is that by seeking these experiences only in such places we will effectively put shackles on God, and a wearisome burden on ourselves.

How many restless seekers have gone from place to place, their spiritual *vita* a shopping list of every popular movement that flashed across the spiritual sky? They may seem filled and satisfied with their latest "answer," but without a continuing connection to God in the ordinariness of their lives, their spirits atrophy. It becomes clearer and clearer with the advent (and then the predictable decline) of each new spiritual "answer" that the pursuit of peak experience is at the very core of what is wrong with too much of what passes as spirituality today. Rather than daring to peer long and hard into that ineffable, bottomless pool that is God, we actually want to see ourselves reflected, upon the surface. We can't bring ourselves to leap fully into that pool, afraid of both its depth and freedom; we would rather simply float along, securely attached to the short tether of our ego.

"The miracle is not to walk on water," writes Thich Nhat Hanh. "The miracle is to walk on the green earth."[7] He tells the story of a man who, desperate to see the Buddha, hurried by a woman in dire need. When he arrived, although there the Buddha was right before him, the man was incapable of seeing him. The same principle runs through the New Testament miracles: they occurred because people involved were open, because they believed not so much in the possibility of God in the hereafter, but in the possibility of God that very moment.

The rain had stopped and a blanket of steam rose up from the earth, a sigh of thankfulness from the saturated clay to the clouds floating by, now white, fluffy, and benign. The sun again blazed brightly in the azure sky for which the Carolinas are justly famous. I began to walk back to the monastery buildings, churning over these thoughts about everyday mysticism, the mysticism of this place, my own myopia about mysticism in the rest of my life.

I thought about our family vacation that summer. It was a specific

---

[7]Thich Nhat Hanh, *Living Buddha, Living Christ*, 53.

moment I remembered, on a hike climbing out of the Grand Canyon. Noah and Daniel, some way ahead of Tracy and myself, walked through a huge hole nature had carved through a piece of shale. This rock had tumbled down from high on the canyon face thousands, perhaps millions of years before. Wind and rain had slowly etched its surface—until finally, one day, a pinhole of light showed through where only darkness had reigned. And there were my sons, men of this time, bearing the traits and formation of so many centuries of ancestors neither I nor they will ever know in this life. Our two boys were caught for an instant in the brilliant morning sun, Noah's blond hair shimmering and white, Daniel's auburn hair aflame with red highlights. Then they were gone, out of the light, through the rock, around the bend.

The week before our trip I had taken the Eucharist to Joan, a valiant woman battling an implacable cancer, back in the hospital because the catheter site through which she received medication and chemotherapy had become infected. Regardless of what she was going through, what setbacks might have occurred—for hers was a sad path inexorably leading to a painful death—she always had a smile and a good word when I visited. After she received communion that morning we both bowed our heads to place ourselves in the presence of God. In that moment I felt an overwhelming desire to somehow convey my affection for her, my respect for her bravery. When I pressed my cheek to hers, so fevered, I felt the sweetness of a tear. It was a tear of gratitude, a tear of understanding, a tear of confidence in God's goodness. How it was that I knew all those things for certain I cannot say; but I did, for I could feel them in that instant, touching a drop of her soul's dew.

These infusions of grace into our lives occur with such regularity that it is somewhat embarrassing to stop and think for just a few moments and be faced with such abundance. It is certainly a lack of generosity to ourselves not to acknowledge them. We think ourselves not worthy of God's continuing presence and concern. God should think about me, communicate with me? Hardly. The hardness of our hearts, our supposed sophistication, sometimes our self-loathing—all conspire to keep our soul in the darkness, away from a light that never dims. For God is in our midst. Ours need not be so much a search for "God" and "meaning," but rather the alert living in the ordinary extraordinariness of each of our lives. After my walk I continued my monastic day. I ate the refectory lunch of pasta and a red sauce. I could taste the individual dots of dried basil and oregano, a flake of red pepper. The apple juice was almost overwhelmingly refreshing. Two carmels, covered in white chocolate, were a perfect dessert. I read for a while. I walked some more. Supper was no more than a bowl of all-bran cereal. What a fine, nutty flavor it had. The milk was rich. The bell for vespers summoned me to church. More reading.

As compline and the monastic day ended with the singing of *Salve Regina*, I watched as the monks emerged from their darkened stalls and filed toward the front of the church where the abbot stood in a shaft of soft light. Each bowed his head to receive Francis's blessing and a sprinkle of holy water. As usual, nothing was hurried; what was there to hurry for? These men know exactly what they will be doing at each hour of the day. Their routine may appear to be an exercise in deadening regularity, but in the monastery there is enough time for everything. Time is not considered a limited commodity; each moment is all the reality that anyone can hope to experience, and that moment is now. And now. And now. A series of opportunities, encounters. Each with its own message. We are invited to listen—and then, if appropriate, respond. Time in a monastery is shaped into a series of frames to experience God—in prayer, in work, in eating, sleeping, talking.

The monks were gone. I stood alone in the darkened church, the moisture of holy water upon my neck.

Time. How crucially time is linked to the mysticism of everyday life. For only when time is understood as precious, but not scarce, do we begin to live. Only when time is broken into discrete segments, and not allowed to become a blur of memories and projections—what I didn't spend enough time doing, what I won't have enough time to accomplish—can we hope to open ourselves to the opportunity of seeing God in the world. How distorted we have allowed time to become, fearing continually that it is running out. But when time is framed it provides an inner structure that brings intensity, awareness, calmness, delight. These wise monks have learned that when time is so regarded, when they live in the now, they transcend the constraints that time normally imposes upon us. In essence, they experience eternity. For what more is eternity than the everpresent now?

On my way to vigils the next morning, I walked out under a canopy of stars so dazzling and luminous there seemed not a spot in the night sky allowed to cower in darkness. The air was moist but fresh, as yet untouched by the day. The mind is in a similar state at this hour, which is precisely why monks and all seekers rise early to take command of the day before it takes command of them. Everyday mysticism was on my mind as the ancient words of the psalms were gently proffered, passed back and forth by each side of the choir, two parsed lines at a time, in the plainsong chant that allows each verse its moment to infuse the heart or imagination of both speaker and hearer. The words were from the Third Psalm:

> *I cried unto the Lord with my voice*
> *And he heard me out of his holy hill.*
> *I laid down and slept; I awaked;*
> *For the Lord sustained me.*

As I rested on those words, a somewhat disconcerting thought came to me. If we manage to become modern mystics—if being a mystic means sensing the presence, power, and beauty of God—we will probably be the last to know. Change is difficult to see, as the ocean teaches us. Only when a wave is crested do we see its power—and in effect it is already dying, losing that power. So it is with mysticism. We rarely can say, as the event is happening, "Yes, this is a mystical moment. God is here!" As the Scripture tells us, we do not see the face of God; we only know God when he has passed by and we, in effect, see the back of his head.

So we must muddle on, trying as best we can to live in the eternal now, going where the good seeds within us are allowed to flourish, avoiding all that would deaden our souls. It is not that God's presence cannot be found everywhere—in the cosmic sense, it can. But for most of us unenlightened ones, we must be more discerning. The monks continually restrict their freedom, their hours of sleeping, their libido, what they read, what they eat, to maintain that "edge" that even the earliest desert fathers and mothers saw as absolutely essential to a life with God—and one's truest self.

The monks daily churn over the words of the psalms, alternately disquieting and comforting; they do deep and regular spiritual reading. They pray, alone and in community. But, unlike pre-Vatican II Trappists who may have had little access to any other than meditative reading, they also read many of the same newspapers and magazines we do. This is a different monastic era, and it was never Benedict's intent that practices become ossified. So modern monks read these publications for entertainment and for information—but they are too cunning not to also read them for inspiration.

Their shrewdness is a lesson to us. If to fill our empty hours we turn to magazines devoted to cigars or wine or the lives of celebrities, those are the seeds that are sown within us. Not that cigars or wine or celebrities are intrinsically bad; they are not. But when our minds are flooded with these evanescent images and desires, when they are numbed by the media's obsession with depictions of excess and deceit, they become accordingly less open to the infusion of graces, the everyday mysticism that Rahner talks about and to which the monastic life is directed.

Our eyes darting over a schedule, a hand yanking back a sleeve so we can see the time. It is seductive, a sign of importance and worth to cram more into our days than is humanly possible. Why then do we find that our senses are not heightened, but actually dulled, by such frantic activity? Life becomes a slurry of faces, events, sounds. There is no frame around them so that we can really focus and perceive. We ache with fatigue that is in some part physical, but in greater part, spiritual. Such a one-dimensional life, limited to what we are, get, and have, is but a shadow of what life can be.

Monks do not watch television. This is not to say that we should not, for we live in an entirely different world—we have different needs both for information and leisure than do cloistered men and women. But the monastic *idea* is still valid if we want to join hearts and minds to God, to provide those openings through which the part of ourselves that is deepest and best might be touched, encouraged, and invigorated rather than cluttered up by the distractions. If we want to be mystics, we cannot build a foundation for a transcendent life on what diminishes and eventually kills the human heart, what clips the wings of the spirit within us that yearns to soar. Yes, it might be easier to be a mystic in a monastery; but the *attitude* that nourishes mysticism is universally available.

Mysticism is a strange part of us. We may feel its lack far more than we know its presence.

Leaving the monastery and returning to my life as husband, father, and writer, I was soon reminded that everyday mysticism is hardly a stream of spiritually enriched moments. It is theoretically—and probably—easier to be a mystic in a monastery; but most of us are not called to live in such places. So we must find wonder and God amidst a far more complex and distracting spiritual landscape than that which monks inhabit. Remembering those times of sweet communion with God, when the most profound depths of our being were touched, we may strive to do everything we can to increase and intensify mystical moments.

Well, we can and we cannot.

As we attempt to live a deeper spiritual life—even when we feel we are becoming more in tune with the mystical dimension of our lives—our horrible, most base selves will shockingly reappear, seemingly negating everything that we are trying to be. Some would say this is the work of the Evil One, the devil. I don't know much about the devil (or for that matter, angels), but I do know that I am composed of conflicting forces—virtue and vice, mysticism and materialism. Who does not want the comforts of this world? Who wouldn't take an easy, drip-dry spirituality that produced the bliss without the attendant cost? Who wants to have constantly to weigh actions and attitudes, what we read and what we say? But keeping the edge requires constant honing. Patience, love, generosity, humility—all extract their cost in those of us still imperfectly aligned with our Maker.

I was a perfect example of this dualism just a few days after returning from my monthly visit to Mepkin. Thankfully I had not come back, as I had months before, armed with the clenched fists of good intentions. Instead I simply tried to slow the speed of my life, to alternately embrace and release time from its normal constraints. I tried to be aware of what were the beauties and blessings of my life.

I live near a beautiful expanse of the Atlantic Ocean. I am surrounded by good friends and acquaintances, reside in a pleasant neighborhood, have a loving wife and pretty good kids. And while I could see splendor and blessedness in all this, I found I was beginning to discover an even deeper and more mystical beauty in an unlikely place—at the hospital, as I took the Eucharist to my patients the next Thursday. Their names stared blankly from a straight column on a computer printout, but their lives, in a strangely unrestricted way, were opened up to me. I listened to each, and each I could hear, differently. Cancer, amputation, viral meningitis—these words allegedly described the patients I visited, but they spoke nothing of the nobility of their souls, their grace, that light which shone in eyes dulled with pain and medication. I could see through huge patches of blood-stained dressings and beyond tubes; heaving chests and wasted limbs were not the measure of people so close to God—whether articulated or not—in their hour of need. They were on holy ground, hovering between what we call life and what we see as death; people stripped bare of any pretense of normalcy, cast before God, weak and vulnerable. Yet his presence showed through them. They were not alone. They were certainly not cursed. In some strange and altogether inexplicable way, they were sacred vessels; in these precious moments they overflowed with a lifetime's abundance of graces. I could see them, bathed in a whole new light. Time may have been running out, but that was merely human time. God's time opened generously to them, abundant, eternal.

Even the elevator ride to begin my rounds on the ninth floor proved to offer moments of grace. A large woman with glowing black skin, so beautiful with a tasteful edge of fine lace at the neck of her flowing dress. A white woman, as thin as the other was stout, her fine cheekbones set off by carefully applied blush and just the right twinkle in her eye as she got off at her floor. The black man in the baseball cap, peering through his bifocals to carefully punch in the floor numbers as people called them out, his hands as determined as Michelangelo's. Three spirits had traveled with me; now they were gone, but I felt a strange warmth and kinship.

"Maybe these crazy occurrences . . . are brief glimpses behind the curtain of existence, soft whispers from the wings, reminding us that we are awaited, we are loved, that our lives are right on course," writes my friend and wise teacher J. Murray Elwood.[8] Frederick Buechner, minister and novelist, imagines them as "momentary glimpses into a mystery of such depth, power and beauty that if we were to see it head on, in any other ways than glimpses, I suspect we would be annihilated."[9]

Then how could it be that the very evening following my hospital rounds I did not see my boys as two pure spirits stepping through that rock at the Grand Canyon, but instead as two miscreants banging around the local building-supply superstore, completely fouling up my attempt for a quick stop to purchase some light bulbs? I had allotted just so much time; my sons had other plans than such efficiency. Buying light bulbs might not have had the makings of a mystical experience, but it didn't have to be like this. Not that children don't have to be reprimanded for horsing around; but like this, with an ugly verbal assault? We came home in a sullen silence, and when poor Tracy tried to mediate the stalemate I erupted again, with a venom I did not know I was capable of. I went to bed disgusted with myself. The aftershock had still not worn off; an unvirtuous hangover rang in my head. Mysticism had a terribly hollow sound.

The next morning—wallowing in my own wretchedness, grasping for something to hold on to—St. Ambrose extended his hand. Simple enough, the passage from his "On the Mysteries" in my breviary called out across the centuries; "Grace can accomplish more than nature."[10] Yes, we can do everything to see the world as holy, but Ambrose was making it

[8]J. Murray Elwood, "When Is Synchronicity a Sign?," *America*, 20 December 1997, 17.
[9]From William Zinsser, "Spiritual Quests," published 1988, quoted in Elwood, 17.
[10]Quoted in *The Liturgy of the Hours*, vol. III, 511.

clear that ultimately the mystic's life must resemble that of a trusting fool. By sheer resolution, we are incapable of this everyday mysticism on our own—monks learn as much early in their formation, and we in the world need equally to learn that finally it comes down not to an act of will, but of the heart. We can guard what we read and how we talk and who we choose for friends, but those are all tied to nature—our imperfect, conflicted selves at work, "as yet unredeemed by grace."

Two great philosophers came to mind as I mulled over Ambrose's words. One, Woody Allen, said: "Ninety percent of life is just showing up." The other was my late friend, Father Joseph Greer, and his pithy assessment: "What is life? Life is lacing up your sneakers every morning and getting out on the court." How open each approach is to grace. That by showing up, by simply walking out on the court, something will come of this inner disposition and readiness. Thomas Merton's desire to please God was all that he could authentically offer. Somehow, some way, the divine contract reads, we will be filled with grace. It is when we refuse to show up or lace up, refuse to desire because of our supposed inadequacies or our fear of further failure, when we refuse to believe in the magnificent possibilities in the sliver of eternity called now, that we shut off access to the source of grace—God.

I thought about this one morning as I was swimming. The reason we gasp for breath as we turn our head out of the water is not because there is insufficient air to breathe. The room is full of air; we only need a tiny bit of it. It is because we have not expelled enough of the old, stale air so as to open our lungs to the freshness of this life-sustaining, abundant essence.

In the mid-1960s, when the Catholic Church was buffeted by winds of both cultural and institutional change, Western monks like the Trappists learned a valuable lesson from Eastern monks, especially the Buddhists. Western monks had prided themselves on austere living, on combating the devil at every opportunity; they adhered to a severe interpretation of "custody of thoughts," vigilant against even the slightest venal notion as they prayed. They placed great stock by the ability to steer a straight, untrammeled course to God. Barriers were constructed and fortified, eyes were steeled, teeth gritted.

Eastern monks, far advanced in the meditation and contemplation the West had pushed aside in favor of more rigorous asceticism, smiled at our Western assertiveness and offered another way. Don't worry if every waking moment was not focused on the divine, they counseled. Don't fight the spurious thoughts that waft into one's consciousness during prayer, meditation, or daily work, they advised. Allow these thoughts to float off just as they had floated in, to make a speedy and peaceful exit. These Eastern monks knew they could not control what came into their minds; rather, with an ease born of great spiritual wisdom and discipline, they sought only to edit what remained there.

The object of contemplation—and of mysticism—is not to pursue God or transcendence as a prize or goal, but to "show up" for the wonders that might be ours. To exhale in order to be able to inhale. To frame each moment, each breath. Merton's most profound mystical experience occurred before Buddhist statues at an outdoor shrine in Polonnaruwa, Sri Lanka, not during his twenty-seven years at Gethsemani as a cloistered Trappist monk.

If we want to be everyday mystics, we—like our brother and sister contemplatives in abbeys and convents—certainly need to be open and alert to the many miracles in our lives. But the yin of that yang is that God must be allowed to do God's share of the work. For if what we achieve spiritually is to be dictated by our nature, our disposition, and our abilities—and not grace, openness, and that "second naivete"—we shall be little more than dry pods from which real life can never spring.

I thought back: my boys in the Grand Canyon, Joan in that hospital bed, my companions on the elevator. I had not sought God; God was there. All I needed to do was open my eyes—and my heart—to recognize the presence.

I returned from my swimming trip and found my boys at the kitchen table, reading the comic pages. My wife was in the pantry, ready to reach up to a cereal box. It was just an instant, but there in an American kitchen, in the silence of a normal morning, the goodness and grace of these people with whom I spend most of my life was apparent. They virtually gleamed in the fluorescent lights. Their efforts at goodness, their patience with a husband and father, was as evident to me as had been the presence of God to Merton at Polonnaruwa. I found I was not breathless or light-headed at all. I simply said good morning. And the day went on.

JANUARY

Chastity

True Freedom

I drove through the familiar gates off Dr. Evans Road, still thrown open to the world on this Friday evening just after 7:00 P.M. It was late in the Trappist day, but barely yet the hour that the rest of humanity ventures out to seek the pleasures of the weekend. Rather than the usual sigh of relief, a duet of low groans echoed in the car.

My good monastic companions, Noah and Daniel, consigned at birth to be life members of my own community, vowed to stability, not given much to detachment, with a faith in just about everything—including their

parents—that fluctuates with alarming swings, had registered their senti-
ments. Quite natural responses, I have convinced myself, of thirteen- and
eleven-year-old American boys. They show little outward evidence of being
solicitous about their religious life; they say, and I believe, that they would
much rather be shopping at Blackbeard's fireworks store in Myrtle Beach or
Grandma's Goodies vintage clothing shop in Charleston. While they might
resist—as boys this age do about practically everything that isn't their own
idea—they still seem to enjoy themselves while they are here on our twice-
yearly visits. They come back with tales to tell their friends—albeit of
alligators and silent lunches, not insights into mysticism and discernment.
Nonetheless, for better or worse, the monastery is a continuing presence,
another kind of stability, in their young lives.

They are on the cusp of becoming young men. The fine hair on their
arms and legs has taken on color. Their voices will soon grow deeper.
Their hormones are beginning to percolate. I looked at them as we quickly
unloaded the car at the gatekeeper's cottage just inside the grounds that the
monastery offers to families and small groups. They are the fruit of my
love—and quite frankly, my lust—for the auburn-haired woman whose
eyes never seem to be dull, even when she is tired, which at that very
moment she was. We took our suitcases into the cottage and drank in its
distinctive damp, low-country fragrance. We were hungry, but the bell had
already rung for compline.

As we hurried along the edge of the cloister garth, we could see stakes
off to the right topped by bright-colored plastic flags flapping in the gentle
evening breeze. For an instant I saw prayer flags at Dharmsala, high in the
Himalayas, where I went twenty years ago to hear the Dalai Lama's remembrances of Thomas Merton for the documentary I'd made on the famous
monk of Gethsemani. The as yet unfunded $5 million building program,
that would bring a new senior wing, library, and expanded refectory, was
underway.

In church, the monks greeted the Wilkes family with far broader smiles
and more pronounced nods than I am ever accorded alone. Not many
children come to Mepkin, and the monks are always happy to see the boys.
For their parts, reluctant weekend monks that they might claim to be, the

boys know it. They took their place in choir, black T-shirts displaying allegiance to the band of the moment, amid monks attired in fashions centuries old.

I am so proud of my sons. I love them so much. And I wonder what kind of men they will be, if I have set them any kind of example that should be followed. What will they take from these monastic visits—from these men, a strange sort of extended family of identically dressed distant uncles? I hope the boys find out what it is to be a man quicker than I did— a real man, a man who is both strong and weak, unstinting and ready to compromise, keeping their own counsel and yet open to change. A man with faith and trust in God, conscious of God's loving mercy, able to see the wonder, beauty, and holiness that trembles all about them. A tall order, I know.

Of course, there is another powerful force they will soon have to reckon with—the force these men in white choir robes attempt to master with the practice of chastity. It is actually not a formal vow for monks, but chastity is implicit in the *Rule*, for without control of this most powerful human drive their lives would result in chaos.

Chastity—isn't this just another of those pious-sounding, quite-impossible-to-live words? Is it not the exclusive, bramble-strewn path for avowed religious, for consecrated virgins, for those with far more holy intentions than these boys might ever muster, or than their father achieved throughout a significant portion of his mature life? Ironically, perhaps, it was chastity that was on my mind as this visit began. I would have to see what these live oaks and the quiet Cooper River had to say about it.

We returned to the guest house and eagerly opened the refrigerator, for it always held a meal, albeit simple, for the wayfarer—Mepkin eggs at a minimum. But this time the *Rule of St. Benedict* regarding treatment of guests notwithstanding,[1] a lone can of soda, a half pound of margarine, and a few inches of milk in a gallon jug stared back at us in the dull light. A massive building project and the small number of able-bodied monks had obviously

---

[1] *The Rule of St. Benedict*, ed. Thomas Fry (Collegeville, Minn.: Liturgical Press, 1981), ch. 53.1; "All guests who present themselves are to be welcomed as Christ, for he himself will say: I was a stranger and you welcomed me. (Matt 25:35)" (253).

taken their toll on the art and practice of monastic hospitality. Thank God we had brought a few boxes of macaroni and cheese. An apple and orange were left from the trip. We went to bed tired and not exactly well-fed pilgrims.

Chastity. As the boys disappeared into the woods after mass the next morning and Tracy sat in the warm sunlight next to the gatekeeper's cottage with a good novel in her hands, I began to follow this delicate thread that runs through monastic life and to contemplate—good monastic word—what it might have to say to our lives.

Benedict, monasticism's spiritual father, surveyed his world at a time of social and moral dissolution, reeling from the protracted collapse of the Roman Empire, to see a confused and frightened people. With mere survival a difficult task, they necessarily had put reading and building aside; but they craved something even more basic that the Romans had provided in reassuring abundance—order. When Benedict began to draw up a way for men to live together in good order so as to pursue God—the very antithesis to the violence and moral abandon of the day—he deduced that while such dangers as acedia, sloth, gluttony, quest for power, pride, and jealousy certainly needed attention, unbridled sexuality (certainly well practiced in his world) was a primary concern. Without a command of one's bodily urges, how could true love of God grow and deep affection for fellow monks be allowed to flourish in these tiny communities? Frankly, how could a fellow keep a clear head about anything?

The cloister itself was a fortress against carnal temptation, quite literally separating monks from the world. Ascetic practices—fasting, limited sleep, hours of spiritual reading, and corporate worship—were designed not only to give glory to God but to construct a carefully balanced day and to gain dominion—quite literally—over the body.

Yet even with such radical departures from the mores of prevailing culture, Benedict's way flourished. Monasteries were not some sort of torture chambers of sensory deprivation. Chastity worked because it was set within a life where certain sacrifices yielded not only spiritual but human satisfactions. The monks enjoyed being together, supported by each other, even as they maintained an emotional distance. Benedict had constructed a pattern of life with a deep sense of silent camaraderie, mutual respect, and purpose that made chastity possible, a pattern that would eventually be replicated in thousands of monasteries. Although they lived in a most structured environment, monks felt they had great autonomy over their lives. The practice of monastic chastity was a key factor in this.

After Benedict's simple way was corrupted in too many monasteries over the centuries—the embrace of secular power and lush living making monasteries little different from royal courts at the dawn of the eleventh century—Bernard of Clairvaux appeared. His reform of Benedictine life, articulating and spreading the vision of the Cistercian founders, reclaimed monasticism's past and foreshadowed its future. Bernard's God was one with whom monks could forge an intimate and loving companionship through a relationship with the God-made-man, Jesus Christ. Community life, his "school of charity," simply living in harmony with fellow monks, and infusing each act—in field, barn, church, or cell—with love and joy; all this was nothing more or less than God's divine plan, portending heavenly bliss.

But it was Bernard's contemporary, Aelred, who truly saw that intimacy was a necessary element of human life, even for monks living within cloister walls. Aelred was twenty years younger than Bernard; and fired by the French monk's vision, he left the Scottish court to join one of Bernard's foundations, the fledgling primitive Cistercian monastery at Rievaulx, England. Friendships were holy, their give and take and practice of charity a means of sanctification, Aelred wrote in his classic, "On Spiritual Friendship." Union with people was union with God. Not only was God to be found in prayer and contemplation, but right next to them in a fellow monk. Chastity was no longer to be seen as a denial of human intimacy; with Aelred, it had taken on a new face.

Friendship and intimacy—the very threads of chastity that Aelred had explored—were regarded as so deep and potentially perilous that other Cistercian reformers saw fit to periodically trim them. With Armand de Rance at La Trappe, they were virtually severed. Aelred was consigned to the back shelves of the scriptorium. Christian churches mirrored this type of fervor, perhaps not as strictly as was practiced in monasteries, but certainly with the same end in mind—to snuff out even a glowing ember of sensuality lest it burst into an all-consuming flame. Male and female aspirants to religious life were prohibited from "particular friendships" and asked to relate to all people with no more than lukewarm equanimity. As the teachings from such a constricted vision of our corporeal selves spread to the world outside the walls, married couples were diligently taught that sex was only for procreation, certainly not for enjoyment or—that feared word—intimacy. As for single people, they were to live a life abstaining from any sensual pleasures until marriage, when they were provided with a narrowly sanctioned outlet for their concupiscence.

Somehow, the world hadn't really discerned what Benedict was saying by mapping out a comprehensive plan for holiness and happiness in his *Rule*. It was what Aelred, throwing his eleventh-century caution to the wind, had boldly proclaimed: that intimate friendships, properly lived, were not only needed by normal human beings, but crucial for their spiritual growth. Chastity did not mean emotional or sensual denial, but rather a wise channeling of this wellspring of life.

In my Catholic mind, chastity had always been intertwined with another word—celibacy. Indeed, the two sometimes seemed to meld into a single concept. Again, I was mistaken. Celibacy, which originated in monasteries but then spread to religious orders, meant that a person never married. It was a matter of pragmatism (how could cloistered men and women be spouses and parents?), economics (church property would remain intact with no heirs), and theology (celibacy mirrored Christ's unmarried life and foreshadowed heaven, where such unions would not exist).

But chastity, as I would only begin to understand much later in life, is as much an attitude as a practice. Chastity is having deep reverence for the mystery of human sexuality and—as monks treat a kitchen pot with the same reverence as an altar chalice—regarding this precious and powerful part of us with a certain veneration. But chastity is not only about sex; there is a second, complementary, and much misunderstood element of chastity. It is called *affectivity*, that aspect of our experience involving feeling and emotion. From love to aversion, tears to laughter, a quickening of sensation to a logy indifference, these are the powerful forces of the heart that accompany us through life. They can be fleeting; they can be deep. Chastity asks for their good and wise employment in our lives.

At the time of this visit I was reading the first volume of Thomas Merton's journals, which covers the period 1939 to 1941—before he entered Gethsemani. He would eventually become a Trappist and live in a monastery for nearly three decades, but on these early pages of his diary he was trying desperately to shed his troubled past and be open to what the God he saw as "mercy within mercy within mercy" might have in store for him. In a short section, written at least a year before he began actively to pursue a religious vocation,[2] Merton provided some insights into chastity that resonated deeply within me. "I have always been struck by the loveliness of a truly chaste person, one in whom chastity and charity are becoming the same thing, so that these people are almost transfigured by a kind of unearthly and peaceful and spontaneous innocence."[3] Merton saw clearly that sexuality and love were intricately interwoven; one without the other was hollow at a minimum, horribly damaging if left unchecked. He had lived a wild life while a student in England; he had even made a young woman pregnant. His quest to assuage the loneliness and lack of purpose in his life by giving his carnality full license had plunged him into despair. He had squandered his emotional patrimony.

Reviewing my own chastity history, I found that in my early years Catholic education had produced a certain clenched-teeth approach to the mystery of sex. Perhaps it is more than can be expected of a young boy turning man (again, I thought of my sons) to believe that this wonderful, exciting power welling up within me was far beyond human capacity to control and had to be flogged into submission. I was certainly no angel, but my sins of the flesh were pretty mild. I lived by the rules and held my sensate self at a distance, as much out of fear of eternal damnation as the desire to be virtuous. Even my years in the Navy were hardly the stuff of salty stories in far-flung ports.

I was a faithful husband in my first marriage, but when it ended I

---

[2]Interestingly enough, Merton would first apply to the Franciscans, who accepted him but then after he told everything about his past—rejected him.

[3]Thomas Merton, *Run to the Mountain, 1939–1941*, vol. 1 of *The Journals of Thomas Merton*, ed. Patrick Hart, O.C.S.O. (New York: HarperCollins, 1995), 48.

found myself released into a wonderland I had never known existed. I took a path that surprised not only me but anyone who had known me. It was the late 1970s and the sexual revolution was in full swing; I quickly enlisted in that ignoble cause. I was some ten years beyond Merton's twenty-seventh year—when he left the world to join the Trappists—but I was headed the other way, hurtling into the world as fast as I could.

"I love you in this moment," I lied over and over again, profaning that precious word, transforming gold to lead with my foolish, empty bromides. Instant intimacy was the gospel I proclaimed. It was not just about sex, but a total diminution of my affective life. Emotions and feelings—my own and those of others—were no more than so many lights in a pinball game. How many could I illuminate? They flashed brightly for an instant, and then were dark.

How was I to find anything at all—someone to love, God, happiness—when I was exploiting the very nature of decent human interactions? Aelred's words about real human relationships were a haunting reminder of how spiritually and emotionally bankrupt was my life: "There is nothing dishonorable, nothing deceptive, nothing feigned; whatever there is, is holy, voluntary and true."[4]

I had a silly grin on my suntanned face most of the time, but it masked an unhappy man. The only times I felt moments of peace were on Sunday mornings at mass when, even through the fog remaining from Saturday night, I knew I was in the presence of a partner, not of the moment, but of eternity—someone who loved me in every moment, someone who loved me first, purely, without constraint, without reason. There, in the coolness of those places—from Long Island, Negril, and Paris to St. Joseph's Church in Greenwich Village where I would eventually be married—I could rest, needing nothing more than simply to be there.

But on Monday—even by Sunday afternoon—I went back to my other life. As I look back, in addition to being the most dissolute, those were the least creative days of my life as a writer. They were vacant, hollow years, during which I was unable to work on much of anything besides fine-

---

[4]Quoted in Katherine M. TePas, "Spiritual Friendship in Aelred of Rievaulx and Mutual Sanctification in Marriage (II)," *Cistercian Studies Quarterly*, 1992:1, 159.

tuning my libido. I defied chastity, mocked it, sneered at its wisdom as the blather of sanctimonious fools. But, strangely, in the divine ecology, it was this time that prepared me to look more deeply into chastity and what it might mean for my soul and life. For, as Merton had, I discovered the depths of my depravity—how great a sinner I could be, given the opportunity. And I also discovered what love was not—that this kind of freedom was in fact a self-imposed prison.

It would be years later that I would read the words of a Buddhist monk whose tradition, seemingly so far from mine, dealt in truths that transcended mere religious boundaries and went to chastity's core. Thich Nhat Hanh wrote:

> We believe in a naive way that having a sexual relationship will make us feel less lonely. But without communication on the level of the heart and spirit, a sexual relationship will only widen the gap and harm us both. . . . Whatever happens to the body also happens to the mind. The sanity of the body is the sanity of the mind; the violation of the body is the violation of the mind.[5]

Tracy was lost in the haze on that landscape of loneliness I so wearily trod. I was exhausted and lonely because I was estranged from God and myself. I thought I could make my body's supposed needs my highest calling—that I could follow its whims and somehow keep my mind clear, that I could shape and reshape my emotions to fit the day's needs. How foolish I was. Chastity was the very foundation of both human and spiritual life; I was doing everything I could to make my foundation out of shifting sands. Until I had control of myself, I would have no control over anything.

It is only because of the grace of God that we married and I stopped that kind of life. Yes, I love this woman, but I did everything to frustrate that love. For almost five years before we married, I waffled and went back to my old ways. Strange to say, perhaps, but it was in married life with

[5]Thich Nhat Hanh, *Living Buddha, Living Christ*, 96–97.

Tracy that I began to understand chastity. Not a dogma-driven chastity, not a chastity that is lived out of fear of divine retribution or even respect for wedded faithfulness, but a chastity that is the ultimate in sexual and sensual freedom. A chastity that embraces every pulsing, hormonal beat and human emotion and does not fear spinning out of control. For when our hearts and minds are chaste, the true beauty of God's creatures is ours to drink in, to enjoy. If there is perfume in the air, do we need to turn our face from it? Should we resolutely ignore a finely tailored suit or an elegant evening gown? No; we can instead see them as God's goodness and presence for us to experience. In my former life, I would try to possess, control, even devour the source of such beauty. I eventually learned that my mind could caress it lightly, like a dove in my hand, and then let it go, unharmed.

True chastity did not come overnight in my marriage and, from my conversations with monks, it does not come merely by entering a monastery. Benedict, Bernard, Aelred, Merton, and Thich Nhat Hanh knew this. Chastity must have a countervalence, a payout, a reward, if our sexual, sensual selves are to be satisfied and not merely resigned to slow desiccation. Chastity deals in a certain kind of excitement, but one so mellow and appealing that licentiousness becomes overheated and greed futile, no longer promising pleasure, but assuring misery.

My marriage is a passionate, contentious, emotional enterprise, far from perfect. With all due respect to those of Italian heritage, we call ours an "Italian" marriage. We squabble and disagree dozens of times each day—and promptly forget what it was that we were fighting about. But like the confines and limitations of a cloistered monastic community, it is, to quote the Scripture, "sufficient unto the day." I need not look over the wall to see what pleasures and ease lie beyond—for if I look, I will surely find them. For the moment. And I could go off to skitter along the surface of life, never probing the pain and pleasure of true love, never really testing myself to see who lies within. It is only when I believe in chastity's liberating and life-enriching power that I can walk out into the world, unafraid of its siren calls.

I have learned this lesson well in my very imperfect marriage. I have learned that ~~only by conscious control of my thoughts, desires, fantasies, and attitudes will I ever hope to gain control over my life.~~ Why? Because they were "bad"? No, it is not that. Leaving moral judgments aside, ~~they made me unsettled, unfocused, cheapened.~~

The long shadow of monastic life—from my first contact with Merton's writing to that very day at Mepkin—promised its own cool shade if I would only step away for a moment from the heat of my absurd, insatiable cravings. It is not that I have become a less passionate man—that is my nature; it will never change. And it is not that the notion of monastic chastity somehow requires emotional blinders. Merton was saying that to me the first time I read *The Seven Storey Mountain* in high school, even when I was not yet ready to listen. My days at Spencer in mid-life allowed me to stop my dizzying, destructive course long enough to take a hard look at it, who I was, and what my future might be. These Mepkin days were providing an extended look at the beauties of monastic life and their possible infusion into my everyday life.

This delicate thread of chastity running through monastic life, which I once thought was little more than sexual suppression, is actually a much more sturdy fiber. It is woven into the warp and woof of life in human communities.

After all, is not chastity modesty? Modesty in conversation, when we need not dominate, but instead invite others to the true intimacy that the honest sharing of thoughts can allow. Modesty in thought and desires—regarding other people, yes, but also extending to the things of this world that we might hungrily seek, mistakenly believing they will bring us deep and lasting satisfaction. Modesty in our very demeanor, so that the innocence and guilelessness that marks these Mepkin monks might also be ours. Modesty in our expectations, both of others and ourselves.

Chastity does not exploit or manipulate other people for one's own pleasure or self-gratification. As I have dignity and uniqueness—as well as quirks and shortcomings that I wish others would only understand—so do the many people who will pass through my life. Are they pawns on my chessboard, or God's creatures and my partners in salvation? Chastity is acceptance, appreciation, wisdom in human relationships.

To be sure, there are other voices we hear, besides chastity's quiet beckoning.

"Adultery on television may be epidemic, but the theme's treatment does not reflect conservatism or a backward-looking approach. Instead, these shows mirror a newly realistic and deeply pessimistic attitude toward marriage in the contemporary world."[6] This is the *New York Times* commenting on television fare, our daily window onto what is purported to be human existence in the "contemporary world." It is not hard to see that if we agree to accept this "newly realistic" approach, we will have lost all concept of what reality is. True reality is God-centered, God-involved, authentic, and good. Chastity brings us back to reality, back to what is best within us, what ultimately liberates and fulfills us.

For me, the necessary construct for chastity in my life is marriage. I adhere, in a slightly altered way, to the adage that if monks were so good they would not need a monastery. We all need some framework in which to place our lives; otherwise the pull and promise of an unthinking, random life will eventually be too much to resist. Others live a full single life; some devote their energies not to the raising of sons or partnership with a spouse, as I do, but to a work that requires extraordinary attention, time, and devotion. Whatever our state or walk of life, all of us need chastity and its attendant manifestation, modesty, if we are not to deteriorate into selfish, lonely boors.

Whatever we choose or life chooses for us, it is important to maintain the monastic perspective, the perspective of all true spirits and seekers: to be in the world, not of it. This requires being absolutely in tune with our nature, needs, and surroundings, while at the same time allowing none of them to dictate our actions. Again, chastity speaks to us and says that if we cherish ourselves and others, in all our interactions, from a mere look to the most intimate physical contact, we never have to fear. We are free to sense, feel, and act because our inner compass will keep us on course.

In the end, the true reward of chastity is confidence—and with it, a new kind of spiritual and practical energy. We can walk in the world with

---

[6]"Straying into Temptation in Prime Time," Caryn James, *New York Times*, 10 August 1997, section 2, 1.

confidence in our ability to be an authentic human being because chastity gives us command of our thoughts, words, and actions. We are not constantly on the edge of panic, afraid the wild beast within will unpredictably run amok. And this, in turn, releases new energy. Our inner resources are not expended in attempts to control, but released to experience truly—to know, to love, to understand.

As Psalm 51 asks: "Create in me a pure heart, O God." This transparency opens the very channels of grace flowing into our lives so that we see God all about us. Chastity constantly clears our palate; each flavor and taste in life is discrete, subtle, not jaded. We are woefully human; we may never be completely chaste. But when—to adapt Merton's words—it is our desire to be chaste, a new way of being is ours.

Early on Sunday morning I walked alone back to the gatekeeper's cottage from vigils. There, as I turned off the road that leads from the cloister and onto the path leading to the main road, I could see the street light that illuminates Mepkin's entrance. I had traversed this asphalt many times during these visits. Walking along ever so slowly, it was as if in the shadows along this road there were countless stations of the cross, stupas, shrines, and vantage points, at each of which I paused to reflect on one of the jewels in monasticism's crown.

And was not chastity a facet of each of them?

Discernment required a clarity of mind unattainable if that mind was clogged with schemes to exploit sensually or manipulate emotionally. How could we practice detachment if we were so attached to our own uncontrolled and ephemeral physical needs? Mysticism seeks a union with God; it is chastity, innocence, which allows such a union. It is unchastity that tries to convince us body and soul can be conveniently separated, each with its own master or mistress. Faith aches for a pure heart in which to flourish. And what of stability? Was chastity not the very essence of stability, entering into each moment with intensity and purity? Surely *conversatio* was the heart of chastity, a continuing awareness of ourselves and a conscientious response to the changing worlds about us.

Finally, bathed in the garish glow from the street light, I looked back toward the darkness of the monastery enclave. There was only darkness and mystery beyond what my two poor eyes could behold from where I stood. But only by leaving supposed safety and the light of the world could those hidden, holy places be entered. And here, in the eighth of my monthly visits, I knew what lay beyond was not darkness after all. It was my soul. It was Mepkin, a place where the symmetry of life beckoned to all who would leave the world for a while so that they might learn and know.

I could not stay, but I could take that with me.

Tracy, the boys, and I went into the refectory kitchen after mass that morning and began to prepare lunch. We had brought along twenty pounds of shrimp, as well as the more exotic vegetables and ingredients—bok choy, black bean sauce, spicy garlic paste, and ginger—that good Szechuan stirfry demands. The boys chopped and peeled, carrying on easy conversations with Brother Edward, our kitchen companion, as well as the various monks and the abbot who wandered through. It was a perfectly normal large family affair, a family at once as exotic as some of our food components, yet ordinary and relaxed. So many exemplary role models of chaste living, yet not a word was spoken about such things. The temperature of peanut oil and the size of the bricks of ice cream that would cap off the meal were more important just now.

The luncheon reading from Charles R. Morris's excellent book *American Catholic* happened to be from the chapter, "The Struggle with Sexuality." Ah yes, the book explained, the Church and its professed celibate leaders, hierarchy and foot soldiers—terrified of this force within them that could not always be handled by Socratic dialogue or even scores of holy hours—have indeed tussled with the force primeval, often applying more heat than light.

The book quoted St. Basil, as he spoke of possible monastic temptation. "Even when rigorous self-restraint is exercised, the glowing complexion of youth can be a source of desire to those around them. If, therefore, anyone is youthful and physically beautiful, let him keep his attractiveness hidden until his appearance reaches a suitable state."[7] The gentle laugh that rippled through the refectory indicated a certain ease once sadly lacking in

---

[7]Quoted in Charles R. Morris, *American Catholic: The Saints and Sinners Who Built America's Most Powerful Church* (New York: Times Books, 1997), 357.

the church. There was Brother Joseph, the reader, more than fifty years a Trappist, carefully enunciating each word, not a convenient mumble or elision to mask the spicy parts, a sly but guileless smile on his face.

What Brother Joseph's look said was that there was no longer a need in monastic life to hide or distort beauty so that it becomes unattractive. Nor was "rigorous self restraint" the answer. A clutched hand tires and eventually drops whatever it is holding. A gentle touch and an easy smile are the monk's hallmarks today.

When we got home from our Mepkin weekend on Sunday night, I walked into my bedroom and looked up to the picture near the mantel. A bride and groom blissfully gazed into each other's eyes, young, hopeful, sure of each other. But on closer examination, the discerning eye notices that the man badly needed a haircut. His hair was not merely stylishly long; it was downright shaggy. Up to the very day that picture had been taken I had been ambivalent, even stubbornly resisting a haircut for one of life's greatest moments. I was resisting a marriage vow that would demand that I look squarely at chastity's sacrifices—which seemed so great—and open myself to its possibilities, then quite unknown.

"What are you looking at, dad?"

It was Noah. I must have been standing there dumbly, staring at the wall.

"Somebody I used to know," I answered.

The next morning I got up long before sunrise. Inordinately early rising is another of the hangovers from monastic visits, where the day begins so early. I went downstairs at 5:00 o'clock, read my breviary, walked the dog, got the paper. It was about 7:00 when I heard Tracy's footfall in our bedroom. As I crept quietly up the stairs so as not to wake the boys, I felt the strangest sensation. It was a tingle, as if I'd touched a live wire with a mild electrical charge. I opened the bedroom door. Tracy looked puzzlingly at me. I was excited simply to see her. Never in my wanton days had I ever felt this way.

Prayer

Mutual Desire

Oh, God, come to my assistance. O, Lord, make haste to help me . . .
. . . Come, ring out our joy to the Lord;
hail the rock who saves us.
Let us come before him, giving thanks,
with songs let us hail the Lord.

Like undaunted sailors, singing familiar sea chanteys, they stood ready to embark in their trusty but fragile boat on still another leg of a journey to explore uncharted waters, the ocean at the outer edges of human con-sciousness. Are our simple tools, so basic, so ancient, really all we need? What will we find? Will we make it, eventually, to our goal on the other side? At a minimum, will we find a safe place when night is falling? Is this what we should be giving our lives to? Is the Living God to whom we call truly with us on our voyage? A rock who saves?

Each member of the crew may have had different questions, but all needed to mouth these familiar words of the psalmist in unison, both to remind themselves and to encourage their more faint-hearted mates.

The two dozen men gathered on a river's edge in South Carolina had risen long before dawn, as their forebears have done for centuries, as their Cistercian comrades around the world would likewise do this very day. As for physical distance, they will not travel far at all. And, if the truth be told, they are men who might not immediately appear to be capable of such an arduous voyage. They are largely past what the world considers their prime. For the most part they are not extraordinary, neither in mind nor body. There is William, attached to thin plastic tubes providing oxy-gen for a heart growing weaker each day. Dale, who wonders if he should be aboard at all. Callistus, Nicholas, and Peter, men well into their mid-dle years, yet here among the youngest and most fit. Seasoned veterans like Robert and Feliciano, whose eyes are closed and to whose lips the words come from memory. Aelred, standing ready with his stringed in-strument to enhance their chanted words. Their good and able captain, Francis, his eyes pinched almost to closing from constant vigilance during the night watch.

What they will eat this day or what work they will do is not as important as what they are doing right now—offering a prayer to their God to sustain them, inform them, inspire them, guide them. The very basis of this life, as their great leaders Benedict and Bernard said so many centuries before to men equally desirous and brave, timorous and limited, is prayer. Those monks of sixth-century Italy and twelfth-century France had fields to clear, walls to build, seeds to plant, personalities to juggle—all pressing needs; but without this connection to God, no work of their hands or heart would really matter in the end. For prayer was their lifeblood, the continually refreshing stream of God's own graces. Without it, they knew they would perish.

In the world in which this order of men first flourished—and, in turn, indelibly imprinted—prayer was a natural part of the day. The tolling of a village or monastery bell proclaimed that work should begin or end, that heads should bow and knees bend to acknowledge the greatness of God and the utter need for his presence in their humble lives. That routine is no more in our modern cities, with our climate-controlled existence; and we are the poorer for it, disoriented for the lack of such reminders. But here at this outpost of the twelfth century at the dawn of the twenty-first—with automobiles in the sheds, electricity coursing through buildings, and fabrics upon their bodies woven from fibers of chemical compounds, not of animals or plants—prayer remains the staple, little altered over the centuries.

Surely the men have changed, at least outwardly. The consciousness they explore, the culture in which they are set, are vastly different. Even so, prayer and only prayer still holds out the true conversion of heart which they seek. Prayer expresses the longing that brought them here in the first place, in fact elevates it. Prayer promises communion with the source of love they hope to embody, the transformation they desire. Theirs is an impractical, dangerous mission, pursued against the prevailing winds of rational thought and public opinion. But like the centuries of equally intrepid, equally impractical monastic explorers gone before them, they have no choice but to seek that place where the earth ends and another reality begins.

A variety of prayer weaves through the monastic day. There are corporate prayers like the psalms and the Eucharist, and *lectio divina,* where private reading of the Bible and other venerable texts is but a pathway to deep prayer. Meditation—from prostrate adoration of the Blessed Sacrament to lotus-position concentration on a mantra—is also practiced. In all, the monk may spend more time formally praying than working, some five-and-a-half hours. But there is more to prayer than duration and format. Monks, like all serious spiritual seekers, aspire to go beyond such temporal restrictions: what they desire is a quantum leap into God's own consciousness and the deep realization of their own mature self-awareness as well. This is the promise held out for those who "pray always," for this is as close a total communion with God as humans can achieve. For monks, it is a foretaste of heaven, a Christian utopia.

In the sleeping world of February—when the last of winter camellias lay limp and immolated on the bush and the customary lushness of Mepkin was mottled with burnt fields and stands of denuded trees—it was time to think about prayer. For on this visit Mepkin resembled not the warm and verdant place of the summer when I had first come here, but the dark night of the soul that John of the Cross so eloquently described— and through which many, save a rare few, must pass. The early morning was damp and cold, no birds yet had awakened to greet the dawn, no light was promised by the black sky. There was time between vigils and mass, darkness and light, to set out upon my own poorly charted waters.

But at the end of my initial period of rumination that morning, I found that a massive bollard of bewilderment held me firmly moored. I spun in place, creaking at pierside. The wind was still; nothing filled my becalmed sails. I was afraid to launch out so ill-prepared onto such treacherously unpredictable waters.

Prayer—and this I could sputter with utmost surety—is misunderstood practically everywhere, in our world, in most of our lives, even at times within monasticism. How should I pray? What should I say? Where? When? For what? Haven't we heard this from others we know? Cries rising, hoping somehow, in some way, to touch the mystery that is God? Are these not the haunting echoes that reverberate in our own souls? For many of us think—or have been led to believe—that some alchemic combination, some closely held secret, must be discovered if we are to achieve the communion with God for which the soul hungers. Precise, Pharisaic ritual is required. Or is it mindless submission?

And as for "praying always"—how can this be possible? It would require all of us to retire to a monastery—incidentally a monastery where someone else did all the work, so that we might be able to fulfill such a lofty mandate. What of spouses, children, parents, jobs—even an occasional game of golf, a trip to the mall, or a vacation at the beach?

In the dull light of a cloudy morning, more murky than the usual mists of the Carolina winter, a man suddenly stood before me. If there was a modern prototype, he was it: driven, multitalented, complicated, boyish, moody, generous, selfish. Plenty of good intentions, skimpy on follow-through. Except for the great difference between the abundance of his abilities and my own less-generous allotment, I could identify well with him. Never enough time. So many demands. Torn in so many directions. Trying to hold on to a vision. Struggling to conquer hubris and fatigue.

The hem of his fine, cream-colored and brocaded vestment, cut on a religious and ancient bias, fell not quite low enough to hide bare, pink ankles peeking out from black street shoes. It was somehow incongruous that his feet—if not of clay, certainly of mortal flesh—should be so stunningly apparent beneath such imposing liturgical regalia. Abbot Francis Kline, his concentration so fixed upon the host he held aloft over the stone altar, intoned the venerable words of consecration. "This is my body given for you. . . . Take this and drink. . . ."

In the unpredictable acoustics of an abbey church, which bend and exchange sounds and silence at whim, still other words were in my ears. "Prayer? Oh, it frustrates us all. We do so much of it, you'd think we'd be so much more holy than we are." They were Brother Stephen's words, spoken the day before as he stood beside his trusty, rusted bike, its handlebar basket brimming with sheets and towels for the new guests who would soon arrive. Our brief conversation ricocheted from the 900th anniversary of the founding of Cîteaux this spring to the Mepkin building fund, the heavy rains that had set back construction, prayer, the travels of the peripatetic and much in demand Abbot Kline, and back to prayer again.

"Prayer asks for constant purification, surrender to the will of God. It's really the toughest part of being a monk, facing yourself in prayer all the time. Yuck! After forty-five years here and hours upon hours of prayer every day, you'd think I would have gotten it. Really!" And then, after the abbot's frenetic life was dolloped into our conversation, "Oh, prayer is absolutely essential to his life," Brother Stephen said, "because, after all, without it . . ." He paused, his eyebrows reaching for a non-existent hairline, his eyes sparkling with the merriment of a man at once detached from things of the world, yet in tune with things of the spirit. ". . . he'd go mad."

Without it, he'd go mad. Is that not exactly the state in which we often find ourselves? Mad. Not angry; crazy. Crazy in our disconnectedness, in our lack of purpose and meaning, in our need for focus and balance in our everyday activities, behind which—if we are instead to believe Benedict, Bernard, Rahner, and a long line of wisdom teachers—God awaits us. Bricks seeking mortar to hold us together. We are wayfarers in a new age of reason and information which has equally emerged as an age of doubt, roiling with absurdity. But it seems also an age in which the spiritual yearning to return to our origins and tap our native goodness resounds in boardroom and bedroom, on city streets and country roads. Perhaps keeping madness at bay was as sobering a point of departure for a consideration of prayer as this pilgrim might ask for on such a shrouded morning.

When Abbot Kline deals with prayer in *Lovers of the Place: Monasticism Loose in the Church,* he does so in his usual quirky, off-center way. His prayer offers not the consolation of a Hallmark card or a Helen Steiner Rice couplet. Angels are not hovering, wings fluttering, cheeks as pink as his exposed ankles. Prayer, he cautions, "resists all attempts at control and prediction of what God may want of us." He extols the virtues of monastic prayer, yet admonishes (as did Benedict) not to confuse length with depth, pointing out that "*lectio divina* never allows us to bathe in our own unrelated sweet thoughts, but always brings us back to God's prophetic word and his saving will in our lives."[1] Esther de Waal, looking at Cistercian life, approaches prayer on a slightly different tack. The Word of God, she writes, ". . . must be heard in the silence of the heart, the place in which it can be welcomed and given space so that it might become creative."[2]

An unpredictable, creative whirlwind—so this is prayer as practiced by Trappist monks whom the world might regard as merrily humming their way through a highly structured, predictable life. It was only a ripple of

[1]Kline, *Lovers of the Place,* 38.
[2]Esther de Waal, *The Way of Simplicity: The Cistercian Tradition* (Traditions of Christian Spirituality Series), (Maryknoll, N.Y.: Orbis Books, 1998), 51.

wind in my own sails, but it was enough finally to free me from the shore against which I had been held fast.

As we read the spiritual classics on prayer, the temptation—and I use the word advisedly—is to try to transmute those experiences literally into our own. Somewhat embarrassingly, I confess to swooning over the lives of the great ones, from Antony to Charles de Foucauld, Hildegard to Simone Weil. But it is puppy love; nothing came of it. When I sought out Thomas Merton at Gethsemani as a high school senior, he was (alas, and fortunately) not available to perpetuate my fantasy of what a life of prayer was all about. But years later he eventually spoke to me, though I was not sitting in that tiny classroom deep within Gethsemani's recesses. Instead, it was by means of an audiotape of one of his now-famous novice conferences. He spoke of St. Teresa of Avila, whose prayer was addressed to, as Merton said, "this little person inside her." The feeling at Gethsemani in those days, he said, was that if monks were not constantly talking to Jesus or otherwise praying, they were somehow lacking. He poked no fun at Teresa. "But, this was a woman of the sixteenth century; you can see what she's getting at."

The men he was addressing were of our century; Merton was advising them not to let piety masquerade as prayerfulness. What Teresa was "getting at" was not necessarily what they were seeking. To pray always was not so much a string of pious words, but—to again summon the wisdom of my spiritual and as yet unmet companion in Britain, Esther de Waal—"Our prayer reflects the way in which we respond to life itself, and so our prayer can only be as good as the way we live."[3] For Merton, prayer was not separated from living. Prayer informed and infused actions; actions, in turn, brought back the need to pray.

It becomes easier to see what "pray always" means when we realize that though we—and our monk friends—take time out specifically to pray, read, or meditate, there needs to be a continuity between those few moments and the many other hours of our day. What prayer asks, as Abbot Francis points out, is that we acknowledge continually the presence of God

[3]Esther de Waal, *Seeking God: The Way of St. Benedict* (Collegeville, Minn.: Liturgical Press, 1984), 153.

and not become lost in our own illusions. We cannot believe that our love has limits—because the One we address in prayer is Limitless Love, offering to us the possibility of being conduits for that love if we only open the channel. Which, again, is found in prayer.

Looking back upon monks I have known over the years, coupled with my reading of Cistercians of both past days and our own, I have learned that to pray always does not imply some sort of glassy-eyed indifference to the world and the people around us, a constant muttering of prayer or mantra. Prayer is at once far more subtle and dynamic than that. In a conversation with Brother Joseph later that morning as the grinder and mill concocted precisely apportioned chicken feed for the Mepkin layers, we talked about prayerful, holy monks he had known in his half-century of Trappist life. They were the simplest, most common of men, never sanctimonious, often smiling. "You just wanted to be around them," he said; "they had that something."

Prayer promises great rewards. It is precarious. It is emotion-filled; it is emotionless. As the Australian Trappist Michael Casey told the Mepkin monks on his visit to the monastery, a crucial word in mystical literature of monasticism is "sometimes." To seek a blissful state is not the object of monastic prayer, though—sometimes—this may occur. Rather, Father Casey pointed out, the foundational teaching in the *Rule of St. Benedict* is that "Prayer should be short and pure, unless perhaps it is prolonged under the inspiration of grace."[4]

Monks learn through years of experience that the prayer with which they entered the monastery is not the prayer that they will say as they grow in the life. It is not unlike marriage. It is not that you stop loving your spouse simply because you do not do the things you did when you were courting. The love can remain fresh and exciting, but it will not long have the flavor of two dreamy-eyed adolescents intoxicated when they are together and bereft when they are apart. Romantic love is not committed love. A deeper union, a total union, will never result when so much of it is lived on the surface. The ardent, well-intentioned young man or woman will not

---

[4] *The Rule of St. Benedict*, ed. Thomas Fry (Collegeville, Minn.: Liturgical Press, 1981), ch. 20.

survive monastic life if his or her prayer life is not, in some ways, bled of sensory affirmation.

We must be careful here. Sitting in the abbey church at Mepkin brings solace to my soul. I feel Jesus Christ within me when I receive the Eucharist. Seeing my wife as I come up the stairs or my boys walking through a Grand Canyon arch surfaces emotions that are embarrassingly powerful. In *lectio divina*, I read the word of God and I feel an amazing presence, demanding I take stock, constantly urging me on. But what wise spiritual teachers say is that in order to touch God we must transcend our desire for sacred supplication. Oddly enough, only in this way can we ever hope to receive it.

The classic reflection on prayer—and, through prayer, the ascent to God—was written by John of the Cross, a contemporary of Teresa whose efforts to reform the Carmelites were met with such rage that he was actually kidnapped by members of his order and harshly imprisoned. It was John of the Cross who gave us the "dark night of the soul," that exquisitely apt term for describing the virtual hell that spiritual seekers may withstand.

It took me several readings of *Dark Night of the Soul*, spaced over many years and seasons of this man's life, to begin to understand what John of the Cross was saying. For me, it comes to this: if we rely on sensual, human satisfactions in our prayer life, we are limited to the yin and yang of our emotional responses to God's presence in our lives. We will continue to view him through the glass darkly, smudged by our passions, not face to face.

This might sound so much fancy spiritual talk, but reduced to stark reality it happens to be true. What is more, casting an eye across other religious traditions it is resoundingly affirmed in their approaches to the divine. Emptying, purification, abandonment are common roads. What we are talking about is this: when all else is stripped away, there we stand, with nothing more or less than our faith in God. We have nothing to bargain with or for. This is the purest, most vulnerable way of uttering "I love you." It is the greatest and most perfect prayer.

Such pure love in prayer has its own rewards. John of the Cross says our love will be returned, a hundredfold, a thousandfold. Not necessarily in some outpouring of bliss—although this may happen—but in a prayer life that is at once peaceful, deep, yet often without the consciousness that one is praying at all. This, then, is being able to "pray always," for progress on the ascent to God is neither measured by time spent in a church (although these are good places to be and may seem to offer the closest point of contact), nor by material rewards (the most inaccurate tool of measurement), nor even by a general sense of well-being (remember Abbot Francis's warning against becoming lost in "our own unrelated sweet thoughts").

Our desire to touch God will be met by God's desire to touch us. In ways we will not comprehend, with a ferocity and a gentleness beyond imagining, it is in the confluence of these two great desires that we are invited to inhabit. This is prayer's uncharted terrain.

My own dark night of the soul came at a strange time in my life, a life that began with an attitude toward prayer mistaken both quantitatively and certainly qualitatively. I was raised in a Catholic Church of precise rituals and predetermined spiritual rewards for specific oblations. The object of prayer was to do it right, a sort of orthopraxy; to hope for a relationship with God was considered absolutely Protestant, and thus aberrant. The Second Vatican Council came and went; although I knew something seismic had happened, I didn't know how to interpret the temblors rumbling through the church and world. I read the spiritual masters eagerly, wanting so badly to tuck myself inside the pages of those books and live the experiences they so eloquently wrote about.

Forces were building up within me that I certainly felt, but I had no idea where they had originated and in what they would result. I would only later see that what was welling up in me was a desire to know God in a more intimate way—or more accurately, at this stage of the game, to know him at all.

The dark night came upon me not, as might be expected, in the depths of my sinfulness as a newly reminted single man in the sybaritic New York of the 1970s and 1980s, but, strangely, in the shadow of a Trappist monastery, the elegant St. Joseph's Abbey at Spencer. There, I turned my back on the world, rose before dawn and lived a life parallel to monks. I had come to see the face of God.

By coincidence, near the time of this visit to Mepkin I had made a trip back to Spencer. As I drove the familiar back roads, knelt in the magnificent abbey church, even marked individual trees that had been my daily sentinels, I could once again feel the searing pain of that year. I had disciplined both mind and body, prayed so earnestly, fasted, took on *lectio divina* with a steely fortitude. I had called out to God from the depths of my soul, with an agony and hunger I'd never before experienced in my life.

But looking back I realized my prayer of those days—while ardent and well-intentioned—was sadly and tragically flawed. I had the end result of that prayer firmly in mind: becoming a Trappist monk. It was only much later that I could see I had been little different from a person praying for business success or acceptance into the right school. I knew what I wanted; I was only praying to God to supply the means to my end. I wanted a life totally committed to God; it seemed so sacrificial and—honestly?—dramatic. A mere marriage seemed an undertaking of considerably less moment.

I began that hermit year, full-fleshed, mouthing abandonment to God, having no idea what that meant. At year's end, I was but a cinder. I experienced the spiritual dissipation of acedia so profound I could barely breathe. I looked at everything seeking meaning, and comprehended nothing. At times I did think I was going mad in the depths of my dark night as options and choices, possibilities and escapes pounded in my brain. Slowly—very slowly—I began to see that if I wanted real control over my life, I needed to abandon it to God—in the prayers of my lips and heart, and in my actions as well. I may not practice it at all well in my life today, but at least I know it to be true. When I seek total control of my life, relying only on my abilities and insights, I know I will be not only frustrated, for it never will work out the way I imagine it should, but sad, because I have lost touch with the God who desires me without all my grand plans. Indeed, only through finally abandoning my insistence on my own plans was I able to perceive that God had plans of his own for me.

The harrowing experience of my dark night irrevocably changed me and my attitude toward prayer.

What I was forced to encounter in my imperfect attempt at prayer was not a God enthroned upon the ark of the covenant, not a God in a temple or even a tabernacle, but a *living* God who demanded a constant conversation, my continuing conversion. I had no history of good acts to rest upon, no good intentions to offer as promissory notes. It was here, now. William of St. Thierry, a twelfth-century Benedictine abbot who eventually became a Cistercian, wrote that "When in your life of faith you are confronted with the deeper mysteries it is natural to become a little frightened."[5] I learned what he meant.

If anything, William was pleasantly understated. Responding in prayer to the mystery that is God is more than a little frightening. When that moment of truth occurs, when we let loose of (or are wrenched from) the allegedly secure hold we have on whatever religious belief we might hold the result is a free fall into God's own consciousness. The spiritual g-forces drain the blood from our faces, the warmth from our hearts, the rationality from our minds, and the cheap grace from our souls. But the result is a taste of that imageless certitude that God is with us as we venture into the hidden parts, working in our lives even when we cannot feel his presence.

Does this leave a person happier, more content with life? Irrevocably changed? Perhaps it does in some ways, but our basic nature remains. I still want to control my destiny. I want adventure in small, predictable, prepackaged forays. I act before I think or pray. In fact, it is often hard to pray at all. I want easy answers that won't ask more of me than I think I can give.

What I realize is this:

I pray not because I expect to be catapulted to great spiritual heights, but because I simply need God to make it through each day.

I start my day with prayer because I know the day will slip away in a mad chase after the ephemeral and quickly spin out of control unless I at least attempt to state that I believe in loving listening.

I pray throughout the day—short prayers, for the most part, little more

---

[5]Quoted in *The Liturgy of the Hours*, vol. III, 1764.

than a flicker of thought. They come when I am blessed and when I am frustrated, when I feel the need for God's presence and when I sense that he is far away—because they are the only way that I can ever hope to balance sacred yearning and secular necessities in my life. With the Israelites, as they quarreled with Moses, I need to call out: "Is God in our midst or not?"[6] Prayer is the only way I can live mindfully, ready to encounter the inward grace present all around me, the unfolding "mysticism of everyday life."

After years of searching and study, and now in these grace-filled months at Mepkin, I found myself reduced to three simple words that described prayer for me: faith, desire, and simplicity. In a sentence: I struggle for the *faith* in God that his *desire* for me far surpasses my abiding *desire* for him, and that *simplicity* marks the surest path to him. I need not go to this monastery, enter a church, open the Bible—although I have found these things most helpful. If I can come to God each day, in each action, with desire and that deep trust which is faith, I need not worry whether God will hear my prayer—or, indeed, whether I am praying at all. For I will be. If those are my intentions, I will be praying always, whether I realize it or not.

Is not prayer talking both to God and, as Rahner advises, speaking to ourselves? Is prayer limited to formal invocations and the reading of the Bible or inspirational books? Or is prayer so fluid that we do not even realize when we are praying or not? Prayer, like chastity, is an attitude, a frame of mind, a disposition; unheroic for the most part, ordinary. As Esther de Waal says, prayer is an approach to life. Prayer is a thousand little thoughts wafted heavenward—or just one directed toward that impatient woman in Office Depot; simple, uncertain, faith-infused desires to make sense of the world, to ease another person's path, to bring love into situations where it is welcome and where it is shunned.

Prayer at once embraces our world and yet constantly measures and weighs it. In prayer we are fully people of our time, and timeless people of God's eternal creation. In prayer we identify fully with the example of the monks, that God is found both in church and the kitchen, equally in the slightest and grandest of actions.

[6]Exodus, 17:7.

If my experience—both in prayer and in love—is any indication, we must resist the temptation to quantify, define, or restrict prayer from blossoming where it will and how it chooses. I will never forget my stupidity and slowness in realizing that something beautifully different was coming into being between Tracy and myself. I could not believe the feelings of ease and comfort, the way we could laugh together, communicate without speaking, enjoy just being in each other's company. And what did I do? I foolishly kept taking the pulse of this flourishing relationship. "How are we doing now? Now? And how about now?" A seed was germinating, and I kept on yanking on the seedling to check its progress. I was frightened by both the beauty and the commitment that such a relationship entailed. Like a child who fears something wonderful could be whisked away at any moment, I wanted—moment to moment—to inventory my storehouse of treasures.

For prayer life, as real life, is lumpy, irregular, constantly bumping into itself. We make the same mistakes over and over again; change occurs so gradually that we cannot perceive it. We expect our prayer life to be otherwise; we envisage it as some sort of constantly ascending path, leading us eventually to "it," where we can rest and be satisfied. As our prayer life stirs alive or begins to flourish, our inclination may be to close our hand tightly so that this skittish bird won't fly away. All we will do is suffocate and crush our desire to know God and clamp down on the flow of graces, unpredictable though they may be.

Both a prayer life and a committed life are rooted in that emptiness deep within us, hoping to be filled. To love and be loved; surely this is the very foundation of monastic prayer, what sustains these intrepid voyagers day in and day out on their journey. They express their love in prayer, and in return God loves them. How, we might ask? How are they rewarded for their prayer? After all, the world doesn't change, money does not automatically come, new vocations are not at hand. And, as Brother Stephen laments, holiness remains elusive.

But prayer itself is its own reward. Monks discover this; those of us outside the walls are equally open to this reality. It is only through prayer that we all can experience God's presence in everyday life. It is only through prayer that we can fully face our inner conflicts, and be opened to the possibilities within us. Even when it is dry and seemingly useless, there is a presence in prayer that we cannot find anywhere else in our lives. Here is where our desire to be one with God—requited or not, depending on the time—is made manifest. Here is the distillation of all it is to be at once human and divine.

Prayer in itself is perhaps the most healthy act—physically and psychologically—that we can perform. What the ancients knew instinctively, modern science now confirms: people who pray and are prayed for live better lives. New institutes exploring the mind-body connection confirm that a regular prayer life is beneficial not only to one's inner peace but to the health of the body, the resistance to disease, the easing of pain. In monastic literature, there are stories of holy monks whose prayerfulness could actually be felt through the wall of the cell next to them. Prayer, though we know not how, is transmittable.

Prayer provides the frequent examination of conscience we need to lead sensible lives. St. Ignatius found in prayer that some thoughts made him happy and others left him sad. Is not this kind of discernment exactly the kind of self-correcting help we all need? Do we not need to see the "fruits of the spirit" clearly displayed so that we can judge which of our actions and dispositions lead to God, and which lead away from him? Do we not need the graceful energy that prayer produces?

I like the appraisal of St. John Vianney, the simple, unsophisticated, and absolutely brilliant parish priest known as the Curé d'Ars:

> Prayer is nothing else than union with God. When one has a heart that is pure and united with God, he is given a kind of serenity and sweetness that makes him ecstatic, a light that surrounds him with marvelous brightness. In this intimate union, God and the soul are fused together like two bits of wax that no one can ever pull apart. This union of God with a tiny creature is a lovely thing. It is a happiness beyond understanding.[7]

[7]Quoted in *The Liturgy of the Hours*, vol. IV, 1269.

Prayer is practical in another way, as monks discover—and so can we. Without prayer, we will find we have little or nothing to offer to the world. We all need time to reflect and refresh ourselves, to gain some perspective on life. Without prayer, we are mariners trimming our sails to the prevailing wind, constantly tacking and jibing but never consulting our compass to see where we actually want to go. What help can we provide others on their journey if we have no idea where we are—and give no thought to where we are going?

Earlier in the year I had given a talk on prayer at St. Raphael's parish in Raleigh, North Carolina, and asked the participants about their prayer lives. I was amazed with the diversity and the profundity of what I heard. One woman prayed in her car on the way to work, out loud so she could hear what she was saying. Another said the rosary, not with the usual mysteries, but with real life experiences: not the crucifixion, but someone with cancer. One man sought out churches wherever he went on his travels to sit before the Blessed Sacrament. "I just like to have Jesus looking at me," he said; "it brings me great peace in an often harried life." Another man read a scripture passage in the morning, and reflected upon it in the circumstances of the day, trying to apply it to what happened. Then, at night, he assessed how successful he had been. And a nurse who worked in pediatric intensive care confronted hour-by-hour problems—shortage of beds or staff, serious cases—by assembling the staff for a quick prayer; it set and reset the tone for the rest of the shift.

One woman told us that she prayed not to God but to her recently deceased husband as an intercessor in heaven. ("I can talk to him easier than to God.") Another returned in her mind to a holy place she had visited to relive that transcendent feeling once more. A special-needs teacher told of asking her children about prayer. "It's when my soul smiles at God," a five-year-old spiritual director told her.

The power, the wisdom of these people! They meet the challenges of the day, cast light into the dark nights of their souls, all with their own combination of faith, desire, simplicity.

I thought back to my own home. One recent evening, a friend of

Noah's had stayed for dinner. I don't know how the topic of religious belief came up, but he said he had never been to church and had no religious training whatsoever. As we sat down at the table, I was wondering, out of courtesy, if we shouldn't dispense with our customary prayer before meals. We join hands around the table and usually take turns at a short prayer. It is the only time we pray as a family, seconds long though it may be. Lately, the boys had been reluctant to pray, in fact sometimes doing their best with a furtive look or heavy sigh to say they wanted to proceed directly to the food.

We sat. There was a moment of hesitation. I felt Noah's hand slide into mine. His other hand reached toward his friend; and he began. It was a wonderful prayer about thanking God for our visitor, wishing blessings upon his family whom none of us knew, asking the hungry, poor, homeless, and friendless somehow be given what they needed.

I spoke very little during that meal.

The shadows of the towering live oaks were lengthening on the Mepkin roadways and paths as my rumination about prayer was coming to a close. There was one term I had somewhat sheepishly and self-consciously avoided, but I did not want the day to end without at least allowing it to bubble to the surface. The word was contemplation. In the spiritual lexicon on prayer it is a term at once mysterious and enticing. It is discussed in a good number of ancient texts on mysticism, and is contained as well within the title of my favorite modern book of spiritual reflections, Thomas Merton's *New Seeds of Contemplation.*

Contemplation—discernment's handmaiden and another of the pillars of monastic life—is often misunderstood as occurring only during intense periods of prayer or meditation, a mystical state reserved, naturally, for mystics. Yet contemplation is far more than that, and far more available to us. Contemplation is the continuous weaving together of our daily lives and God's creative spirit. Contemplation blends vision and action so that each is formed and influenced by the other. Either without the other is incomplete, whether for contemplation or for life itself. It becomes apparent that contemplation is not restricted to cloistered Trappist monasteries, but rather is, as Abbot Francis has written, but one of "the gifts of the monastic spiritual craft. [It] can be exercised within or without the walls of a monastery."[8]

It is contemplation that both John of the Cross and the anonymous author of the spiritual classic, *Cloud of Unknowing,* pronounced as the true purpose and summit of prayer. Yet for centuries this rudimentary concept was subsumed by a religious culture that put entirely too much stock in form, forgetting what the actual dynamic of prayer really hoped to yield. It was Merton who helped bring contemplation back into more popular use, but with a refreshing difference. Contemplation was not the exclusive province of only the cloistered or sainted ones in our midst, Merton said; it was accessible to all.

Contemplation, Merton discovered through his own struggle in prayer, is not so much a method as a gift to which one is naturally drawn. In contemplation, "The soul, aided by ordinary grace, works in the familiar, natural mode. . . . One makes use of all the resources . . . in order to focus a simple affective gaze on God."[9] Required was "a prayer of silence, simplicity, contemplative and meditative unity, a deep personal integration in an attentive, watchful listening of 'heart.' "

Contemplation forms the person, creates a life style and approach, that "habit of being" of which Flannery O'Connor wrote. Contemplation is a focus on God's presence. It is a stillness and receptivity that transcend our normal unsettledness and unceasing activity—both for monks and those of us who attempt to be monks in the world. In the words of the Apostle Paul, "We do not know how we are to pray but the Spirit himself pleads for us with impossible longings."

All these wonderful thoughts of prayer and contemplation were floating around in my mind when Brother Joseph headed me off on my way to compline and placed a sheet of paper into my hands. "Where is the holy monk in this picture?" he asked puckishly. It was a cartoon depicting a long line of monks entering church. Their terribly serious faces were inclined in obvious prayer, eyes were cast down. Except for one, who had put two fingers behind the head of the monk in front of him. The slanting light in

[8]Kline, *Lovers of the Place,* 48.
[9]Thomas Merton, *What Is Contemplation?* (Springfield, Ill.: Templegate, 1981), 25–26.

the cloister—about the same angle as that in which Brother Joseph and I now stood—cast a shadow of a rabbit's head onto the church wall. The mischievous monk had a huge smile on his face.

"Let me guess," my words trailed off.

The lights were not yet turned on in the church when I entered. A few monks were already there, sitting or standing in the shadow of choir stalls. I looked at their faces, cast in darkness. In the hollow crevices beneath their eyebrows, I could see that their eyes were closed. Contemplation? Who could know? They could have been thinking how bloody tired they were, or wondering whether the mating hoot owls would keep them awake as they had last night. Or about egg production, or what might be prepared for lunch the next day, or why a headache hadn't responded to the ibuprofen. Or perhaps there was a passage from Scripture that had inspired them that day, or some act by a fellow monk that had warmed them. Or perhaps they were lost in some personal reverie about family, a loved one, a friend, and feeling terribly lonely.

What the spiritual masters and the wise monks down through the ages tell us is that any and all of these are opportunities for contemplation, for communion with God. As Merton said, in desiring to please God, we have pleased him. In trying to reach him, we already have.

Outside, the bell for compline sounded. I looked around. The other monks were in place. They turned toward the altar to sing.

Now in the fading light of day, Maker of all, to you we pray, that in your ever watchful love you guard and guide us from above. Help and defend us through the night. Danger and terror put to flight. Never let evil have its way. Preserve us for another day.

With these lines, so familiar to them, still another monastic day was coming to an end. The Mepkin monks had come full circle, returning exactly to the place from which they had set off early that morning. Each day in the monastery they seek a glimpse of heavenly bliss, balanced, lovely. Each would have to judge for himself how he had fared on the high seas of an ancient rice plantation that day.

But the verses allow for no hand-wringing for chances missed, or miles untraveled; they only make the simple request that they be preserved for another day, in order to set out again. After singing the *Salve Regina*, they moved, single-file, toward the front of the church. There, each monk bent at the waist for Abbot Francis's blessing. Sleep was now at hand, rest to ready them for the morrow's ventures. The last footfall echoed and finally the church was quiet.

As I traveled north after vigils the next morning, my companion on audiotape was the actor Peter Coyote, reading the Book of Job. His gravelly voice, the tale of the Bible's most tested man, and my thoughts about prayer all hovered about me as I headed toward home and the other—and much larger—part of my life, the part not lived at a monastery. The story was so excruciating, so assaultingly unfair, I was tempted to turn it off. Enough reflection! I had to get on with my life.

There was the perfectly upstanding Job, the model of decency and patience, doggedly along his pilgrim's journey—and seemingly set upon by a God who apparently wants to break him. Finally a scream rises in Job's long-suffering throat: Look at me! I am a good man! How can you persist in this punishment? What more can you ask of me?

The windows were open to the cool air. A fog was rising from the damp Carolina soil; the earthy, fresh smell of morning, yet untouched and unaided by the sun, filled the car.

It is clear, Job. It is clear, Paul. Can't you see? God wants none of your supposed rectitude. None of your fine intentions, your grand plans. He knows you, all of you. And he wants you, all of you, the blemishes as well.

The ultimate essence of the universe wants the insignificant, magnificent speck that is each of us, unadorned. In prayer, that is what we offer to him.

Listen. Listen to your son in prayer. Listen to God's murmuring on the wind and on the street. Say little. Be still and know.

MARCH

Vocation . . .

. . . *Within Vocation Within Vocation* . . .

The psalms of Lauds left their lips to echo in the rafters high above, but a waystation on the ascent to God. Pleading words, confident words, downtrodden and triumphant words at once wafted heavenward and turned inward so that God's dominion might be acknowledged and humankind's need poured forth.

The mass following was both regal and simple, mystery and magnificence understated by the priests and brothers in flowing white choir robes, encircling the altar of their Lord. They recited the ancient prayers in

unison, reliving the ancient sacrifice prefigured by Melchizedek and per-
fected that Passover night in Jerusalem. Food for the journey shared, communal support tendered. The mass ended just after eight. It was time to
turn to the tasks at hand, the *labora* after the *ora*. The front door of the
church swung open.

There, separated from that holy space by no more than a three-inch
thickness of oak, lay another world. Sultry models proclaimed the cults of
such modern deities as Calvin Klein and Donna Karan. Finlandia vodka
promised agreeable friends and a good time for no more effort than the
trip to the next bar or liquor store. True paradise awaited in the Caribbean.
Worried about the price? With MasterCard, needs are addressed immediately and costs deferred. Estee Lauder will make you beautiful. Crest will
make your teeth sparkle.

I hesitated on the steps of St. Vincent Ferrar church on Lexington
Avenue and East 66th Street and took a deep breath. The incense in my
nostrils was supplanted by a rich mixture of coffee and bacon, bus exhaust,
and expensive perfume. Ah, New York. So many years before, arriving at
Columbia University and on the threshold of my New York writing days, I
pulled my car to a screeching, traffic-stopping halt on the middle span of
the George Washington bridge, stepped out, and maniacally screamed that
this city would know me before long. But, alas, if the people hurrying by
the church steps were any indication, those words had dissipated quicker
than a morning mist over the Hudson River. New York did not know me
at all. So much for youthful excess and mature reality.

My monastic sanctuary and template for life were hundreds of miles to
the south and, with Lands' End canvas bag in hand, wearing a reasonably
well-cut blue blazer, khaki trousers, and trench coat, I was but another
hopeful soul offering himself in this other city of dreams.

I had made these rounds many times before, to the offices of newspaper, magazine, and book publishers, television stations, and networks.
Merging into the stream of fast-moving humanity heading downtown on
Lexington, I thought of Paul the itinerant tent-maker of Christ's time,
traveling from town to town, offering the work of his hands for pay while
in pursuit of a larger vocation and another kind of reward. I thought of my

own father, also Paul, who presented his calloused hands and strong back for work—any work at any price—during the Depression, a time when "vocation" was not exactly the first word on most workingmen's lips. Along the way I saw an aging man, Everyman, a sweaty brow beneath a poorly fitting toupee, shirttail erupting from his belt as he wheeled a huge suitcase stuffed with his line of goods along the Lexington sidewalk. Mine in a canvas bag; Everyman's in a battered case—each of us presenting what we had to offer to the marketplace.

I faced a full schedule: a blur of conferences with various editors; breakfast, lunch, and dinner meetings. I don't get to New York that often, so I had crammed a daunting list into fourteen waking hours. But looking ahead, as I planned my schedule from Carolina, I wanted this day to be different from my other trips to New York. As I would be going about my workday, the Mepkin monks would be going about theirs, each of us in pursuit of our particular vocation. I wanted the spirit of the monastery to be with me, monastic wisdom to be my guide.

Throughout the day, monks continually pause to refocus on what they are doing and to discern whether it and they are pleasing to God. After these many months of exposure to monastic ways and *ora*, I, too, wanted to be monastically mindful of how I went about my *labora*. But I knew if I had any chance to do this, I had to take as much care in finding both time and a place to pause as I needed to take to arrive on time at the right place for my appointments. To address that need head on, I had a simple plan: I would find a church to visit between as many of my stops as possible.

I was able to begin the day with a leisurely, contemplative mass with the Dominican friars at St. Vincent's. Other church visits throughout the day varied from just a few moments to five minutes at the most. My periods of reflection on that busy day presented for my consideration a man composed of various parts of integrity and disingenuousness, clarity and confusion, total honesty and an honesty a shade or two (imperceptible to any but himself) this side of total. It was, not so remarkably, exactly who I am.

In midafternoon, as I peered into the cool darkness of St. Paul the Apostle (appropriately enough) on West 59th Street and Columbus Avenue, my own shirttail by now unfurled, my mind sailed back to Mepkin and the open book in the church foyer. Within it, after the names of the abbey's major contributors, was a quote from Thomas Merton's *New Seeds of Contemplation:*

> Let there always be quiet, dark churches in which [people] can find refuge . . . Houses of God filled with his silent presence. There, even when they do not know how to pray, at least they can be still and breathe easily.[1]

How well that captured my state of mind just then. I had sought refuge, but for the most part it had been difficult to pray. I had hurtled through the day, trying at each of these stops not to dwell on my failures or shortcomings, resisting the temptation to offer *quid pro quo* supplications, simply trying—perhaps just the problem—to be still and breathe easily in that silent presence. "I am here with you. Be with me now and when I walk back out onto the street." With such an elemental supplication, I was focusing as best I could on God, not on the meeting just past or the appointment just ahead. I had the sense that if I was in tune with God, the events of the day would—for better or worse—find their way to the best resolution, regardless of how they appeared to me moment to moment.

While we may treasure the reflectiveness that comes naturally in places like Mepkin, we may equally regard it as a luxury we can ill afford in the rest of our lives—especially our work lives. There is hardly a minute in our workday that is not already overcommitted, we plead. If anything, we may feel the need to jam in still more to 1) survive, 2) advance, or 3) simply do what we do better. Yet even our protests are evidence of another voice within us, the voice of our mindful selves. It has something different to say: Be still. Go slow. Look. Be. Somehow we sense that if we want to live a life at once more fully human and more nearly divine—an enlightened, spiritual life—we cannot simply consign our spiritual health to the few

[1]Thomas Merton, *New Seeds of Contemplation* (New York: New Directions, 1961), 82.

hours most of our lives ever give us at whatever holy places we may have discovered.

Although the world may tell us that success, as measured by the size of a paycheck, is all the reward we need in our chosen (or, at times, unchosen) vocation, our souls tell us something quite different. There must be more to our lives than work. Not one of us would willingly agree to be reduced to a soul the size of the job we have. But this says at least as much about our work as it says about us; we want, and lack, work that feeds the soul— or at least will not stunt its growth.

If monastic wisdom has anything at all to say to our modern working world, it is that our labors, humble or vaunted, are potentially an unending source of holiness, purification, and grace. Monk or mechanic, computer programmer, writer, forest ranger, stockbroker—all can be worthy, even sacred, vocations. "Vocation" is not a word that applies only to those in religious life; there is a God in heaven who looks down mercifully upon us, loves us and apportions to each tasks and opportunities in this life.

Yet, finding a vocation—and meaning within that vocation—does not always come easily or naturally. This is no different for monks than it is for the rest of us. It is often difficult to look beneath the blurry surface to see the inner meaning and worth of a vocation we have chosen, or that—a harder task—fate or necessity have chosen for us. Equally, we may not always be so pleased to see who we are as we go about our work; the very thought of looking at our spiritual selves in our working lives is a threatening one, and so we turn away. It may seem an impossible chore to lift up the work of our hands and minds to God. Me? In my line of work?

Monastic wisdom flies in the face of many popular notions about both the kind of work we do and how we perform it. As Benedict decreed, a pot in the kitchen was to be no less venerated than a chalice on the altar. For Benedict, all types of work held the potential of offering intimacy with God, as well as personal happiness—and therefore obliging our best effort. Work was not something at odds with or set aside from our spiritual selves, begrudgingly done simply to provide for bodily needs, regarded as some-how inferior to time spent in prayer or meditating upon the words or omniscience of God. Each of us has been given a unique part in the vast and ongoing co-creation and sanctification of this world; prayer alone, in the end, just isn't enough to accomplish that.

Indeed, monasticism would never claim that being a monk is one's true vocation. Rather, being a self-in-union-with-God is the true vocation. That, of course, might result in certain persons finding their home in a monastery. It is as fundamental as this: God summons us to *being*, not doing. It is in the discovery of our true selves, and the alignment of the self, whatever it might be, with God, that the deepest meaning of life on earth is found.

Crucial to the foundation of the monastic approach to work is the approach we take to that work. The upshot of this is that primary value is not placed on the results of our efforts. Rather, the monastic approach looks to that one aspect over which we ultimately always have control, whether living in a monastery or the world. This is our intention or attitude, or—in Merton's words—our desire. As St. Bernard concluded, "Our works do not pass away, as they seem to do; rather they are scattered like temporal seeds of eternity. The fool will be astonished when he sees a great harvest shooting up from a little seed—good or bad harvest according to the different quality of the sowing."[2]

Mine turned out to be a day with more disappointments than affirmations, more enervation than inspiration, more humiliation than acclamation; I had little idea of the quality of my sowing. But with each church visit I found myself—how can I say it? Refreshed? Grounded? Centered? Calmed? It was certainly not because of some gimlet-eyed focus on the specifics of what I was trying to accomplish. Rather, each visit provided a quiet, sometimes pretty generic reminder of who I was and how I needed to approach each encounter, subway ride, walk across town. I spoke with powerful editors in glassed-in offices and ordered coffee from a counter clerk in a deli. I saw opportunities for grace, some of which I missed, some of which I allowed. I was at turns kind and impatient, loving and stupid.

The day ended after 10:00 P.M. By now the Mepkin monks were long in their beds. At this hour open churches are not that easy to find in

---

[2]Bernard of Clairvaux, *Sermo de Conversione ad Clericos* 17; *Sancti Bernardi opera*, vol. 4, p. 90, ed. J. Leclercq, H. M. Rochais, C. H. Talbot. Rome: Cistercian, 1957–77.

Manhattan, so on a ride up Broadway I sat quietly in the back seat of my private chapel, a Yellow cab. I could not remember the prayers of compline; I could barely remember where I was heading just then. It had certainly been an imperfect day. Yet tired though I was, a certain calm presence was also with me. Was I finally able to pray? All I know is that a feeling of extraordinary gratefulness flowed over me as I recounted the hours of my workday liturgy. It had been a generous, strangely easy day. Successful? I couldn't yet say. Certainly it had been filled with a mixture of intensity and detachment, the decidedly secular and hopefully sacred. And, I realized— quite the opposite of what I had tried to do in my first nine months at Mepkin—I would be taking the world back to Mepkin, rather than attempting to bring Mepkin into the world. Seeds of contemplation planted by the banks of the great city by the Hudson would be transported back to a village of a few dozen men by the banks of the Cooper so that I could see what their sprouts might yield.

When next I traveled to the monastery, I had my car window opened to the early morning air. Just outside Wilmington, the banks of the Brunswick River radiated their damp, musky, fecund odor; this the birthplace of so much life, so many important links in the food chain. Then, wood burning from a campfire, bread being baked just outside Myrtle Beach, oil of leaking crankcases in a Georgetown junkyard. A fish just caught in the Wadboo River, honeysuckle opening up to breathe another day, undifferentiated sour and sweet smells. Every few miles, a fresh array presented itself. Mankind and host Earth, at work, at rest.

After this olfactory prelude, I was confronted upon arriving at Mepkin with the fact that my days here had not been similarly open to the totality or balance of monastic life. While I had been talking a good line about integrating work life and a prayer life, in fact I had neatly separated the two during my days at the monastery. I had been so solicitous to take time to pray and read, and had consciously avoided doing any sort of work there.

This is not all that exceptional, for monastic visitors are actually encouraged not to work. The invitation to those of us from the outside world is to "share the quiet of the life." We are invited to retreat in order to regain our bearings, speak to God, and allow him to enlighten us. I had decided that work was a diversion I should not allow myself during my Mepkin visits. But as I looked about the community gathering for mass one morning, it became all the more apparent that I should reconsider such an arbitrary restriction. The average age of the Mepkin monks is in the high 60s. It had recently risen a little again, not by addition, but by subtraction; Brother Dale, one of their strongest, youngest members, had left, finally deciding—after more than a decade here and at Gethsemani—this was not his true vocation. After mass, I followed the monks into the chapter room just off the sanctuary where they received their assignment from Brother John. I presented myself as ready for any work.

The good brother patted me on the shoulder. "Oh, no Paul; you rest. Just rest while you're with us. That's your job." At first, I was crestfallen; then, with monastic detachment, resigned. Finally, I was touched.

These men who obviously have so much that needed to be done retain the ability to keep work in perspective. They have thousands of acres to watch over, buildings in need of repair, aging monks in the infirmary, 35,000 chickens to tend, a $5 million building project less than half paid for. Yet the visitor is not looked upon as a potential pair of helpful hands, but as Christ in their midst, come in need of rest.

With all this said, it did not escape me that, impetuous zealot that I can be, perhaps I needed to do some work more than the work needed me to do it. In monasteries, things never quite turn out as the ardent soul would have them. I was left to mull over work in my mind, not perform it with my hands.

There were two words I was using interchangeably—work and vocation, but as I thought about them that morning I knew I needed to pull them apart in my mind and examine them separately for a while. As best I could make the distinction, vocation is the nature of what we do, the type of work, perhaps even the title we have (nurse, cook, nuclear physicist, monk). Work, on the other hand, involved the actual, practical performance.

The monastic fathers believed that when one found one's true vocation, that person also had already found something fundamentally true about himself or herself. In this theology of work, they saw the hand of God. It was not that each person had to find the one specific job or place in which uniquely they could find happiness and unity with God. But there certainly were forces within us—basic urges, talents, disposition, invitations from God—that had to be reconciled.

Abbot Francis serves as a perfect example. Here is an organ prodigy who might have gone on to a brilliant career; instead he turned to a life where his music plays a decided second fiddle. Who knows; he might have been far more successful as an organist than as monk and abbot. There was something else in the mix, something that compelled him away from even this remarkable gift and the opportunities it presented. He once recalled, reflecting on the experience, that if he hadn't responded to the monastic call, "I [would have been] forever poorer for it. God touched my heart, and I couldn't deny it."[3]

That is but one path. Monastic and other wise spiritual writers would never maintain that the finger of God only points to the cloister. St. Francis de Sales, a man of conciliation in an age that preferred contention, claimed that a deep, rich, personal spiritual life was not the exclusive right of monks and nuns, but was available to everyone: "When God the creator made all things, he commanded the plants to bring forth fruit each according to its own kind . . . each one in accord with his character, his station and his calling." Would it be proper, he asked, "for a bishop to want to lead a solitary life like a Carthusian . . . or for a working man to spend his whole day in church?"[4]

To speak of having (or, worse, seeking) a vocation can understandably get people nervous. It seems to summon us to a higher standard, continuous discernment—not merely an occupation, but a task that has transcendent value and worth. Stripped of all rationalizations, this is exactly what a vocation is. But we need to look further and deeper.

Look at a Trappist monk and we see vocation. Look at countless men and women around us performing menial work and we see toil. Look a little harder, to see those who struggle daily merely to find enough to eat,

<hr />

[3]"God Touched My Heart," *North Carolina Catholic*, 9 November 1997, 3.
[4]From *The Introduction to the Devout Life*, quoted in *The Liturgy of the Hours*, vol. III, 1318.

and we see sheer survival. Somehow, by lumping all this together, many of us excuse ourselves from the challenge of living vocationally. If we are doing all right for ourselves, we fear any distraction. If we are barely getting by in the material world, we have no time for the spiritual.

The reality confronting most people reading this page—and its writer—is that they have some measure of choice in what they do with their lives and how they earn a living. It is not a matter of survival. It is a choice many have never exercised; yet if Benedict is right, it is only by daring to exercise that choice that our spirits can enjoy, and flourish from, our labors. Some may not have discovered their vocation, many others the vocation *within* their vocation. Instead of acknowledging the yearning of their souls, they instead apply such measures as the size of their bank balance, the number of bedrooms in their collection of residences, the growth of their retirement plan, or the make and model of their car as holding the meaning of life or the essence of fulfillment. How can the soul soar with pride at what the body and mind are doing for a third of the day or more if that body and mind are but another commodity, divorced from the soul and sold to the highest bidder? Many of us know—and the rest of us suspect—that even those who pursue what is outwardly a most worthy vocation often find it bereft of any grace-giving potential. How are we to know the fullness of this word "vocation," in order some day to use it to describe not just what we do, but who we are?

There is a gem of great value to be found in monastic literature, one brilliant enough to pierce the darkness of our confusion and lighten the way to our vocation—or our vocation within a vocation. In searching for what we are to do with our lives, spiritual masters call upon us to do as they have done—to look to the "fruits of the spirit." This is a far simpler and more accessible process than might be imagined, a combination of mysticism and faith, psychology and gut feeling. Again, the divine alignment.

What is it that truly makes you happy? How do you feel after a day of doing what you do for a living? What part of it made you feel the best? Can you remember a job that satisfied you just by doing it? Moments when you felt at peace? Where were you; what were you doing? What is it that you do as an avocation that you wish you could do as a—now the word is easier to use—vocation? The answers to these questions are all "fruits of the spirit." Men and women who approach and enter upon monastic life ask themselves questions like these. We, who never will be monks, can do likewise, for the result of such a confrontation with ourselves can actually be much the same thing they seek—a vocation big enough for our souls.

"Fruits of the spirit" are the most trustworthy indicators of who we truly are, not the person others would have us be. Does anyone else know the deepest desires of our hearts and souls? When we listen to the divine call that summons each of us—in vastly different ways, to be sure—to holiness and excellence, we are listening to that hunger within us that wants to be fulfilled. There is a secret in our heart to be discovered.

And secret is exactly what it may be, for a vocation does not always present itself boldly and clearly. It can be more a question than an answer. Thomas Merton saw this in the life of St. Stephen Harding, the third abbot of Cîteaux and (along with St. Bernard, St. Robert, and St. Alberic) a founder of the Cistercians. "The vocation was not clear or well-defined," Merton wrote of Stephen, "it was just an urge, a persistent inward ache, a striving after something which he could not quite define. All in all, it can be summed up as a strong awareness that he was not in the place God had destined for him."[5]

God, everpresent in the world, we may think of as a light that shines whether we see it or not. Discovering one's vocation might be compared to being struck by that light. The light was there all along, but either we had not faced it or felt its glow. But keeping ourselves protected and hidden in the darkness is exhausting. Our shields, once so effective, no longer keep us from perceiving that light. Once we have been struck by that light, the whole world is changed—forever.

This is what brings men and women to monastic life. The world, even their families, might consider such a life a waste, aberrant; yet something within them knows that they must go into the desert, seeking more of that light. Many of us try, in a similar way, to move toward where that light

[5]Thomas Merton, "Saint Stephen Harding: Third Abbot of Cîteaux and Founder of the Cistercian Order," *Cistercian Studies Quarterly* 33(3) (1998), 266.

leads—no, not to monastic life, but to work that will engage not only our hands and intellect but our heart as well.

With the dizzying number of possible career paths open to us—especially since the education explosion that followed World War II—it is not surprising so many people find that living is exactly what they can't do in what they do for a living. "Vocation" is not a word they would readily employ to describe what occupies their time. Their line of work, while providing very well for their material needs and perhaps offering prestige or acclaim, is simply not big enough for their souls. Six- and seven-figure incomes do not assure happiness. We all have to look hard at what it is we do in order to find out whether it is the place God calls us to be right now. It is not enough to say that so-and-so does this or that. Each of us must confront who we are, what talents and desires we have, so that we can find not only what is financially rewarding or prestigious, but what it is that will truly fulfill us.

This surely does not mean that monastic wisdom and its reliance on "fruits of the spirit" will turn us into a legion of monks and social workers. Quite the reverse; if there is no holiness in Silicon Valley, on Wall Street or Madison Avenue, on ranches and in convenience stores, in factories and laboratories, then a penurious God has restricted himself to select places rather than permeating the world. Nor does it mean that there is only one calling that we must find or face the risk of life-long misery. Similarly, it does not mean that life necessarily holds but a single vocation. Certainly not; a series of vocations spread throughout a life is perhaps more normal than a single one, doggedly pursued.

Just after my visit of the previous month, Brother Dale had returned to the world to continue his training toward certification as a registered nurse. I know that he left somewhat disappointed in himself that he could not continue in monastic life—and, perhaps, frustrated with the community. "Why can't they change?" he continually asked himself as over the years he was confronted with the ordinariness—and sometimes obtuseness—of the monks with whom he lived. Finally he found that neither the monks nor he needed to change, but rather that each needed to go about the life to which God had called them. Dale had once been asked how he wanted to be known. Almost without thinking, he said, "Compassionate and kind." My guess is that this good young man will be exactly that as a nurse—perhaps a nurse-monk, informed by his years of monastic life.

There are many trails up the mountain of perfection, along which people proceed at different speeds, performing different tasks. Does a hungry traveler not need a Big Mac prepared well and served with a smile? Does the person in pain not need a medication introduced to her doctor by a pharmaceutical salesperson, created by a research scientist who depends on the laboratory custodian? Shouldn't the retirement income of a school teacher be increased by a wise stockbroker? Doesn't a baby need a loving hand to steady those first, tentative steps?

Theresa Mancuso was a cloistered nun who then became a research analyst in a New York probation department. Looking back on her monastic life she wonders just where God was closest: "I baked cheesecakes and bread, I built cabinets and furniture, grew vegetables and cooked for the community. I tended guests and prepared the hospitality we offered to strangers. . . . Was it more purifying to my soul or more pleasing to God than these hours before the computer researching and writing about criminal justice? Who can say that one is somehow more pleasing to God than another?"[6]

Some people sense they have found their calling—or, at least their calling for now. But many have not. What is a soul to do in the interim, an interim during which many years—even an entire lifetime—might unfold? Seemingly so different, people in both these situations must rise each morning, live each day. Whether they sense or long for a feeling of alignment with God's will and ways what are they to do? The question hung in the air before me like incense. It seemed to be all about work's practical application.

At that moment there was a barely audible knock at the door of my small cell, as if an oversized moth was seeking entrance with the answer. There was Brother John—with a roll of screen, staple gun, hammer, and screwdriver. He grinned his gap-toothed grin. If I wanted to, the screens on

[6]Theresa Mancuso, "Monasticism Outside Cloister," *Review for Religious*, May–June, 1992, 333.

the back door of the refectory kitchen could be replaced. It was the most gentle invitation to work I had ever received. My ruminations on the nature of work would have to wait while I actually did some.

I walked toward the refectory, past the construction site for the new library. Nature had made light of man's work, an hour-long downpour filling in what the latest in earth-moving machines had taken days to excavate. Lessons abound. I traveled on to my work site.

I am not the handiest of men, but I sized up the tall door and figured I would at least give it a try. I took the door off its hinges and carefully laid it on the ground. As my hands traced over the dusty, brown-painted wood, I found I was neither nervous about my abilities nor in any special hurry. It just wasn't the way things were done around here. In other places throughout the abbey, monks were grading eggs, mowing lawns, caring for the infirm, sitting before a computer screen on behalf of "Earth Healer," weeding a garden. If my reading of monastic literature and observations of the Mepkin monks were at all accurate, each person was at once invested in the work at hand, yet detached from it.

As I began to remove the molding, I found my mind defiantly trying to make more of the situation. There were dozens of other damaged screens that needed repair, one of them right outside my room. If I hurried just a bit, I could do not only this one, but one or two others. Wouldn't Brother John be impressed? I rapidly moved the screwdriver along, but in my haste struck a nail. The screwdriver leaped out of my grip, gouging my other hand before it tumbled to the ground. I immediately saw what I was doing. What more needed to be done wasn't the point. Within the divine and human ecosystem that was this monastery, at this time, on this day, I first had *this* screen to replace, as well as I could. I picked up the screwdriver once more.

By carefully sliding the screwdriver beneath the molding strips I was able to remove them without a crack. I peeled off the old screen and the staples that had held it in place. I cut the roll of new screen and began stapling, starting at the middle of the top and bottom of the door. My hand traced over the smooth mesh, ironing out any ripples as I continued to staple. The tiny molding nails so gently removed eased back into their original holes with just a few taps from my hammer. With a smudge of olive oil cadged from the pantry, the pins slid into the hinges. Well, it wasn't perfect—a slight sag at the screen's midsection precluded that—but it didn't look half-bad, and at least it would keep insects out of the refectory. Encouraged by my modest success, I was ready to go on to the next damaged screen. The bell sounded for sext. My short career as a screen repairman was on hold. It was time for prayer.

The next morning found my fellow Ohioan, Brother Nicholas, a bit uninspired on the noon menu. I suggested, then helped him prepare, a favorite rice-cheese-spinach casserole, prepared a lemon-zest salad dressing for Brother Callistus's fresh garden greens, and put a fresh cranberry relish through the food processor. On my way to the library that afternoon I saw Brother Lawrence struggling in the dust of acoustical tiles and battens of fiberglass insulation he was removing from the shell of the old infirmary, which was about to be torn down. How would they be used again? I asked this unassuming sixty-nine-year-old man whose five decades of monastic life have so handsomely chiseled his face. He didn't know, he replied; he just couldn't bear to see them go to waste. I agreed.

When I showered that evening, I had a strange sensation—besides the tingling of fiberglass in my hands and on my neck. Although my contribution had been pathetically small, I had a sense of being part of this community in a way I had never felt before. I had given myself over to the rhythm of this place, putting my own agenda aside. I could not share in their vocation, but I could participate in their work, both with my hands and in my prayer. What was more, there wasn't—and didn't need to be—any direct benefit to me from any of it. I had contributed to a meal silently eaten by the monks, and scavenged stacks of building materials that may do no more than gather still more dust in a farm shed and be thrown out some day. I chanted the psalms, read Scripture, attended the Eucharist, prayed alone in my room. I napped after the noon meal. I could point to no great accomplishments at all. And it didn't matter.

Who knows? That lemon-zest salad dressing might have been absolutely ambrosial to a certain monk in need of a little temporal sapidity; the building materials might prove crucial on some day in the future; my screen might be the last line of defense against a venomous wasp or disease-bearing fly. My prayers could have been the beginning of a new personal enlightenment, breaking through a barrier to an outpouring of grace.

But I doubt it.

What I did know was that I wanted (more in the kitchen, less on the screen) to do what I was doing with as much competence as I could muster, and with—if I might borrow Thomas Merton's words—a desire to please God. Of course, I had no idea whether I pleased him at all, but if I can rely on Merton, the desire to please God was both a reasonable start and its own reward. It was enough for God—and, as it turned out, for me—that I just wanted to be the best me I could be.

Yes, a vocation that can satisfy the enormous hunger within our souls is important, but what we do within it—or as we muddle through life in search of it—is even more important. As Merton looked around the monastic community at Gethsemani, it was not the choir monks with the finest voices working in important jobs that he felt were living the most authentic Trappist life; instead it was the simple lay brothers who silently and lovingly went about their daily chores.

All of us know people miserable in apparently fabulous jobs—while others, doing apparently mundane work, seem to find in them a sense of mission and vocation. A typist I knew in New York lived and worked in the tiniest apartment, one most people would consider confining, claustrophobic. But her spirit soared as her fingers flew over the keyboard, smoothing out this young writer's mistakes and excesses. There is a memorable toll collector at Exit 13 on the Massachusetts Turnpike, who greets each driver as a treasured guest. A McDonald's manager in my adopted home city of Wilmington, North Carolina, who calls out "my brother," "my sister," to each customer with warm authenticity.

In my own life I can look back to the dozens of jobs I have had and picture exactly how I performed them at various times, depending on my attitude. When I was a hospital orderly during college, I could place a bed pan gently under trembling thighs, or thrust it efficiently into the same position.

Whether we are orderlies or orchestra conductors, either we befriend our work—seeing in it the opportunity for moral excellence and a continual outpouring of heavenly grace—or we become its victims. As the Benedictine David Steindl-Rast writes,

> Work, if we don't approach it consciously, will suck us into its demands. Then we become slaves, no matter how high up we are on the ladder. . . . Even people who have jobs they don't like and find meaningless can still be free within them . . . by reminding themselves deliberately and often, why they do them. As long as we do work out of love for those whom we love, we do it for a good reason. Love is the best reason for our labors. Love makes what we do and suffer rise like music, like a soaring line of chant.[7]

In order to allow our work to rise up like that chant, sometimes we need to see the vocation within our vocation, a way to approach and apply what we do so that it is more than a mere means to an end. This was dramatically illustrated to me when my wife returned from a morning walk with a neighbor, who has a mortgage-loan business. Tracy had started an after-school program in the arts for underprivileged kids, and after hearing about it our neighbor sheepishly admitted feeling that her own work was not so altruistic. But as the conversation continued, she described with genuine affection some of the low-income families for whom she'd bent the rules to make sure they obtained the home loan they needed. A plastic surgeon I know spends most of his year making a lot of money with tummy tucks, eyelid reshaping, and cellulite removal; but for two weeks a year he's in the jungles of the Dominican Republic, performing hundreds of surgeries, restoring cleft palates, resurfacing horribly disfiguring scars, and otherwise giving people a new life. Are these not saints in our midst, bringing hope and dignity to others?

My own efforts to integrate work and vocation have traveled a tortuous path. In the Catholic world of my youth, to "have a vocation" meant only one thing—the religious life. The rest of us merely worked. While the

---

[7]Steindl-Rast with Lebell, *The Music of Silence*, 60–61.

social encyclicals of such recent popes as Leo XIII (d. 1903) had ex
the virtues of the work of all people, the idea had not filtered down
most parishes. There remained a hierarchy in human vocations, with priests
at the highest level, nuns a decided step below—and a few steps below, us.
Like most good Catholic boys I naturally wanted to be a priest, for my
work to be closest to God. But—again like most Catholic boys—my
teenage hormones advised me that ordination was not without its sacrifices.

I became a writer not because of any altruistic desire to inform or
inspire the world, but simply because, being too small and untalented for
sports at Cathedral Latin School, I found I could earn a letter by writing
for the newspaper. I eventually studied journalism at Marquette University,
but I really had no idea of pursuing it as a career. It was not until I looked
out the porthole window of a Navy destroyer while docked in Karachi,
Pakistan that I began to see writing as my vocation. In my hands was a copy
of the *Karachi Dawn*, a daily newspaper, telling me that things were just fine
in this country. On the dock were lepers, people with ghastly elephantiasis,
children suffering from deformities and diseases I had never seen before. I
made the connection: I was a journalist; I could tell the truth about what
was really happening in the world.

After two newspaper jobs and that graduate year at Columbia, I settled
in New York to begin a free-lance career. I wrote for some of the better
magazines of the day, primarily profiles of celebrities, movie stars, and
sports figures. My work went reasonably well, but something was sadly
missing. No sooner did a story of mine appear on glossy pages than a
hollow feeling set in. I did not know "fruits of the spirit," at least not by
that name, but I did know that writing had to be more than this.

I met a priest in Brooklyn who looked after an assorted collection of
drunks and shut-ins, the diseased and infirm of mind and body, and found
his life far more interesting than visits to movie sets, locker rooms, or
lunches at fancy East Side restaurants. I wrote a story about him—which,
incidentally, was never published—and my life and writing took an abrupt
turn. But even after I began writing books primarily about religious belief, I
still had the feeling I was missing my vocation. The hollowness continued
to haunt me. Inspired by that priest, I helped to start a Catholic Worker

lly living with a group of homeless men in a shabby apart-
out to abandon my writing for a life dedicated to the poor
at the Trappist monastery in Spencer forced me to look in
hat I saw was a hollow-eyed, unhappy man trying to become
was not destined to be. Father Mark Delery, who would
become my spiritual director during my hermit year at Spencer, pointed
out that writing was also worthwhile—that God wanted each of us to
discover our calling, not become martyrs to our own egos. I was hung up
on the idea of vocation; he was talking about the inherent dignity of work.
Ego was very much involved in my pursuit of a vocation, even for what
might seem an abdication of worldly ambitions and a rapid trip in down-
ward mobility. What I sought—mistakenly—was an idealized place on this
earth, one where I would definitively prove my worth. God calls some to be
Trappist monks or to work in Calcutta slums, others to be high-tech CEOs
or used-car salespeople. His love and acceptance are not predicated upon
the supposed merits of what we do; they are always there—that ubiquitous
light—wherever we are and whatever we are doing, so long as we are doing
our best to be our true selves.

The signs are always there if we look for them. I remember watching a
videotape of myself on a morning talk show I hosted one summer in
Baltimore. It was exciting, well paid, an opportunity for some modest fame.
I was told I was actually not that bad at it—perhaps I could make it a
career. But when I looked at that man with his glib remarks and too-ready
smile, I knew that if I had to face him for the rest of my life I would hate
myself. I have proposed many foolish projects that were never accepted,
waited for phone calls that never came, written words that will never be
published—and when I look back all I can do is thank God that my
determination was at turns blunted, tempered, or miraculously redirected.

Rather than looking deeply for the "fruits of the spirit," too often we
interpret surface rewards and ephemeral accomplishments—even acclaim
and acceptance—as the true signals that what we are doing is pleasing to
God. Within the monastery, everything is done to frustrate such an approach. The whole idea is to demolish the ego while at the same time
exalting a monk's sense of intrinsic worth, regardless of his abilities. If a

monk has a special talent, more than likely he will be given a job—at least initially—that does *not* utilize it. This puts work in its proper place, not allowing it to distract him from the task of continually seeking out his vocation. For if a man comes to a monastery to be a "successful" monk, he has come to the wrong place. There is more to life in a monastery—and in the world—than that.

And yet monasticism is not a foolish bully about this. When Abbot Francis left his music behind to join the Trappists, eventually his abbot took him aside. "We're really not getting the best of you. Half of you is still outside."[8] He was allowed to practice, and then to perform publicly. Merton felt his writing life was over when he entered Gethsemani and even somewhat idolized the contemplative life as its opposite. But he found "the kind of work I once feared because I thought it would interfere with 'solitude' is, in fact, the only true path to solitude. . . . Once God has called you to solitude, everything you touch leads you further into solitude. Everything that affects you builds you into a hermit, as long as you do not insist on doing the work yourself and building your own kind of hermitage."[9]

This monastic approach might not be exactly applicable to those of us outside monastery walls. But very few of us have not been tempted to regard our work as our god, one demanding great devotion and expecting costly sacrifices before its altar. As Thich Nhat Hanh has written, "People of our time tend to overwork, even when they are not in great need of money. We seem to take refuge in our work in order to avoid confronting our real sorrow and inner turmoil. We express our love and care for others by working hard, but if we do not have time for the people we love, if we cannot make ourselves available to them, how can we say that we love them?"[10] The fascinating (and troubling) research finding[11] that people are beginning to find the workplace their true home where they want to spend more time—and their home a place of work that they want to escape—

[8]"God Touched My Heart," *North Carolina Catholic*, 9 November 1997, 3.
[9]Merton, *Entering the Silence*, 463.
[10]Thich Nhat Hanh, *Living Buddha, Living Christ*, 94.
[11]Arlie Hochschild, *The Time Bind* (New York: Metropolitan Books, 1997).

indicates that we are sadly out of balance. For, even when we have the most worthwhile vocations (yes, there are workaholic monks as well as executives, exterminators, and factory workers), we are little more than pawns if we cannot see into the very nature of work and vocation.

The suicide of a friend of mine tragically made the point. J. Anthony Lukas was an acclaimed journalist and author, a two-time winner of the Pulitzer Prize. But when a book on which he had spent years did not turn out as well as he had hoped, he killed himself a few months before its publication. He had suffered from depression; perhaps that demon finally wore him down. But his frustration with his own abilities and worth as a writer must certainly had contributed. What a shameful waste to lose so masterful a craftsman as Tony—who wrote compassionately about people caught in the vortex of their humanity and their society—to the vagaries of the success of one mere book.

I thought about this when I paid a visit to a man in the hospital after he had suffered a heart attack. He is an ambitious man, a good man, but seemed always in a hurry; there were so many projects he was involved in. He could become intensely angry with those with whom he worked, in essence blaming them for the stress that had led to the heart attack. His wife confidently said it was not his cholesterol, weight, or level of exercise that needed correction; he would not in fact have to change anything, she said, but "get rid of the stress." This was and was not the answer. Work must be seen in the context of life in relationship with God and fellow human beings, embraced—and held at a distance. Aligned.

My life has none of the high drama of being either a street worker with the poor or a Trappist monk. My adrenaline is not racing every waking minute; my schedule is not always full. The world may or may not benefit from my words, but they are hardly so important that they are my primary reason for living. I hope the kind of writing I do is what I should be doing—at least for now. I hope I have a generosity of spirit and faith, both when my writing is going well and when it is not. I hope I will continually try to discern what are the "fruits of the spirit" and respond appropriately both to rejection and acceptance. And, as the great wind of God's spirit blows where it will, I must be open to a tomorrow where there may be a very different kind of work for me to do.

For what often happens—it has happened to me, and may well happen again and again—is that we need to find not just our vocation, but the vocation *within* the vocation. We need to find that certain way that best attunes us to God, to what is the most authentic in us within the frame of our daily work. This was the case with St. Benedict, for whom being a solitary was not enough; he found he had to share his vision with others who came to him. Could it be he wanted company? St. Bernard could not merely be a monk, but needed to be a certain kind of monk. It is no different in all walks of life; we must brush aside the externals, joining what is best and most whole in us to that which is our share in the unfolding creation of the world.

I returned to my home and my computer to continue my own vocation as a writer—and, as had been the case throughout this year, to be continually educated by life, a life that now had some thin, barely noticeable monastic threads woven ever so slightly through it. On a Saturday morning, my son Noah demonstrated his lack of enthusiasm for doing his chores by irately swinging an extension cord through the air. This would not have been such a big deal had the plug not met, then shattered, the Plexiglas window of our front door. I was furious (so much for monastic detachment and self-control) and so was he—especially after we picked up a new piece for which he had to pay $41.15.

There was a silent, uneasy truce between father and son, neither of them wanting to be outside on a chilly North Carolina night for a task so senselessly made necessary. We took the door off its hinges and laid it on the walk. I worked a screwdriver beneath the molding and then showed Noah how to ease it along gently so as not to bend the nails or crack the wood. We exchanged a few tentative words on technique. The four pieces of molding—one of them an ornate, carved piece that had me worried—came out flawlessly. We took out the old pieces of Plexiglas and placed the new piece over the frame. Noah moved it into place. He marveled that our measurements, after all, had been right. I began to squeeze the clear caulking around the perimeter. Noah reached for the caulking gun and, after a few early excesses, expertly completed the task.

I held the molding in place as Noah tapped the nails back into their respective holes. We cleaned up the excess caulking and eased the door back onto its hinges. We washed both sides.

"Nice job, huh?" Noah said.

"It sure was," I replied. My arm over his shoulder, we went inside, two monk-novices who had done the best they could when presented with a highly imperfect work situation—and had a Coke to celebrate the end of our *labora*.

Community

Many Churches

Behold how good and how pleasant it is for
brethren to dwell together in unity.

The words of Psalm 133 at noontime prayer that Friday at Mepkin were apt testimony to the "angelic life," as the monastic way has been called. The calmly parsed words, while sung without a hint of intonation or emphasis—and certainly without any false boosterism—seemed to soar overhead while yet gently enfolding us as we stood in the choir stalls. The school of love and compassion was proclaimed, the sanctuary of understanding and companionship that the *Rule of St. Benedict* aspired to bring into being. There were no visitors in the abbey church, as is often the case at noontime prayer; just the monks and their by now frequent guest. I felt a sweet communion with the two dozen men around me.

And later, as practical testimony that it could be just so, I had found these words of St. Aelred, the famous abbot of Rievaulx:

> The day before yesterday, when I was going round the cloister of the monastery, then sitting with the brethren in a loving circle, as though amid the delights of paradise, I admired the leaves, the flowers, and the fruit of every tree. I found no one in that great number whom I did not love, and whom I did not believe loved me. I was filled with such a joy as passes all the delights of the world. For I felt as though my spirit was transfused into them all, and their affection into me, so that I could say with the prophet: "Behold how good and how pleasant it is for brethren to dwell together in unity."[1]

I had experienced how good and pleasant such monastic togetherness could be earlier that morning—not in cloister garth or church, not accompanied by a celestial chorus, but serenaded by the rhythmic pulsing of a conveyor belt. Appearing for morning work assignments in the chapter room, I had been called to a new, if temporary, vocation: to be a member of the morning egg crew. My job in the abbey's grading house was off-loading flats of eggs so that a marvelous contraption of rubber-tipped fingers could then swoop down to transfer them gently on the first step of a journey through cleansing, candling, grading, separation into neat choir-like rows, and eventually their final rest in a cardboard shipping crate.

It was a factory scene, but for the details of setting easily replicated anywhere in the world. Only the workers were somewhat out of the ordi-

[1] Quoted in Esther de Waal, *The Way of Simplicity: The Cistercian Tradition* (Maryknoll, N.Y.: Orbis, 1998), 124; de Waal in turn is quoting Pauline Matarasso, *The Cistercian World: Monastic Writings of the Twelfth Century* (Harmondsworth: Penguin Books, 1993), 184.

nary. For here was Father Aelred, of beautiful voice and fine guitar; and there was Sister Louise, a strange addition to a decidedly male world, yet now so naturally a part of it. She was "between" Trappistine convents and was given refuge here. There was Brother Nicholas, the "egg abbot" running the show, and Calvin Myers, a retired Methodist minister from Colorado; Father Malachi, half a century a Trappist; a visiting layman, who also happened to be a neurosurgeon; and myself. Brother Lawrence, my friend in the salvation of acoustical tile and fiberglass insulation, wheeled in racks of eggs fresh from the hen houses.

It was a wonderful morning. We laughed at the stupidest egg "yokes," helped each other out when a gooey mess or too many small, medium, or large taxed one of the lines. Pee wees were especially difficult; like eager but poorly formed novices these tiny first offerings of new layers didn't know their place, and kept fouling the assembly line. Through it all, the very kind of work that people might consider drudgery was anything but.

There were long periods of silence when we were left to our own thoughts. My mind wandered, freed by the gentle rhythm of the machinery, the repetitive motions of this kind of *labora*. I found myself imparting good karma on those thousands of white oblong spheres, visualizing their presence in a Piggly Wiggly shopping cart or scrambled before a hungry kid, in pancakes and pineapple upside-down cakes, poached in Eggs Benedict (how appropriate!) with a cup of cappuccino in a Charleston restaurant, in the mess hall line at Charleston Air Force base, a steady abbey customer.

I thought of Simone Weil, that saintly, tortured woman in German-occupied France who left the community of intellectuals to join a community of factory workers. There, amidst the clatter and the dirt of the factory floor, she looked into the faces of her coworkers and saw the face of God. Men and women come to the monastery for similar reasons. Why not in an egg-grading house as well? I looked around me. Yes, indeed.

It was an altogether peaceful morning. At times it was routine and mindless, yet there was a quality about it quite different from the other factories in which I had worked during college days—making cans and beer and electric power tools. There was a community spirit here, each of us supported by the presence of the others, all focused on a simple goal: sending to market a good product, one that sustains the Mepkin community.

According to Benedict, Bernard, and other great monastic lights, this time together was as perfect a prayer as the most triumphal liturgy, this community as purposeful about doing God's work as any within the cloister. These three hours on our feet watching over tumbling eggs could be as grace-filled as three hours on our knees before the Blessed Sacrament. For the *Rule* to which these Trappists conform their lives is not some abstract treatise on the intricacies of personal piety or a theological labyrinth to be navigated in search of God; rather, it is a quite pragmatic approach to daily life. Everything—if we were only open to it—had meaning. The sacramental encounter with God and Christ was possible in the circumstances—*all* the circumstances, to the discerning soul—of daily life. After our shift, as Brother Callistus and I walked back toward the cloistered area, I touched on this subject; his reply was a *basso profundo* laugh of dismissal. "Look, man, I don't want to go around spouting platitudes about splattered eggs and your aching back and mine. Life is so much misery anyhow, isn't it? Either we see through it to God or we don't. But if we can just recognize our smallness, our utter dependency on God, don't you think he'll come to our little group in the workplace and sanctify it?"

Supporting such an all-encompassing view of potential holiness, the principle of community is at the very foundation of monastic life. It is in essence the idea that through their intentions (their will infused with grace, to put it in other words) mere mortals—though proceeding individually on often disparate paths and with vastly varying talents—can attain in a group personal sanctification and wholeness in ways they could not achieve alone. They cannot only survive through cooperation, but flourish. Support was essential in any great pursuit, and its application in loving friendship—one of Bernard's great contributions to monastic life—was a crucial component in the economy of human salvation. By giving over oneself to the group, the tiny mustard seed that is the individual is sown upon fertile ground, there to burst its shell and grow to fullness and fruition. Holding on to that mustard seed in the tightly clenched fist of our selfishness condemns it to a smothering death.

Lest we be dreamy-eyed or romantic—neither of which have any place in the monastic system of values, past or present—community life is not always the paean to cooperation and synchronicity that this occasional visitor experienced at Mepkin Abbey that Friday morning in the postmodern epoch. The "loving circle" is not always made complete; filial affection is not manifested each day. As Walter Daniel, St. Aelred's biographer, recalled:

> And, as we two sat alone in the room, a monk entered, mad with rage, a real wild bull in full charge. He came upon Aelred, bellowing and grimacing, seized his mat and jerked it up with the father on it and hurled this father of a hundred monks and five hundred lay brothers into the fire among the coals, shouting: "You wretch, now I am going to kill you . . ."[2]

In one modern Trappist monastery—name charitably withheld—one irritated monk smashed another, a more solicitous type, squarely in the jaw merely for trying to free the arm of his choir robe from the edge of his stall. Fights in the monastery fields are not unheard of; neither is profanity that would make a teamster blanch. So, not so much to our surprise, there are two sides to the community coin, even within cloistered religious societies. Brilliant, elliptical, spirit-filled, but certainly impatient St. Bernard saw in monks living, working, and praying together a path to salvation and a wellspring of God's graces. He also assessed *actual* community life: *Vita communis poenitentia maxima*—"Community, my greatest penance."

At Mepkin, while there is a commonality of purpose and vocation, there are significant tensions below the serene surface and divergent views of how Trappist life should be lived. One monk told me there was a feeling, especially among older monks, that the order had ossified in the nineteenth and twentieth centuries, sailing along on its fairly recent patrimony for too long. A reformulation was in order. But what was it to be? Ironically, perhaps, it is this older generation of monks that is more open to change

---

[2] Walter Daniel, *The Life of Aelred of Rievaulx*, trans. F. M. Powicke (London: Thomas Nelson, 1950), 69.

and a more flexible (while still Cisterian and cloistered) lifestyle. Formed in an era of exact discipline and multitudinous strictures, they now bristle against the imposition of too many rules.

Younger monks, most of them having lived in the world during the wild and wooly 1970s, seem to seek a more structured life. How much freedom—and in what circumstances? How can discipline be had without clear rules? How should good order be maintained? How does fraternal charity stack up against what we now know of human psychology? What will happen if age-old traditions are bent, seemingly to conform with the prevailing winds of the day? These are the questions facing the Mepkin monks.

On my trip to Mepkin the day before, I had listened to an audiotape of Alexis de Tocqueville's *Democracy in America*. He marveled at the regulated but free atmosphere found in the New World. There were rules and constraints, but the populace had internalized their basic thrust, rather than having to live under a capricious punitive code and military control.

Abbot Francis seeks a similar internalization of Trappist ways for the Mepkin community. As an example, he points to a plywood wall once constructed around the path leading to the church from the refectory so that the monks would be shielded from the world. It was an unattractive way to maintain the integrity of the cloister, and when he was elected abbot he had it torn down. If the monks could not preserve their interiority without this wall, Francis surmised, they were mistaking monastic form for monastic content.

Within the various communities we inhabit, and indeed in our society as a whole, we are undergoing similar change—and are faced with a quite similar dilemma. Working in community, thinking about the good of the whole, while navigating on the shifting winds endemic to an era of dizzying change—it is an extraordinarily difficult proposition. We crave the kind of community life—imperfect though it may be—that we see in such a place as Mepkin. In fact, simply to take part in such a community is the reason that brings many either to join or visit a monastery. We want to feel the support of a group based on shared values and tightly focused on a goal of enduring worth.

With the peculiarly American exaltation of individuality, with our increasing suspicions of any moral absolutes, we have reached a point at which shared values are no longer commonplace in our culture. The deification of personal rights exacts a toll in the coin of community needs—especially when common decency, much less morality, becomes a matter of personal taste and prerogative. Proclaiming vociferously the self-evident rightness of our point of view and way of life, we become more and more alienated from others. If we are right, someone must be wrong. Communities mutate into interest groups; cooperation is no longer the grease in the machinery of civil life but a poison to be avoided at all costs. We concentrate on the promulgation of certain views and the obliteration of any that disagree. Our fortress mentality, foretold in David Riesman's *The Lonely Crowd* of the 1950s—and in no so small way shaped by a terrified reaction to the tumultuous 1960s and 1970s—finds us caught in the paradox of craving the succor and support of community while doing everything we can to obliterate it.

No one need tell us that we cannot have it both ways. Either we are willing to give over part of ourselves for the common good of the various groups in which we live our lives, or we can remain an island of self-concern and self-righteousness. What is right and decent has been replaced by what is legal—or what we can get away with. The form may be there; but what of the content? No wonder so many people feel so alienated today.

A monastic community like Mepkin stands in increasingly stark contrast to prevailing societal norms. It offers a different template for our lives. Composed of individuals, it stands for the triumph and ultimate wisdom of the common good. Give what you can; be given what you require. And it says that if a person wants to be close to God, to find their true selves, to flourish and not merely survive, a different way must prevail, an overarching communal attitude that reaches into every corner and every action of their lives. The simple fact is that Christianity, Judaism, and Islam all teach an inherently communal ideal of faith. Christianity and monasticism demand the most difficult sacrifice of those who live in Western cultures—that of individual ego. But they hold out the promise of another way of life, true liberation from the tyranny of self.

As I walked about in the warm April air one afternoon during this visit, paying homage to a stand of small but hearty tomato plants that Brother Callistus was nurturing behind the Earth Healer quonset huts, I became even more aware that within this monastic community there were many smaller communities. The group at the grading house was only one. There are the office monks, business monks, kitchen monks, hospitality monks, maintenance monks, farm monks. And so it is, I realized, with us. We have a base community—for most of us, it is a family. We may also have a spiritual home and community, a place like Mepkin. But then as we go into the workplace or traveling or shopping, still other communities present themselves. Some are fleeting, others more permanent. But each is the stage upon which we live, offering opportunities for grace, redemption, and happiness—or, in contrast, promising alienation and the poisoning of our spirits. From a monastery on the banks of the Cooper, another vision of life is quietly being lived—and offered to the rest of us in both example and human incertitude.

Before we throw up our hands and say "impossible" or "with the way things are today?," it is somewhat comforting to look back to the situation confronting St. Benedict—and to realize that he encountered many of the same problems that seem to us so insurmountable. As Esther de Waal writes, "The world into which St. Benedict was born was a troubled, torn apart, uncertain world. It knew little of safety or of security, and the church was almost as troubled as the secular powers. It was a world without landmarks. It had this in common with the twentieth century: life was an urgent struggle to make sense of what was happening."[3] The imperial reach and power of Rome—the only order most people knew—had fallen, and people tried to isolate themselves from the ensuing chaos. It was a dog-eat-dog world. Self-proclaimed holy men and women wandered the countryside, denouncing the all too evident wickedness of human nature; only by escape from contact with others could anyone be saved.

Benedict would not allow the Christian vision to be set aside, regardless of the extreme forces pulling at either pole in society. His idealism chal-

[3]Esther de Waal, *Seeking God: The Way of St. Benedict*, 15.

lenged the perceptions of the day. He wanted to establish a new kind of landmark, one that would not be swept away, even in the midst of epochal changes in political system and government. His true genius was to see that it was in the relationship of one individual to another, and another, and another—not of apprentice to holy man, as was popular at the time, or only to God—that promised endless possibilities of transformation. He could see that selfishness and self-seeking turned people away from God, and rather than aiding in wholeness and holiness actually inhibited both. Benedict proclaimed that God could be met in everyday circumstances, in everyday encounters. If a heavenly paradise was to be recreated on earth, it could not be abstract, theoretical, or merely concerned with pious practices. It had to be a product of interaction with other people.

Yes, community life could be rife with tension; but it was only through facing the intricacies, failings, and transcendence of human beings that we are tempered, educated, and ultimately fulfilled. It might seem a dizzying, impossible order: that I must be attuned to the needs of each community I encounter and sensitive to the individuals within it. Yet if we look deeply into Benedict and Bernard, it may not be so impossible after all. In fact, it can become a quite natural habit of being, if we—both prayerfully and rationally—allow such an outlook to flower. For there is nothing in the spirit of the *Rule* that asks people to foolishly expend their energies in a fruitless quest for perfect relationships in community. This does not mean, to be sure, that the standard set is not a high one. What the *Rule* calls for is stated quite well in chapter 72: "The monks are to bear with patience the weaknesses of others, whether of body or behavior. . . . Let them be charitable towards their brothers with true affection."

For fear of terrifying ourselves, it might be useful while reading and digesting those words not to begin by imagining being called to such excellence, but rather to place ourselves on the other side of the equation. Is this not how each of us would want to be treated when we are an intemperate or foolish spouse, parent, worker? When we wait impatiently in a crowded doctor's office, are late for the next appointment, or are disappointed over not getting something we so fervently prayed for?

It is only when we realize the profound effect those with whom we interact have upon us that we begin to understand the necessity of a communal outlook. Monastic communities seem so idealized as communities that we tend to put them aside as impractical for lay people. Yet Benedict's and then Bernard's monasteries were based upon something as basic as common concern. Exercising this concern within the context of tiny communities of monks, they accomplished the amazing feat of reclaiming civility and civilization in their day. In our day—perhaps a time of similar social breakdown?—Mepkin's glow, the quiet witness of a small band of men rising, sleeping, working, and praying by the quiet banks of the Cooper River, can infuse our lives in ways at once venerable yet fresh.

The monk's hunger is the same as our hunger for supportive relationships—or communities. It springs from deep within the mystery of human nature. We are not meant to be alone; we are not islands. The monks of Mepkin have emotions and needs and idiosyncrasies, as do we. We approach our various communities—family, work, church, social groupings—hoping that they will meet those needs. The monks do the same as they enter a monastery. How wonderful the promise! For them, of a loving, understanding monastic community with a singleness of vision; for us, the security, the continuity of a family or other grouping.

Yet while both monks and those of us outside the walls may find comfort and solace in our various communities, we inevitably also experience disappointment. There are many reasons for this; one is primary. We have enthroned the *thought* of community, not comprehended its *reality*. Simply put, we seek the benefits without the willingness to pay the price. I wish to receive—compassion, understanding, forgiveness, love; yet, parsimoniously, I withhold them.

Oddly enough, while community life asks for the constant deferral of personal needs and desires, the seeming sublimation of ego, no one else in the community is more important to the mix than I am. For what is a community, but so many "I"s? What makes some groups work so well and meet the needs of its members, while others are so corrosive to the human spirit? It is the work of the many "I"s within—one of which is each Mepkin monk, and each one of us.

The "I" is at once dominant and, paradoxically, unimportant.

While we hunger for the solace and security that a healthy community provides, even when we find it we are ultimately alone. This, too, is a paradox, and one that may seem to promise little more than disappointment. But in the end, any group or community of which we are a part shares but a small part of us. We have our own demons and angels, thoughts and needs. We are unique, different from all others. Although we may want to blend ourselves with them, losing ourselves to the community, we can never do so entirely. The key is neither to triumph in our individuality and stand aside from human interaction, nor to attempt to submerge our identities in a group. The key is to find our real self, see our real self within these communities—what we can provide, what we require. Our limitations, abilities, and areas for growth comprise this "I," and it is this "I" we offer to the community, clothed in its coat of many colors. Imperfect though we may be, this is all we have. As best we can, we are invited to delight in virtue, know its power, seek its wisdom—and shudder with the expectancy of who we might become. The kingdom within us—our relationship to and quest for God—flows out to mingle with and sanctify the kingdom among us. Monks spend their lives facing who they are, as they stand before the members of their community and before the throne of God. We are no different.

Some would-be monks forever search for the "ideal" monastery, only to discover that none of those seeming paradises ever turn out to be so. Disillusioned, they trek on, their dream always one step ahead of wherever they are. Many of us have been on similar quests in our lives, seeking the ideal while never willing to confront—and transform—the ordinary, the mundane, the routine that comprises so much of life.

It was perhaps a bit strange that the next day at vigils, during a quiet morning's meditation on the meaning of community, my mind locked on a phrase of Peter Maurin's, the man who, along with Dorothy Day, started the Catholic Worker movement. Peter never talked about creating ideal Catholic Worker communities, but rather "places where it is easy to be good."

I know that I need to be in such places.

I must be careful about the communities of which I am a part. When I have the choice, I do not want to be in places or with people who are corrosive to the human spirit. I am simply too weak. I don't want to be where laughter at the expense of others is easy, where moral values are not at least part of the equation, where people are respected not for what they have, but for who they are. My days are not generally spent (except at Mepkin) in religious settings. Hardly. But I hope many of them will involve places, groups, and people that at turns nurture, challenge, affirm, and support me. This doesn't mean I seek out only cheering sections; not at all. But if I find myself in communities that work against the monastic vision of mutual respect, care, openness, and concern, I must look hard at them and myself to find if this is where I really should be. This involves, to use a monastic term, discretion in my choice of affiliations.

While discretion—where we spend our time and with whom—is a significant component of a monastically inspired life in the secular world, we often find ourselves in situations that are, to put it mildly, less than desirable—or, at least on the surface, morally (or monastically) neutral. While the Trappist ethos asks the brethren to sacrifice for each other, seek the common good, and defer at times to the will of the community, the mandate is not simply to suffer through bad situations for the greater honor and glory of God and for the salvation of one's immortal soul. The community, too—its life, its health, its functioning—is always under careful scrutiny. We—if we base our outlook on how the best of modern monastic groups function (and Mepkin, I think, stands as a good example)—are asked to assess with care and candor our various communities as healthy or dysfunctional. It is not the job of each monk to attempt frantically to make every situation perfect or, when in their community setting, to accede to the demands of every other monk without reservation. Neither is it our calling to do so in our communities.

In one article I read on community life during this visit, the accent decidedly was not on silently and blindly bearing with another's faults.[4]

---

[4]Joel Giallanza, "Community—Healthy or Dysfunctional?" *Review for Religious*, (56) (1997), 587ff.

Jesus' "Render unto Caesar the things that are Caesar's, and to God the things that are God's" was the pragmatic rallying cry. Appropriateness and balance were the bywords. Unfair expectations—whether of one's self or one's community—were to be avoided. Communities come in many varieties, reflecting the needs in God's kingdom; the message was to choose carefully some communities for support, and to try—when it is possible and within reason—to make other communities better through your actions. And as for the rest, peacefully leave them to God.

Monastic wisdom bids us not to exhaust ourselves in the search for perfection, but rather to find those communities that stand for what we want to believe in—even if we are not yet full believers. As Thich Nhat Hanh said, simply by professing that we want to be something we have made an important first step. These are not necessarily communities that comfort us and agree with our approach to life; those that confront us may even be more help in our spiritual and human growth. We recognize such places when we find communities that are home to selfless individuals, communities where there is an easy interchange, where people are neither ashamed to ask nor hesitant to give—where asking provides others the opportunity to open themselves.

The point is to recognize that we need to be encouraged. Communities that work well can inspire, and are often models worthy of emulation. When Abbot Francis returned from a visit to a poor Trappistine convent at Esmeraldas in Ecuador, his stories of their happiness and generosity in the midst of their struggles had a profound impact on the Mepkin monks and caused them to reevaluate their community life.

Monastic wisdom—and Abbot Francis would be first to affirm this— also warns against mistaking efficiency for intimacy in our most vital communities. Simply because a monastery or a family runs smoothly one may not presume that individuals are truly investing themselves. Precision and speed are for fine cars and computers, not groups of people.

The idea is not to have some grand, overarching ideal for community life; it is enough to start with small things, small actions. If you have prepared with many small, seemingly insignificant acts, you'll be surprised how normal your response will be when the great moments arrive, or when great sacrifices are called for. "The qualities of love and unity in a community must be personal and individual before they can exist communally."[5]

As I looked back over my year at Mepkin I could see that monks, in the least self-conscious way, are constantly trying to make life better for members of their community. Scouring pots for a brother who made a great—but messy—noon meal; putting egg cartons onto a busy line; hoisting a grain sack; offering a cold drink in a steaming, fetid chicken house; holding back a cutting remark that, while true, would injure more than instruct. These are gracious, human, attractive, unself-conscious examples of practical monastic life and spirituality. It is St. Therese's "little way," possible for any who might be sufficiently unafraid to want to be a profound force in a confused and love-starved world, who are open to God's initiatives and constant invitations, who hunger to see his presence in others and sense it in themselves. It is exactly the quality that makes monasteries so appealing to the visitor. It is in the air we breathe as soon as we come through the gates of these holy places.

As I neared the end of my monastic year, it was fitting that community should be so often on my mind. After all, of what value is a life of the spirit if it is not lived out with others? What if I know Benedict's *Rule* by heart, pray earnestly on my monthly trips to Mepkin, yet express nothing of monasticism's wisdom and power in the real circumstances of my life?

Cistercian monks wear their white tunic and black-hooded scapular as both symbol and reminder of their calling. My choir robe in the world might not be so visibly apparent, but it needed be no less clear to me. What I needed was, unadorned as it might sound, a right mind. Monks wish for the best in each other; they try to bring peace, ease conflict, assist, care, love; they live so as to treasure God's creation. For those who aspire to live a monastic life in the world, the mandate is no different. One group of lay people working to create a Cistercian "school of charity" in their own lives together have framed the task well: "Regardless of whether our community consists of other family members, co-workers, neighbors, fellow parishioners, or monastic brethren, we all share a basic responsibility to

<hr>

[5]Giallanza, 596.

foster attitudes and behaviors that are based on Christ's teachings about how we ought to live together."[6]

We can find a deep asceticism, a true, self-correcting, all-encompassing spirituality in the full range of communal interactions—from the most intimate and significant to those which pass with barely more notice than a single flutter of a butterfly's wings. Here is where holiness lies; community is the point through which all roads eventually pass. Was this not the distillation of this year at Mepkin?

Is it not in community that we strive to be constantly converted—the *conversatio* that monks vow and we want to emulate. Is not *stability* a keystone of community life, keeping us from flitting from one place to another, seeking the unattainable perfect while remaining imperfect ourselves? Is not *detachment* a crucial quality if we want to be separated from the thin veneer of ego so that the beauty and goodness and truth within us might be revealed—both to others and ourselves? And is not the *mysticism* of everyday life revealed with others, in others, at family meals, in supermarkets and airline terminals—in Sunday worship and a Tuesday night city council meeting?

Community is faith's testing ground, where a belief in God—sometimes palpable, most times barely discernible—boldly confronts the situations of daily life and proclaims that each of us, in ways great and small, has the power to bring that divine presence into the world. Community draws us out of ourselves, loosening the chains that bind us to our opinions, our desires, even our self-destructive ways of doing things—and freeing us to become aware of higher goals, the bigger picture, a greater need. In community we find at once hidden, yet readily available paths and possibilities that would never have opened to us had we blindly continued along our own way. Community is a purging flame, separating the dross of our hubris from the gold in us that can only make a difference if it is used in service of others. Community is the warmth of companionship in pursuit of a goal.

Some in our day would counter that the distributive, other-directed,

---

[6]"Lay Response to the Reflections of Dom Bernardo on Charismatic Associations," *Cistercian Studies Quarterly* (1997:2), 238.

other-concerned thinking of monastic spirituality works negatively. Certainly it runs against the wisdom of late-twentieth-century American values, a gospel that proclaims the primacy of individual needs and fears that self-sacrifice precludes true emotional health and maturity. Yet strangely, in practice we find just the opposite is true. Working toward the common good is as beneficial psychologically as it is spiritually. In addressing needs beyond our own, we in turn—oftentimes unknowingly—embrace our own deepest desires. Fatherhood is a perfect example for me. This "vocation" was quite low on my list of things to do with my life, yet the early years with two infant sons completely changed me, reordered my priorities. By giving myself to my children, I received in return a much more focused self. I gave time away—yet found I had more of it.

Monastic spirituality is prophetically in perfect alignment with what we have learned of human psychology in the past century. Human beings have a built-in need to feel part of something larger than themselves, to pursue a higher calling. This can never be achieved by the relentless pursuit of only what we desire. While we seem to avoid and fight it, we have an innate desire for togetherness, for inclusion—to be in harmony not only with God, but with his creation. Our modern ethic, which proclaims the individual, teaches us to fear losing our sense of self most of all. But fear not; there is always enough ego to go around. We will not turn into mindless communards.

Merton, writing about the mystical life from the seclusion of Gethsemani, concluded: "A man cannot enter into the deepest level of himself and pass through that center into God, unless he is able to pass entirely out of himself and empty himself and give himself to other people in the purity of a selfless love."[7] Years later, on a busy street corner, he truly found what he was alluding to.

In Louisville, at the corner of Fourth and Walnut, in the center of the shopping area, I was suddenly overwhelmed with the realization that I loved all these people. That they were mine, and I theirs. It

[7]Merton, *New Seeds of Contemplation*, 64.

was a life waking from a dream of separateness, of spurious self isolation in a special world; the world of renunciation and supposed holiness. The conception of separation from the world that we have in the monastery too easily presents itself as a complete illusion. The illusion, that by making vows, we become a different species of being.[8]

As I drove through the morning blackness the next day, how I wanted to embody those words. How I wanted to live what I had been learning in the library, on quiet walks, in the grading house, in the church of Mepkin Abbey. Although I would never wear their cowl and live as they did, monasticism loomed before me on the darkened highway, no longer an illusion, but accessible if. . . .

That "if" hung in the air as I listened to a tape of Merton lecturing to the Gethsemani novices on "Love and Purity of Heart." The ever-capacious Merton demonstrated the need for community and for monks to exist for each other by talking about a Sartre play in which three selfish people are condemned to the hell of staying together, in the same room, for eternity. To lock ourselves in self-involvement was hell; to give ourselves away was a taste of paradise, part of the divine plan.

The big word, "if." *If* I were able to put aside my petty desires, my towering impatience, my desire for others to act as I would have them do, my selfishness. *If*, instead, I was able to allow the ember of my own self-giving, fanned to a rich glow in this community, to grow into a true flame. *If* I would make a conscious effort to call upon this repository of monastic wisdom and practice as I went back into the world. How well I knew— how well we all know—that our human nature makes it difficult at best to look continually beyond our wants to the needs of others, to think communally in the most intimate and permanent as well as the casual and evanescent communities in which we find ourselves.

Be that as it may, I wanted to try. And while my approach over the next days was perhaps too broad, revealing a distinctly undisciplined and undis-

[8]Thomas Merton, *Conjectures of a Guilty Bystander* (Garden City, N.Y.: Doubleday Image, 1968), 156–57.

cerning mind, I slowly began to see communities all around me, beckoning me to live out the gospel message, the Trappist way, the way of true self-discovery, wonder and enhancement, happiness. God.

I boarded a United Airlines flight, headed for Chicago. As I put my bag in the overhead bin, I scanned the plane. Yes, I *did* love all these people. Packed like human sardines into this silver tube, we were a community with a quite definite goal: to reach our destination safely, and hopefully on time. But each of us on that plane—by the way we allowed a person into a seat, helped the flight attendant by passing a drink across, offered a smile to the weariest among us if we had one to give—made that thrown-together, very short-term community either a blessed or a barely tolerable gathering. The graces could flow, or not; it was up to each of us.

I did my best. I touched a particularly harried man on the shoulder and said something I hoped was not too inane. I met the flight attendant's eyes with a sincere "thank you." I put my papers in a neat stack for the cleaning crew. I thought of this as my community for those two hours. While I don't know if I did anything so differently, it was a wonderful flight, with a bit of reading, a nap, an easy smile here or there. I arrived at O'Hare airport refreshed, not travel-worn.

In a faculty meeting at the university where I teach part-time, the topics were quite different from those of a chapter meeting at Mepkin. But the members of an academic community require the same skills as the monks—to listen, to be honest but not cruel, to keep focused on the common good and not their own agenda, to care for each other. It took me a while, but the need for these skills in building an effective working community became plain here, too—as one of my fellow faculty members, not one of my favorites, was being worked over (somewhat deservedly) with great vehemence and at great length. I said something positive about my colleague, with a light enough touch not to be pandering. The mood in the room, on its way to being ugly, was shifted ever so slightly with those few words.

Monks and university departments must make tough decisions, but grace can still be in the air if we remember that sometimes we will be on the winning side, and sometimes on the other. If we expect compassion, we must be ready to offer compassion. The group of many "I"s is forcefully altered, when it becomes a "we," moved by genuine concern for both the goals of the group as well as the needs, strengths, and weaknesses of its members.

The votes in that meeting actually went against what I had hoped for, but a community spirit had prevailed. All I could do was offer a silent prayer of thanks at the resounding defeat of my ego.

As I walked into the hospital for my Thursday-morning rounds as a Eucharistic minister, I saw that this also was a community. The woman spraying the door and wiping it clean, that young mentally challenged girl whisking the mail through the corridors, the surgeons in their blue scrubs between operations, the woman at the switchboard, the nurse at the chart desk. We were a community of healing, each doing his or her part so that the mind, body, and spirit of the patients in our care might be restored, bolstered, sanctified. There was a staggering list of thirty-five patients on the list that morning. Grace flowed where impatience or fatigue might have once reigned.

The tiny, premature infant in the ICU incubator virtually radiated, allowing the nurses the opportunity to care for her and for me to say a small prayer, my hand pressed to the plastic walls of her protective home. The handsome young man whose red blood count had dropped to zero; we could pray together for the healing of anemia—his pronounced and physical, mine held in reserve, for this was his moment to be lifted up to God. Our needs were not exactly the same, but in that moment each of us, I believe, confronted his profound deficiencies and acknowledged our mutual need for God's presence. My friend Mary from the parish, in so much pain, her hot cheek against mine. How sweet was the embrace of two pilgrims— one upright and walking this moment, the other, for now, in her bed.

Sacramental encounters, each of them. Just as Bernard, font of Cistercian wisdom, had promised.

So one night at supper, with my wife and two sons gathered around me for supper and my heart filled with all that I had experienced, I struggled to express my growing sense of community in our prayer before dinner. I offered a prayer of thanksgiving for this and all our communities. That we might see God in others. That. . . .

And the boys snickered.

In an instant, my attempt at imparting a sense of communal bliss was shattered. Their laughter was but a mere distant rumble heralding the thunder that burst from my mouth. I shoved myself away from the table and stormed out the front door. I hadn't even reached the sidewalk when I broke down in tears. What a scene: this grown man walking down his tree-lined street in the early evening, sobbing. I was embarrassed; I was crest-fallen. My Mepkin year had been a sham, so much pious talk and musings, so little real follow through. I had learned nothing at all if such an ordinary, childish reaction, could evoke that response.

A heavy rain had fallen and puddles dotted my path. The trees dripped with moisture, their tears blending with my own. Now it was *my* face that was feverish, not Mary's. Although the air was still at ground level, the clouds overhead were moving rapidly across the sky. With blurred vision, I looked up—at what, for what, I don't know. First, there was a glimmer of light, then a ray. For an instant, I was back at Mepkin, beneath the live oaks, brushing aside the Spanish moss along the peaceful, tree-lined approach to the cloister. Then a blazing stream of evening sunlight pierced the clouds and cascaded down through even more familiar trees—the trees of my neighborhood.

A rabbi I once wrote about taught me that Jews constantly recite the psalms in order to make the words become a part of them, instantly available for application in life's circumstances. Other lines—phrases and sayings from the Mepkin year—came spilling into my mind. I could not then quote them word for word as I do now, but their essence was there:

. . . that the strong have something to yearn for and the weak nothing to run from.[9]

For when God loves, all he desires is to be loved in return.[10]

[9] *The Rule of St. Benedict,* 283 (RB64).

For in sacrifice you take no delight,
burnt offering from me you would refuse.
My sacrifice, a contrite spirit.
A humbled, contrite heart you will not spurn.[11]

No matter what happens, be gentle with yourself.[12]

The monastic challenge stood there before me—but equally, the monastic promise. The monastic way. A way of life for ordinary men and
women, not angels and saints. How great the vision; how imperfect my
execution. This was not the two-hour flight or hospital rounds. Neither
was it the easy smile of a monk to the new and eager visitor, or a kind word
a Trappist might offer when shopping in Monck's Corner. This was daily
life within my real community, as my community members deal with their
own humanity. This was Benedict living a new way of life in harmony with
the dailiness of community life. So much grace at hand, so many false
steps.

I stopped. Not another step away. The sun broke through cloud after
cloud until the street was drenched, not with rain, but with light. I pulled
out my handkerchief and walked back into my house and toward the table.

This was not the first time I had left the family table in irritation. In
the past, when I returned, a pall would have descended upon my family.
This time it would not be so, I vowed, if I was truly to be a member of this
community. I had been tested and I had failed, but. . . . What were those
lines in Esther de Waal's fine book on the Cistercians I had been reading?
She had quoted Gilbert of Hoyland, a twelfth-century Cistercian abbot:
"And there is no dwelling together in unity unless it be in love, love which
brings those with a common way of life under the same roof." And then
she had gone on: "There is a double movement within love—the love of
sharing and the sharing of love, two movements, which cannot be separated

[10]Quoted in *The Liturgy of the Hours*, vol. IV, 1333.
[11]Psalm 51.
[12]Ellsberg, *All Saints: Daily Reflections on Saints, Prophets, and Witnesses for Our Time* (New York: Crossroad, 1997), 357.

one from the other." And then, coming back to Gilbert: "Love, by a certain instinctive moment, longs to pour itself forth and transfer the good it possesses to someone it loves with all its love; it longs to have it in common, to take the other as a companion."[13]

If I loved anyone, it was these three people. If I had any lasting companions in my life, here they were. We dwelled under the same roof, and would for many years. I came back to the table and apologized. So did my boys. I made sure that "long look" was off my face and asked about school—only to have the conversation quickly launch into discussion of curfews, concerts they wanted to attend, how "everybody has more privileges than we do." Instead of countering with my battery of arguments, I simply listened. This was my place of conversion, this was my monastery. And these were my community members trying to discern how they are to live their lives, to find their way, in the world. They made some valid points; my temperature was down and my ears were open.

And there was Daniel, talking about a priest who had visited his St. Mary's School classroom and had pretty much squelched any other than the most doctrinaire answers to the complex problems that face the modern church. Form ruled over content. But Daniel was not about to buy that approach. "Why don't we have the right to make things right?" this wise and brave young man said.

The next day loomed as a busy one for me: a book review and an article were overdue, calls had to be made, and I had a bunch of those errands that can eat up the better part of the day. The boys and I were also to volunteer at a local soup kitchen. Why today, of all days? Noah and Daniel awoke early, got the paper, and discovered it was also a perfect day for surfing.

Surfing! No computer, no phone, hours wasted. My mind tallied up the minuses—and then I looked at them, thirteen and eleven, standing there in their baggy T-shirts that pass as nightwear. I hesitated. They said nothing.

We grabbed some bagels with lox cream-cheese spread and were at

[13]de Waal, 120.

Wrightsville Beach in a half hour. A blood-red sun was just edging over the horizon. They went into the water; I settled into my beach chair. I was able to sketch out both the review and article on a legal pad—and was amazed it took so little time. I looked up from my work, out onto the Atlantic. It was a good surf day indeed; clean, three-foot waves. There, on the silver-drenched surface, were both of them, side by side, riding the same wave in one felicitous moment that is still etched in my brain.

In the monastic day, work is constantly interrupted by prayer so that the monks can regain focus on what they are really doing on the face of the earth. I stuffed the legal pad back in the beach bag and reached for the book I'd been reading, *Dark Night of the Soul,* by St. John of the Cross. It is not an easy read—especially when a father is watching his surfing sons—and I had been slogging through it for the past few weeks, a page at a time. I finally concentrated for a moment. And there it was:

> It is a characteristic of the power and vehemence of love that all things seem possible to it, and it believes all to be of the same mind as itself.[14]

Yes, it *was* possible.

We went to the Good Shepherd Soup Kitchen and helped feed some eighty members of our very extended Wilmington family. There came into our midst a moment of grace in the person of a former Buddhist monk who now survived in a strange new land by handing out flyers for a local pizza shop. Each sheet he formed elegantly into a delicate origami shape. My boys stood there speechless at this miracle in shabby clothes. Throughout the morning Noah and Daniel were as friendly and respectful of their guests as a maitre d' at a fine restaurant, as solicitous as junior executives inviting the boss over for dinner. It was a holy time, a sacramental encounter.

But then, so was surfing.

[14]John of the Cross, *Dark Night of the Soul,* trans. E. Allison Peers, 3rd rev. ed. (Garden City, N.Y.: Doubleday, 1959), 143.

MAY

The Simple Path

Monastic Wisdom for Everyday Life

In the pale early morning light on what promised to be a brilliant, cloud-less May day, I walked the now familiar road out from the cloister to the fertile low country fields that rim the Cooper. Trappist monks had worked this loam and marl soil for decades; Henry Laurens (a Revolutionary War general), willing settlers, and indentured slaves before them. Now that there were too few monks, a few local farmers still in dairy or beef cattle were the new stewards. The field to my left, which last year yielded a rich harvest of corn, now brought forth only blotches of weed, a ghastly and profitless green. There was only an occasional stalk of corn, spindly, forlorn. These byproducts of a bygone season stood in mute testimony to the eternal verities: a field must be prepared anew, crops spaced when they are planted, then nurtured, fertilized, and carefully tended. Harmful influences must be held at bay and natural qualities allowed to evolve. Even the good, random seed has no better chance of succeeding than, say, the best of good, random human intentions. Neither alone—seed nor intention—has the ability or power to withstand the assaults of wind and weather, or to prosper from the blessings of the seasons and finally come to fruition.

When I sat in choir for mass that morning, it would have been easy to come to a similarly fallow appraisal of these choir-robed stalks of Mepkin Abbey. There were three fewer of them than when I had started my visits a year ago, and the majority of those remaining had their best harvest years behind them. Brother Paul was now in a wheelchair. Brother William's congestive heart failure was at such an acute stage he rarely came to the hours—and when he did he wearily wheeled a canister of oxygen behind him. Brother Boniface's slippers slid so slowly along the tile floor that each inching movement seemed perhaps his last. Brother Peter, the last novice, was gone. There were no more shimmering white tunics brightening the day to both portend and assure the future.

Were these more than mere mortal signs? Was God dead, as he had been pronounced during the tumultuous seventies? Was monasticism about to succumb, swallowed like a furtive minnow by the great killer whale of secularism? That grand pursuit of the ineffable that has characterized our earthly condition at least since our brains developed to the point that we realized there was something beyond food, drink, shelter and reproduction—was it at an end?

To the casual observer, the scene in the abbey church might have hinted at a landscape as unpromising as that field near the Earth Healer quonset huts. But a more discerning eye than this was required.

For there, in the midst of men whose number is shrinking, was an unheard of and unprecedented long-term visitor—Sister Louise, a Trappistine nun. In choir stalls designed for monks alone, some ten visitors stood in place. In the egg-grading house that morning, five Duke University students—only one of them Catholic, and an admittedly nominal one at that—went to work. Two lay people, volunteers, climbed onto tractors, mowing the lawns. Other guest rooms were filled with a variety of people—some, but not all, Catholics.

Beyond these few thousand acres of sanctuary and fourscore professed and nonprofessed seekers, beyond the walls of the monasteries, was a world out of breath, a virtual nation of seekers. Which of those seekers beyond the walls did not want to live fully (in words perhaps more familiar to them, "optimize"), with a certain sense of awe and reverence (no longer limited to "religion," they might choose "spiritually"), expressing and receiving love ("love" is exactly the operative word, illusive as it may be), in peace (once again, a word they would use)? Perhaps Karin Culp, a Methodist minister who was visiting from Charleston, spoke not only for herself: "Why do I come here? I need a structure for my spiritual life and nothing I've found provides it like monasticism. But I'm frustrated. I feel like I have my nose pressed against the glass. I want to take monasticism into my life, but I don't know how to do it. So I keep coming back, trying to learn, trying to practice what I learn."

She noted that her church had offered a eucharistic service only six times a year when she arrived. It was not enough, she felt, once she had been exposed to daily mass with the monks. Eucharist is now a monthly occurrence at her church; the week before, at a newly instituted Monday-night Eucharist, the dozen regulars even chanted a psalm. By the tenth verse, they sounded like veteran monks. It was not exactly the Methodist way, but her congregation was thriving on such a mixed spiritual diet.

It is not difficult to see that something is mutating within monasticism—American monasticism at least. Much of it is blurry, quite different, even exotic. The piercing cry for meaning is not going unheard behind cloister walls. And monasticism's answer is strangely—mystically—universal, transreligious, nondoctrinal, nondogmatic, pure, human. The lessons of Old Testament prophets and the gospel message of those professing a decidedly new testament have taken on a new relevance in what is called a post-Christian period. Monasticism, which while resting on the bedrock of tradition and practice has been in dialogue with varying cultures for centuries, stands ready to address these times. Healthy sprouts—not the scorched stubble in the Mepkin fields—are fighting their way to a new day's sources of heat and light, plunging their roots to ancient nutrients for continuing sustenance. The choking weeds of cynicism, self-doubt, and hubris that seem to grow so thick in every age can—monasticism contends—be controlled. Within the once self-contained organism of the most disciplined, stylized, and institutional manifestations of Christian belief, something—in Abbot Francis Kline's words—is indeed breaking loose. Seeds blown to the winds are falling on fertile ground. Lines are blurring between the sacred and secular to a degree that would make both Rahner and Merton—even Benedict and Bernard—smile. Lay people are entering the monastic world and carrying their experiences there into the world outside. Oblate groups linked to monasteries are springing up all over the country. Monastic literature is dramatically again in demand. Monastery guest rooms are often booked many months in advance. The abbey's Charleston experiment of lay people living the monastic day in the secular world was on hold (due to the building program and the reality of too few monks for too many obligations), but the idea was exactly right. Such a group already exists in the center of Paris; another in Rome. It is only a matter of time until such a group appears in America. Perhaps it has already. Monasticism, never apparently in the vanguard, typically so slow to change, is breathtakingly out in front of us, blazing a trail. Once again it is drawing seekers to its almost madly ambitious goal—nothing less than piercing the human heart and God's heart as well, so that divine connection might be made not only in heaven, but on earth as well. As a recent theological commentator on Cistercian life has suggested, "It may be, in the last analysis, that monasticism can again provide to the world something that it has offered in its beginnings: a counter-cultural movement that stands as both a prophetic sign against the excesses of society and an alternative to those who remain serious and faithful to the desire for God."[1]

During my Mepkin days it was not that I had discovered something so

---

[1] Lawrence Cunningham, "The Monastic Charism: A Lay View," *Cistercian Studies Quarterly,* 1989:3, 251.

hidden or so new. Nor had I undergone some sort of dramatic conversion. I would have welcomed either, or both; but neither occurred. Instead, what I had found beneath the brambles of my life was a simple path, monastic wisdom for everyday life.

Was I a different man from that eager, fervent soul who first had come through the gates a year ago? I could not honestly say that I was. Certainly I did not know that much more about the mystical life. But I had learned that trying to get an accurate reading of one's spiritual temperature was ultimately useless. Words from the *Dark Night of the Soul*, my recent reading, still hung with me: "Usually, when the soul is receiving fresh advantage and profit, this comes by a way that it least understands—indeed, it quite commonly believes that it is losing ground."[2] All I could hope for was what my computer told me as the text of one word-processing program was being translated into another: "Conversion in process."

I did not know if advantage and profit were mine; I hoped so. What I did know for sure was that when I was losing ground I could sense it all too readily: my stupid acts of ego and arrogance confronted me instantly, demanding repentance and *conversatio*. I had been offered in this year a new set of tools—sturdy, yet fine and precise—for use in my family life, work life, community life, spiritual life. The issue was whether, and how, I would choose to employ them.

But whatever it was about monasticism I had learned here at Mepkin, I had discovered it in a most personal way, the fresh way that is the blessing granted all novices. My life-long affection for this venerable tradition, which has punctuated the fits and starts of my checkered spiritual life, had led me to the sustained encounter of this year—and now I would be going from it, if not a changed man, at least a somewhat more knowing one. As balmy winds blew up from the Cooper and across the Luce graves, rustling the huge swags of Spanish moss on the great live oaks and faintly whispering about the cloister garth that constitutes the epicenter of Trappist life in this little-known place, it was time to undertake some kind of an accounting. My twelve months of attempts to penetrate monastic mysteries was at

---

[2]John of the Cross, *Dark Night of the Soul*, 154.

an end. The file folders—both actual and mental—into which I had jammed quotes and thoughts and articles for still other aspects of monastic life would have to await another day.

Certainly, I quickly realized, I had barely scratched the surface. So much yet explored. I had to face the distinct possibility that I might have, after all, missed the very essence of this life. What of the magic of silence that stilled the soul? What about solitude, the gateway to self-understanding? Why is it that simplicity—that radical, monastic simplicity—has a subversive, cleansing appeal? Or that poverty allows us to see our real wealth? Or that discipline structures a life such that freedom can be fully embraced?

It was tempting to go further into these aspects of monastic life. But I realized that once I yielded, I would find still more spiritual threads to follow. Scrolling can be done as well with spirituality's possibilities as with life's miseries. It is both the writer's and the seeker's temptation: to continue research rather than begin the arduous task of putting what has been learned on paper or into practice. Those concerns that had seemed so pressing a year ago had taken care of themselves in God's time, without any assistance from me. I had been additionally blessed. Had any great successes come my way, had I heard a siren song, I might not have continued to plod along a pilgrim's path. I had written some words, my children had been fed, tires had been bought, utility bills paid, my basic needs had been taken care of.

Now that the year was at an end and I had at least an inkling of perspective, I had to conclude that a strange thing had happened. In essence, Mepkin had deconstructed my view of monasticism. This outpost representing the grand bulwark of Western civilization and Christian spirituality had not so much crumbled, but fallen away. The mystery of this life was no longer so mysterious. As if in a boat yard, I had laid plank upon plank and, seeing the many holes, sealed them with pitch. That drydock had now fallen away and now my rickety, imperfect bark was about to be set afloat. I could not claim to know any shipbuilding theory. I knew only what I had crafted, humble vessel that it was. I knew very little about a grand institution or pattern, but something of a simple way of life.

In a strange way, I wanted not so much to go forward with my life, but to be able to go back to those first moments here at Mepkin when insights and warm revelations seemed to come, as they do to the naive and open mind, with ease. I wanted to rest secure in that sweet reverie, to cling to those tender moments. But I could feel my fingers slipping away. It was not an altogether bad feeling, for I equally sensed that I did not have to grasp those tender mercies as tightly (and sometimes frantically) as I had before. I had to move on.

I could now see that the monastery's shadow is a long one, reaching far beyond the expanse of well-trimmed grass that rings these buildings. As monasteries have quietly influenced humanity throughout history, I had felt the power of this place. Now the question was: Would I also cast my own small shadow? Would I exhibit monastic spirituality in my everyday life? Only, I knew, if I could remember what monasticism is really about.

Monks spend no time in a renunciation or even a critique of the world. They don't preach; they are not missionaries. Their only work is to trans-form—not through any modern form of communication or coercion, but by the way that Benedict and Bernard espoused: the example of their lives, the creation and maintenance of a place on this earth showing by example that gospel values are basic human values—values that make both earthly and cosmic sense. As the spirit of God daily touches our faces and hearts ever so lightly, it is the work of these Mepkin Trappists—in their own small but most significant way—to discern what humankind's response to God should be in this particular time. Monks are a crucial component in our world, keepers of a rich spiritual tradition; but they are also only one community in a network that encircles the globe, "networks of the heart" as the Trappist abbot Armand Veilleux so aptly calls them, both nourishing and feeding from each other.

What monks seek is what is in the heart of every person who seeks unity with the supreme presence that is the essence of life, of love, of goodness, of happiness. Trappists might seem to have a rarified way of expressing that desire—but then again, I would have to say after my year with them, it was not so unique at all. They are nonconformists, to be sure; but are we better off as conformists, blithely spinning in the prevailing societal winds that so harshly buffet our souls? "Monasticism may well find itself on the fringe, but it is a vital fringe."[3]

Lawrence Cunningham, a theology professor and friend, posed a hypothetical situation to students at a state university where he once taught. Suppose there was a transcendent reality (called God in the Christian tradition) and a group of people wanted to make the "approachability, the knowability, and communication with that transcendent reality the main focus of their lives."[4] How would they proceed? His class decided there must be strong aspiration for that goal, and not upon material success, which would only divert them. Furthermore, a discipline that went beyond mere ethical behavior would be essential to safeguard against self-delusion or ego-tripping—in other words, discernment. The students wondered whether service to the world also needed to be a part of this life—or, alternatively, whether the pursuit itself was service enough.

It is obvious that their answers were a near blueprint for monastic life—which only confirms monasticism's universal appeal and its wise, balanced approach to perennial issues and universal longing. Monasticism addresses what is fundamental to a human being. Reflecting again on monasticism's origins, it was comforting to remember that this way of life was not the creation of medieval bishops or theologians trying to so institutionalize belief that it could be more efficiently monitored. Christian monasticism sprang from a deep yearning in lay people, opening their arms and hearts to the love of God so that the aching deep within could be healed, and the uncertainty of the human condition—if not resolved—at least be boldly faced.

Taking on tunic and scapular does not guarantee holiness. No monk—within the monastery or without—knows if his or her life is at all efficacious. That is why Trappist monks rarely speak about their spiritual lives. If any allude to holiness, you can be sure it has eluded them. The seeker never arrives at the goal, or if a goal seems to be reached, it is but a way

---

[3]Donald K. Swaerer and Grover A. Zinn, "Monasticism East and West: An Inquiry," *Japanese Religion* 7 (1971) 29–50; quoted in Jean Leclercq, "Monasticism and One World," *Cistercian Studies Quarterly* 21 (4) (1986), 289.
[4]Cunningham, "The Monastic Charism," 243.

station en route to another goal. The Buddhists advise that if the seeker finds the Buddha, the Buddha is to be killed. Monasticism deals in mysteries, and that should hardly surprise; for what is God, and what are we? Precise mathematical formulae? Provable syllogisms? Hardly.

Equally, monasticism is not some sort of spiritual lottery. Benedict fully *expected* God to be experienced in the dailiness of monastic life. But God's light would only shine, he believed, through the clear panes of those whose hearts and minds were not clouded with their own wishes and plans. In our time, Benedict's wisdom beautifully synchronizes with the modern quest for the experiential, the bold, seemingly impossible quest. Whether or not we see results from our efforts is not the measure. The desire to please God *does* please God. The good journey, the road less traveled, is its own reward. All that is required of us is that our hunger is never abated and our desire never cooled. And our reward will be rich, even in the very act of desiring. We can and will feel God's presence in our lives.

As impressive as the Trappist way might be, as universal the need that the monastic approach addresses, it is decidedly not the only model for a spiritually rich life. Nor does Christian monasticism say something to the human condition that monks of other traditions—or even some solitary hermit in a simple cabin somewhere—do not also confront. A twelve-step program offers its own path, usually outside traditional religious constructs, but not unaware of the sheer logic of human frailty and divine transcendence. The way to holiness and transcendence may be through a narrow passageway, but that is not to say that there are not many paths, each with its own passageway.

Christian monasticism offers *a* way to God, not *the* way. And looking back over my lifetime, I realize I did not choose it; it chose me. Monasticism resonated with me, with my imperfect, impulsive self, because it encompasses all human activity and asks that the disparate parts and moments of our lives be not merely tolerated, or managed, but sanctified. Nothing is outside its purview, wisdom, or experience. While monasticism is mystical and mysterious, it is also imminently practical. It makes great demands. It grants even greater allowances. It gives us the wherewithal to live in the trust that this universe is God's province, that we need not cower in fear of being condemned to so many years in an alien, intimidating world. It is a way to live life that not only links each of us with the divine, but forges links between each of us and others through our actions and thoughts—thereby linking us all to God.

Through visits to a place like Mepkin, monasticism is accessible here and now. Like the bubbling holy-water font in the abbey church, it is forever fresh, replenishing. I can read of Cîteaux and Monte Casino; but to visit a place where monasticism is being lived out today, to puzzle with monks who are also confronting modernity, is a source of both inspiration and comfort. I can, in essence, pass through that pane of glass Karin described, if only for hours or days. Here, in the presence of God and each other, utilizing the marvelous monastic example that has guided so many before us, we can read the signs of the times and discern our respective futures. What is superficial and evanescent, what is meaningful and lasting. Certain qualities of monasticism, and indeed of human beings, do not change from age to age, but endure to find expression in their own time. Today, we have an information age; then, there were the Dark Ages or an industrial age, the dissolution of *ancien régime* or dawning of global exploration. Each presents different demands and opportunities.

In a monastery, there is mutual support, but not the mandate that God be pursued in exactly this way or that. In a monastery of celibates, birth pangs are expected and not anesthetized. In a monastery, life is hardly renounced, but lived to the fullest—all in the rich glow of grace and expectation and openness. What better qualities for a full life can there be?

This is monasticism's promise for those who approach it hoping to penetrate its mysteries and understand its astounding pragmatism. When Thomas Merton first came to Gethsemani some nine months before he joined, he triumphantly called it "the center of America," the place that was "holding this country together."[5] But already he could see it was not a place to admire; rather, as with all abbeys, it was a place to be *used*. This was not a place for saints, but for sinners who hoped to become saints. Self-denial,

[5]Merton, *Run to the Mountain*, 333 (entry for 7 April 1941).

prayer, and labor could become their own perverted gods, if not employed properly.

Merton saw that if humans were to thrive in such an environment, they had to go beyond doing penance for past wrongs or even focusing their hopes on the assurance of eternal reward. "However hard it is, it is still a form of play . . . we must . . . do things not because they are physically necessary, but freely, as if arbitrarily, almost: for love."[6] This is key, not only to Trappist life, but to our spiritual life as well. For whatever we do only from obligation is a bitter pill indeed. Such actions lack the intensity that will and passion alone can provide. After a period of time, if our spirit and our action is not continuously replenished by the wellspring of love, atrophy and death result. My life is ample testimony to that.

The freedom of which Merton speaks of is, surprisingly but unquestionably, at the very heart of Trappist life. It seems an anomaly that men and women living a cloistered life, following a regimented schedule for waking, sleeping, working, meeting, eating, and praying, could be so free. But free they are—perhaps more than we are. The very structure of monastic life gives them the ability to live each part of it fully; their careful approach to material things loosens the bonds that entangle so many of us. The monks seek that which will truly satisfy their minds and wills. They will not settle for less.

And, while heaven is a possibility, the search for the divine is not—as a great chorus of monastic writers of the Christian tradition and equally prescient voices within the world's religions repeatedly tell us—some stratospheric projection into another world. The other shore is this shore, the Buddha instructed those whose gaze was always to nirvana beyond the present. The Pure Land that we search for is already in the human heart, providing a place of rest for those wise enough—guileless enough, really—to claim it.

Trappist monks seek their Pure Land within the confines of a monastery. For the rest of us, our Pure Land can be our homes, our workplaces, our trips to the supermarket and our sitting in town council

[6]Ibid., 336

meetings. In our highly secularized world, where there are precious few readily apparent signs that God is in our midst, this is oftentimes difficult to comprehend; how often I have failed to see it. And as much as I have always admired Trappists and grew to respect them even more at Mepkin, it seems to me—though it might be presumptuous to say such a thing—that to be a monk *outside* a monastery is a far braver act than being a monk *within* one. To take that spirit born of these holy places into a world not at all as holy is an art form, one infused with the spirit of play, adventure, and love. To live the Trappist way, the monastic ethos, is a heady challenge indeed.

There is an ancient Jewish proverb that warns the further you go from Mount Sinai—where God gave Moses the Ten Commandments and the structure for life—the weaker you become. What this really says in our time is that the further we are diverted or detached from the real meaning of life, from our real selves, the less able we are to truly live.

A small number of men and women will be clothed in Trappist garb, but the rest of us in the world can wear it just as well—invisible as cloth, but visible as action, attitude, desire, love, *conversatio.* Not everyone should enter a monastery. But everyone seeking God can live, invisibly clothed, a monastic life. Married, single, old, young, here is a lifestyle that—at least from this pilgrim's vantage point—is both exhilarating and comforting. As Theresa Mancuso writes: "If monasticism is the search for truth and harmony with the universe, a search for God hidden beneath all the layers of reality that cover everything and everybody, then those who search are truly monks."[7] Each of us, monk within the cloister and monk in the world, is attempting to become whole. So was Pachomius when he went to the old hermit Palamon in the Egyptian desert, who promised "to labor with you until you get to know yourself." The search for wholeness, which is the search for God, is ultimately personal, a search for the true self. It is not institutional, enlightened but not driven by dogma or doctrine. All of us, as Armand Veilleux says, must "go through the path of their own heart."[8]

[7]Theresa Mancuso, "A Monastic Way in the World," *Review for Religious* 51 (3) (1992), 334.
[8]Armand Veilleux, "Networks of the Heart," in *Blessed Simplicity: The Monk as Universal Archetype*, ed. Raimundo Panikkar (New York: Seabury Press, 1982), 143.

This is the invitation extended to—let us be so bold as to say this—the new monk. The new monk, who will never enter traditional institutions, is yet impelled by the attractions of a life built upon principles that are thoroughly monastic. Our path requires, as any initiation to a new (or renewed) way of life, a different consciousness. We must disrupt old ways, shattering the planes upon which we have unwittingly built lives that do not bring us the happiness, the fulfillment, the transcendence for which we hunger. We need not turn our back and flee to a monastery; rather we must turn toward the world, our lives, our work, our community, our loved one, in a new way. The Pure Land beckons.

On the last morning of my Mepkin year, I arose for vigils at 3:00 A.M. I walked slowly along that roadway, lined with those now familiar lights that had once so blinded and disoriented me, toward the abbey church. As Psalm 95 was again wafted heavenward and also volleyed tenderly from one side of the choir to the other, I looked out at my good companions. Their holiness inspired me, but as I scanned their faces it was their ordinariness that impressed me even more. Confused, broken, incomplete men, with all their foibles, daily they tried so hard to be good to one another, to live the high Trappist ideal, to be worthy in the eyes of God. And they failed—they failed repeatedly. They were seeking the Absolute, knowing that the Absolute was ultimately simple—so simple that even they could not see it. But they went on, from prayer to work to bed, with faith that their best efforts were pleasing to an understanding God.

How I loved them.

After vigils, I walked into the sacristy. I had asked Father Aelred to save portions of the previous day's Eucharist so I could take the sanctified bread back to the patients I would visit at the hospital that day. The two pyx, golden in color, lay on the countertop. Behind them was a large, framed picture of the Atlas Trappists who had been murdered. In the soft fluorescent light, they seemed a quiet, living presence there in this place where priests vest for mass, not dead at all. I opened one of the pyx. Chips of brown wafer. Bits of broken, unleavened bread for souls broken open by pain and disease. Food for their journey.

I walked out into the warm air of that May morning. I had no need to bid farewell to monk or monastery, for I would be back. Again and again. Who would ever say goodbye to such a place as this?

In the refectory I filled my travel mug with coffee for my own journey and toasted two slices of Brother Boniface's bread. On the bulletin board was a notice. It explained why the abbot was not at vigils this morning; he was in New York in search of building funds. The notice also mentioned that the day before, cell phone at his ear on Fifth Avenue, he had absent-mindedly wandered outside the cement barriers designed to bring order to the chaos of Manhattan intersections. He had been told quite sternly, by a city policeman, to abide not by the rule of Benedict, but of Mayor Giuliani.

As I neared my car a strange glow caught my eye, suspended as it was between the tiny road-marker lights and the sparkling canopy of stars. A lone magnolia blossom glimmered in the darkness, a sign that another season had passed and the rich fragrance of these huge, short-lived blossoms would again be upon the land. I inhaled, deeply. Yes, the sweetness was on the night air. Could a single blossom be so redolent? What choirs of magnolias hummed quietly from the darkness to back this sterling solo performer at center stage?

As I drove beneath the live oaks, outlined against the night sky, I found myself overwhelmed with a feeling of sheer indebtedness—that I have such a place to go to, that I can enjoy the luxury of coming away from my life in order to see it more clearly. And I was grateful that the pruning of this past year had not been a punishment at all, but instead portended new growth, new life in the days ahead. I was grateful for the surprises of the year, that in its very unpredictability I had been awakened in ways I could never had imagined. My life would continue to be unpredictable, I was sure, but it was that very quality which would keep me alert to God's mysterious presence at work in the world.

I turned left out of the gates and onto Dr. Evans Road. For the first hour or so of my journey home, I resisted turning on the BBC World Service—that hushed, authoritative voice among the blare of overnight talk shows, religious and music programs—to find out what the world had been up to in my absence. I had a tape beside me but I did not play it; I listened instead to the silence of my soul.

Each time I begin these trips, in my dazed early morning state, it is as if I am going into the land of Oz, a strange and expectant voyage. Each time I am hopeful that this time I will have learned something profound, unlocked the door to my soul, put the pieces together in a way that will not fall apart again. But there had been no apocalyptic revelation. I would go back into my life, and God would test me and come to me in the most ordinary ways—just as he would do with the monks of Mepkin.

Finally, I pushed in the audiotape. It was Kahil Gibran's *The Prophet*, a book I first read many years before. And I heard these words:

"I speak to you only of what is already in your heart."

Afterword

In the ensuing months, as the tides of the Cooper River gently rose and fell, so did life at Mepkin Abbey. A few men left monastic life; others came. The number of monks remained somewhat stable, although Father Feliciano began to experience back pain and had to limit his work. Sister Louise moved on to a Trappistine convent.

Of more significance, Brother William's condition continued to deteriorate and finally he abandoned his cell and asked for an infirmary room on what he called, with the impetuous smile that was his trademark throughout forty-four years of monastic life, "death row." As Brother William grew weaker, Brother Edward asked if there was anything special he wanted. There was.

A few days later, Brother Edward appeared in the infirmary with a thick filet mignon, done medium well, with all the trimmings, and a frosty bottle of Budweiser. Brother William ate remarkably well. He was dead within forty-eight hours. He was buried on a hillock overlooking the Cooper near the abbey church—in his long-sleeved choir robe, as is Trappist custom.

After so many months of work on a foundation, the new library rose up on firm concrete pillars from the red clay, promising to be both beautiful and utilitarian.

And, speaking of utilitarian, yes, Brother Joseph received a new belt. He wears it only on special occasions these days, preferring the one he received a half century ago. It is still held together by an almost imperceptible shred of leather.

Acknowledgments

My thanks to my editor, Eric Major, who believed in this book from the beginning. Thanks also to my agent, Gordon Kato, and copy editor Mark Edington.

Many others contributed their *labora*—from those who did the typesetting, proofing, and printing to those who helped in the various stages of publishing. Some of you I know, some I do not. My thanks for your excellent work.

My affection for the Mepkin monks continues to deepen through the years. They have always welcomed me as a friend. Special thanks to Father Aelred Hagan, O.C.S.O., who kindly read a version of the manuscript.